# *Praise for Spreen*

"I'm inspired by legendary police commissioner and former sheriff Johannes Spreen, who, while working in Detroit during the tense racial times of the late 1960s stated, 'It takes a team, you and your police.' His community-partnership approach encouraged people to work together, and it was successful." Buckeye Police Chief Dan Saban

"I was accorded the priceless gift of serving with Commissioner Spreen as a New York City Police Department officer, sergeant, lieutenant, and captain. As we studied together for higher rank, I was most impressed with his ability to speak and write in a manner that produced understanding and other beneficial results. These attributes are certain to bring forth a book which, in the light of Commissioner Spreen's broad experiences, will enrich the lives of readers who are part of, or in support of, the field of criminal justice." William J. McCullough, Colonel, U.S. Army; President, Looseleaf Law Publications; and author of *Minuteman/Activist* and *Hold Your Audience*.

"Johannes Spreen was a police officer extraordinary; a man who helped restructure and develop New York City Police Academy training leading to a college program, a 'West Point' for police officers—now John Jay College for Criminal Justice. Johannes Spreen is a man of enthusiasm, indeed a prophet; always ahead of his time and a friend for over 60 years." Rudolph P. Blaum, Retired Captain, New York City Police Department, served in the operation and development of the New York Police Service College Program, now John Jay College. He is Former President of the American Education Association in Center Moriches, New York.

"Johannes Spreen has extraordinary credentials and a range of knowledge that will achieve great results." Dr. Isaiah "Ike" McKinnon, Former Detroit Chief of Police, and Professor, University of Detroit, Mercy.

*"Thanks for your dedicated service. Very nice indeed."* Sheriff Joe Arpaio, Maricopa County, Arizona.

*"To somebody who knows more than what's written here and who's lived through it all."* Professor Len Sherman, co-author of Sheriff Arpaio's book, *America's Toughest Sheriff*.

*"I want to take this opportunity to thank you very sincerely for the help you have given me and our own Police Chief while you were in office in Detroit. The scooter patrol innovation that you instituted in the $12^{th}$ precinct worked effectively for you, and based upon your recommendations, we here in Flint utilized it to a great advantage."* Mayor Donald R. Cronin of Flint, Michigan

*"It's almost incredible the task you faced coming to Detroit as Police Commissioner exactly one year after the disaster which this little book describes. The fact that a year later you had achieved such major breakthroughs in building a bridge between the police and Detroit citizens, and healing many of the wounds within the Department, makes your tenure as Detroit's Police Commissioner one of the most significant in the city's history. We remember you with gratitude."* Rev. Dr. Hubert Locke, author of *The Detroit Riot of 1967*.

*"We have always felt here at the Greater Detroit Chamber of Commerce that you were the man to guide us out of the wilderness of law and order problems. Our committees and the members of the staff have enjoyed greatly their association with you. We have admired your work and hope the new innovations you introduced and ideas you developed will continue to contribute effectively to the situation here in Detroit."* Dwight Havens, President of the Greater Detroit Chamber of Commerce

*"I felt an obligation to tell you that I think you performed an outstanding service for the community of Detroit. So many times people in public service seem to get nothing but abuse. To me you gave every indication of dedication to your profession.*

*The causes of crime are pride, greed, envy, and lust. To eradicate these is more in line with my work than yours and if there is greater love of God among our people*

*then crime will lessen. Once a man looks upon his fellow man as a person created by God and knows he must live that way then he will treat his neighbor as one of noble birth regardless of the color of his skin or the size of his bankroll. Poverty of this world's goods may be one thing which helps a person to find riches in crime but I do know for certain that poverty of the love of God causes crime."* Father William Breandan of St. Dominic's Church, Detroit.

# CONFESSIONS OF AN AMERICAN SHERIFF

*To Carol
Best Wishes*

# CONFESSIONS OF AN AMERICAN SHERIFF

◆

The Nicest Sheriff in America?

*Johannes F. Spreen*
With Dr. Diane Holloway

iUniverse, Inc.
New York Lincoln Shanghai

# CONFESSIONS OF AN AMERICAN SHERIFF
### The Nicest Sheriff in America?

Copyright © 2007 by Johannes F. Spreen

All rights reserved. No part of this book may be used or reproduced by any means, graphic, electronic, or mechanical, including photocopying, recording, taping or by any information storage retrieval system without the written permission of the publisher except in the case of brief quotations embodied in critical articles and reviews.

iUniverse books may be ordered through booksellers or by contacting:

iUniverse
2021 Pine Lake Road, Suite 100
Lincoln, NE 68512
www.iuniverse.com
1-800-Authors (1-800-288-4677)

The views expressed in this work are solely those of the author and do not necessarily reflect the views of the publisher, and the publisher hereby disclaims any responsibility for them.

ISBN: 978-0-595-44462-5 (pbk)
ISBN: 978-0-595-88789-7 (ebk)

Printed in the United States of America

*I dedicate this book to the men and women in law enforcement who give so much of themselves to protect others. I particularly single out sheriffs and sheriff's departments, who endure the additional burdens of often being overlooked, undermanned, and underpaid. This includes you, Jay, who allowed me to ventilate about the political problems which encumber sheriffs.*

*I also dedicate this book to my good wife, Sallie, for her love, support and encouragement in this project and upon whom I depend so much, and to my wonderful daughter, Elizabeth Diane Spreen. These women have both made my life very worthwhile.*

# Contents

Illustrations . . . . . . . . . . . . . . . . . . . . . . . . . . . . . . . . . . . . . . . . . . . . . . . . xix
Prologue: Why I Wrote This Book Now . . . . . . . . . . . . . . . . . . . . . . . . 1
Introduction . . . . . . . . . . . . . . . . . . . . . . . . . . . . . . . . . . . . . . . . . . . . . . 5

## Part I — Before Being Sheriff

Before Being Sheriff . . . . . . . . . . . . . . . . . . . . . . . . . . . . . . . . . . . . . 11
Why I Left as Police Commissioner . . . . . . . . . . . . . . . . . . . . . . . . 15
City Council Members Had Their Own Agendas . . . . . . . . . . . . . . 15
Council Decisions Were Not Made Publicly . . . . . . . . . . . . . . . . . . 16
Results of "Studies" of the Detroit Police Department . . . . . . . . . . 17
Praise for the Scooter Program . . . . . . . . . . . . . . . . . . . . . . . . . . . . 18
Media Problems as Police Commissioner . . . . . . . . . . . . . . . . . . . . 23
Was It Time to Get Out of Dodge? . . . . . . . . . . . . . . . . . . . . . . . . . 26
Leveling with City Councilmen and Citizens . . . . . . . . . . . . . . . . . 27
I Was a Quitter! . . . . . . . . . . . . . . . . . . . . . . . . . . . . . . . . . . . . . . . . 28
Responses to Removing Myself as Detroit Police Commissioner . . . 31
Leaving Detroit with Class . . . . . . . . . . . . . . . . . . . . . . . . . . . . . . . 38
My Newspaper Articles . . . . . . . . . . . . . . . . . . . . . . . . . . . . . . . . . . 41
British Police Training Conference . . . . . . . . . . . . . . . . . . . . . . . . . 42
Report to Prosecuting Attorney of Oakland County on Police Protection in
  Oakland County . . . . . . . . . . . . . . . . . . . . . . . . . . . . . . . . . . . . . 45
My Announcement to Run for Sheriff . . . . . . . . . . . . . . . . . . . . . . 52
Why I Decided to Run for Sheriff . . . . . . . . . . . . . . . . . . . . . . . . . . 54
My First Venture into Politics . . . . . . . . . . . . . . . . . . . . . . . . . . . . . 59
What's Wrong with the Sheriff's Department? . . . . . . . . . . . . . . . . 62

Civilian Groups Can Help Law Enforcement . . . . . . . . . . . . . . . . . . . . . . . . . . 64
Spreen Campaign Headquarters. . . . . . . . . . . . . . . . . . . . . . . . . . . . . . . . . . 68

# Part II    *Being Sheriff*

## 1973 . . . . . . . . . . . . . . . . . . . . . . . . . . . . . . . . . . . . . . . . . . . . . . . . . . . . . . . . . . . 71
Changing the Sheriff's Program. . . . . . . . . . . . . . . . . . . . . . . . . . . . . . . . . . 72
An Early Lesson in Party Politics . . . . . . . . . . . . . . . . . . . . . . . . . . . . . . . . . 72
There Were No Rules of Conduct. . . . . . . . . . . . . . . . . . . . . . . . . . . . . . . . 73
What Ever Happened to Teamwork?. . . . . . . . . . . . . . . . . . . . . . . . . . . . . 74

## 1974 . . . . . . . . . . . . . . . . . . . . . . . . . . . . . . . . . . . . . . . . . . . . . . . . . . . . . . . . . . . 77
The Sheriff Don't Get No Respect! . . . . . . . . . . . . . . . . . . . . . . . . . . . . . . . 78
Commissioners Didn't Listen . . . . . . . . . . . . . . . . . . . . . . . . . . . . . . . . . . . 78
Being Popular Doesn't Always Help . . . . . . . . . . . . . . . . . . . . . . . . . . . . . 79
Trouble with a Rotten Apple. . . . . . . . . . . . . . . . . . . . . . . . . . . . . . . . . . . . 79
Replacing My Undersheriff . . . . . . . . . . . . . . . . . . . . . . . . . . . . . . . . . . . . . 80
Acceptance of My New Undersheriff. . . . . . . . . . . . . . . . . . . . . . . . . . . . . 81

## 1975 . . . . . . . . . . . . . . . . . . . . . . . . . . . . . . . . . . . . . . . . . . . . . . . . . . . . . . . . . . . 82
Longer Sentences for Crimes Using Guns . . . . . . . . . . . . . . . . . . . . . . . . 83
Improper Use of Deputies by Politicians . . . . . . . . . . . . . . . . . . . . . . . . . 86
No Local Support for Grants. . . . . . . . . . . . . . . . . . . . . . . . . . . . . . . . . . . . 87
I Was Investigated for "Gathering Intelligence". . . . . . . . . . . . . . . . . . . . 87
I Asked the State to Investigate Me . . . . . . . . . . . . . . . . . . . . . . . . . . . . . . 88
I Answered the Charge Against Me . . . . . . . . . . . . . . . . . . . . . . . . . . . . . . 90
I Finally Got My First Grant. . . . . . . . . . . . . . . . . . . . . . . . . . . . . . . . . . . . 91
Press Urges End of Probe. . . . . . . . . . . . . . . . . . . . . . . . . . . . . . . . . . . . . . 92
The Investigation Cleared the Department and Me. . . . . . . . . . . . . . . . 92
Commissioners Should Investigate Their Own . . . . . . . . . . . . . . . . . . . 94
Media Urged County to Stop Wasting Tax Dollars. . . . . . . . . . . . . . . . . 95

## 1976 . . . . . . . . . . . . . . . . . . . . . . . . . . . . . . . . . . . . . . . . . . . . . . . . . . . . . . . . . . . 97
Contract Policing Was Increasing . . . . . . . . . . . . . . . . . . . . . . . . . . . . . . . 98
The Pros and Cons of Contract Policing . . . . . . . . . . . . . . . . . . . . . . . . . 99
Open House at the Sheriff's Department. . . . . . . . . . . . . . . . . . . . . . . . 100

Does the Sheriff's Office Have What?................................100
Trying to Be Non-Political...............................................101
My Announcement to Run for a Second Term....................102
Plans to Contain Three Sources of Crime.............................102
Expansion Plans............................................................104
The Umbrella Concept of Police Services.............................105
Stopping Big Shots from Obstructing Justice........................105
Giving Publicity for Individual Anti-Crime Efforts.................106
Asking the Public to Support a K-9 Corps...........................107
Joining a Prosecutor Candidate for Election.........................107
Organizing Crime Watches and Patrols................................108
Opening a Reserve Program...............................................109
We Led the Michigan State Fair.........................................110
Swearing In Deputies Every Four Years...............................112

# 1977.........................................................................113
Sheriff Patrols Welcomed.................................................114
Police Executives Must Set Examples Even If It Means Going to Jail..........115
My Toothbrush and Walter Cronkite..................................121
The Case of the Deputy I Fired..........................................122
The Day They Turned Crime Over to Public Relations.......123
Michigan Sheriffs' Association Commended Me....................123
Unions and Lawyers.......................................................124
Police Administrators and Unions.....................................126
The Child Killer Investigation..........................................127
Rebuttal to Criticisms by Prosecutor Patterson....................136
Professionalism and Ethics...............................................136
Police Chiefs Thought I Was Taking Over.........................144
My Proposal to Support Local Police................................145
First Female Patrol Officer in Oakland County Sheriff's Department..........147

# 1978.........................................................................149
Asking Support from Sheriffs for Gubernatorial Run...........150
I Was Sued for $2.25 Million...........................................151
Poor Choice for My Defense............................................153

| | |
|---|---|
| The Sheriff's Role | 153 |
| Harmonizing Law Enforcement Efforts | 154 |
| Cleared of Contempt | 157 |
| Uncooperative County Commissioners | 157 |

## 1979 .................................................. 159

| | |
|---|---|
| Objections to Media Coverage | 160 |
| The Past and Future Sheriff | 161 |
| Law Enforcement Coordination | 168 |
| Reassuring My Deputies About Their Jobs | 173 |

## 1980 .................................................. 175

| | |
|---|---|
| Law Enforcement Life | 176 |
| Comments by Opposing Sheriff's Candidates | 179 |
| Invitation for Schools to Participate in ESCAPE | 179 |
| New ESCAPE Program | 180 |
| Auto Theft Training Seminar | 181 |
| Improvements in the ESCAPE Program | 181 |
| The Day I Nearly Got Shot | 184 |
| Criticisms by Opponents Running for Sheriff | 184 |
| Problems with Organized Crime Strike Force | 185 |
| Jail Overcrowding—No Simple Solution | 187 |
| Organized Crime Task Force Subsidized | 188 |
| Should I Get Involved with the Strike Force? | 189 |

## 1981 .................................................. 190

| | |
|---|---|
| Involving Citizens in the Sheriff's Department | 191 |
| Reorganized Crime Unit Still a Problem | 192 |
| Closed Schools Could Be Minimum Security Prisons | 193 |
| Our County Jail Was Full | 194 |
| Overtime Deputies Raised Concerns | 194 |
| Police Chiefs and Sheriffs—Partners | 195 |
| Politicians, Jails and the Mentally Ill | 200 |
| Our New Scooter Patrol | 208 |
| Resignation of My Undersheriff | 210 |

My Wife Was a News Item.............................................211
My Wife's Problems Became My Problems.............................213
My Posse Rode Again...............................................214

## 1982.............................................................216

I Could Add 38 Positions..........................................217
Honoring Our Volunteers and Employees.............................218
An Audit Cleared Me Again.........................................221
We Were Given a Bus...............................................222
Our ESCAPE Program Won Awards.....................................222
Our Jail Was Busting..............................................224
My Wife Kept Making News..........................................225
Short-handed and Over-crowded Jails...............................226
My Wife's Political Group Was Disliked............................227

## 1983.............................................................228

My Request to Regain 27 Deputies..................................229
My Wife Tried to Help.............................................229
Facts About Losing My Deputies....................................230
Prosecutor Uses Tricks to Reduce Debt.............................231
Competition for the Sheriff's Job.................................232
My Wife Becomes News—Again!.......................................232
Informing Commissioners of Overcrowded Jail.......................233
Jail Inmate Sues Sheriff's Office.................................234
Volunteer Gets Praise.............................................235
Crime Dog McGruff.................................................235
Judge Beer's Double Life..........................................236

## 1984.............................................................237

I Decided to Run For County Executive.............................238
Heat Builds for County Executive Race.............................239
Support for Me as County Executive................................242
No More Room......................................................242
Overtime Hours Became an Issue....................................243
I Lost the Election for County Executive..........................244

## Part III   *After Being Sheriff*

    A Legacy? .................................................... 249

    Community Policing: It Takes a Team ............................ 251

    Politics Today ................................................ 252

Epilogue ........................................................ 255

Synopsis ........................................................ 261

About the Authors ............................................... 265

# *Acknowledgements*

How and where does one begin writing acknowledgements? This was a tough nut to crack for me. I cannot begin to express the kindnesses, generosity, thoughtfulness, sacrifices, and lessons of the myriad of individuals who have contributed to this book.

From my very earliest years, I must give my dear parents credit for struggling to leave Germany and make a new start in America.

Over the last several decades, many wonderful people have assisted me to become who I am and help in the eventual completion of my career, my life, my writings, and this book.

I will be forever grateful to all my family members including my wives, Elinor—deceased mother of my daughter, Betty, and my current wife, dear Sallie, for their encouragement and support.

However, the single most determining person in completing this book was none other than my collaborator extraordinaire and co-author, Dr. Diane Holloway. Diane's patience, savvy, and guidance helped me put together my decades of research, recollections, and information.

I also want to thank Bob Cheney for his excellent proofreading and suggestions. And finally, I want to thank Ron Amack of iUniverse who has helped me publish so many books and has expressed confidence and excellent recommendations for these last four years.

# Illustrations

Cover: Oakland County Sheriff Johannes F. Spreen giving "deputy" badges to children.
Photo 1: A Detroit Police car with the slogan on the trunk "Protectors of Liberty."
Photo 2: Southern Police Institute graduates around 1956.
Photo 3: My wife, Elinor, and my daughter Betty in my New York City Police Department uniform about 1961 upon promotion to captain.
Photo 4: Governor William Milliken toured the Detroit Police Department on March 20, 1969, and tried out a scooter.
Photo 5: Detroit youth and police on July 22, 1969, when we opened a building for the PAYS program.
Photo 6: Showing Detroit police sergeants public information literature to be displayed in all precincts.
Photo 7: The Detroit Scooter Patrol interacting with children on May 14, 1969, at St. Agnes School.
Photo 8: Scooters used by the Detroit Police Department to patrol and train on Belle Isle.
Photo 9: Playing ping pong with Detroit youth in Buck Up Our Youth program.
Photo 10: Buck Up Your Police Department showing that we had raised $42,200 by that time.
Photo 11: Buck Up Your Police Department project results.
Photo 12: At the office in the spring of 1979, running for third term.
Photo 13: *The National Sheriff* journal cover.
Photo 14: Sheriff Spreen and Crime Dog McGruff at ESCAPE program and Big Boy.
Photo 15: Sheriff's posse of Shriners around 1980.
Photo 16: Volunteers working at Elias Brothers Restaurant to raise money for ESCAPE program around 1981.
Photo 17: Selling hot dogs to raise money for ESCAPE program.
Photo 18: Sheriff's deputies dressed as Crime Dog McGruff and his two offsprings—Ruff and Reddi at 1982 Superbowl.

Photo 19: Back cover, Johannes F. Spreen when he was appointed Police Commissioner of Detroit.

# Prologue: Why I Wrote This Book Now

I've decided at the age of 87, I do have definite opinions and have decided to state them. I've also decided to express my views in the form of letters to a Deputy Chief of a Texas county.

In 1996, I purchased a book, *America's Toughest Sheriff.* Sheriff Joe Arpaio and Len Sherman put a darned good book together. People should read it. In his introduction, co-author Len Sherman writes about Sheriff Arpaio, his history and his ideas. Arpaio, elected in 1992, had been in office three years by the time he wrote this book. He is still the sheriff. Controversial? Yes. However, he was easily re-elected no doubt because of this book and his ideas, holding office now for some 14 years.

Len Sherman's introduction is powerful, showing that the book is about much more than crime fighting. It's about belief in ourselves, belief in America, its values and its promises.

Think about this—Sherman's powerful paragraph.

> Government is not the enemy. Politics is not the enemy. Even political parties are not the enemy. They are all mere instruments of our collective will, and when that will falters, all those institutions and those ideas falter.

I knew Len Sherman before. We were both professors and met at conferences. What grabbed me were these continuing words:

> So if the government can no longer be depended upon to perform fairly and efficiently, and politicians and political parties are creaky and corrupted, then we must reinvigorate those organizations and those concepts with integrity and purpose, and jettison whatever and whoever cannot be redeemed.

I would have liked for Len Sherman to help me with a book. I met with Len at his Scottsdale home for about two hours, bringing him several boxes of material. However, Len told me then, and rightfully, that as I had been out of law enforcement for about 20 years, that it would be difficult to create a hook, peg, or angle to cater to the fancy of readers.

When *America's Toughest Sheriff* came out, I had it signed by Joe and Len Sherman. This is what Sheriff Arpaio stated on March 27, 1996: "To Sheriff Spreen. Thanks for your dedicated service. Very nice indeed."

I was completely surprised and pleased by Len Sherman's remarks as follows:

"To somebody who knows more than what's written here and who's lived through it all."

I agree with much (not all) of what Sheriff Arpaio said in his book and most of what he has done since. I also felt that way as sheriff in Oakland County, Michigan, for twelve years.

Although wooed by both parties as a Republican and Democrat, I ran as a Democrat. But as a result, I felt the lash of partisan politics.

While I did not get Len Sherman to work with me on this book about my sheriff career—the twelve toughest years of my police career—I did find a great person later. She was the first president of the West Valley Authors Association in Arizona, Dr. Diane Holloway, who has an excellent background and reputation, and great editing skills. We have worked together on four previous books on law enforcement and police work. She is with me on this one.

It is interesting to me that Joe Arpaio states that "being sheriff is the best job I've ever had." For me, being sheriff was the toughest job I've ever had. Sheriff Joe says: "Now I don't have to answer to any bureaucracy or chain of command. Now I answer directly to the people who elected me."

I felt the same way. I did not feel like a politician. I liked what the Republicans said to me when they were wooing me—"You have a four-year contract with the people." I liked that—being a law enforcement representative for the people. But whoa! I did not run their way—I ran as a Democrat and became an anathema. I was told by the chairman of the Republican Committee, Arthur Elliott, that I would not be funded if I ran as a Democrat—which became true.

Sheriff Joe was happy in his job. I was not. I thought I could be a law enforcement representative for the people, regardless of politics. How naïve I was. I was elected three times. I was the only Democrat serving at the county level elected by the people, surviving the Nixon landslide and the Reagan landslide, and becoming the only Democrat for twelve entire years. But consider the political situation. There were 27 county commissioners, mostly Republicans.

Two years after I became sheriff, a new position—county executive—was put in and was narrowly won by a Republican—Dan Murphy. Lots of problems ensued for me later. I don't know how many commissioners (supervisors) Maricopa County has for Joe Arpaio to contend with and I don't recall that they have a county executive. I resented the political niggardly mess from those who said I would have a four-year contract with the people. I was sincere. I was qualified. I had studied and practiced police work and law enforcement for over 30 years only to be stymied by vicious partisan politicians.

But then one gets hardened and tested in the crucible of vicious politics—if you can emerge safely. This book chronicles my story and my battles.

America's "toughest sheriff"—Joe Arpaio—is portrayed as a controversial, provocative and interesting man. Years ago, the media used the same terms about me, among other terms, of course. Years ago, also as sheriff, I went on desert training maneuvers twice with Paul Blubaum, a former sheriff of Maricopa County.

The title of this book is *Confessions of an American Sheriff—the Nicest Sheriff in America?* In view of the state of crime, corruption, and politics in this country now, it is my feeling that this book will offer information and insights from inside the political crucible—nicest sheriff or not. And I confess, one learns from problems, mistakes, and errors (to be elaborated on later). As a student of government, law enforcement, and politics by experience, and as a professor, my views may be of help to others.

My wife, Sallie, said "Sheriff Arpaio is proud of locking up all criminals come hell or high water, but isn't the prevention of crime a better course to pursue for the protection of people?"

Yes, that has always been my view and my goal. These pages are permeated with those concepts that I used and still live by. This is the "hook" or "peg" or "angle" that prompted this book, now!

And a guy 6'5"—250 pounds—who writes about love must either be a nut or be on to something. You decide!

# *Introduction*

I will use a talk I gave at an Arizona Police Chiefs' meeting on December 21, 2006, as the introduction to this book. This summary of my life and my orientation should serve as a good introduction for what is to come in my book.

Fellow Chiefs, Law Enforcement Officials and Friends, I want to thank Chief Dan Saban for this invitation and for allowing me to bring my Chief of Police, my wife, Sallie.

My title today is "American Law Enforcement Does Not Serve or Protect." That raises some hackles, right? You might think who the heck is this guy, 87 years old—some kind of a nut? Well, I've been called a nut, a dreamer, a visionary, and worse.

I've had 44 years in law enforcement. I don't even like the term "law enforcement." I like the term "policing."

As an old guy, I've been there. I've done that. I've survived damn near everything. Now at my age, I'm not afraid to speak up.

As a young guy, I was an athlete. Pretty good in baseball, tennis, race walk, swimming, won medals. As you get older, the body goes but the mind is still involved. You've got to keep active. I taught memory courses. Then when I was 82, I decided to write some books.

I've written *American Police Dilemma* in 2003, *American Law Enforcement* in 2004, and *Who Killed Detroit: Other Cities Beware* in 2005. Because of that subtitle, other cities beware, we just wrote *Who Killed New Orleans* in 2005, and that just received first prize in non-fiction at the Arizona Authors Association. Then just to keep busy, I came up with a book not on law enforcement. It's a book for children aged 7-14 years about a young Indian brave and his sweetheart. I called it the *Saga of Thunderbird and Dancing Star,* published in 2006.

Let me take you very quickly through 44 years of law enforcement. I spent 25½ years in the New York Police Department and retired as chief of operations. I put in the two-wheeled scooters in 1964-1965. I was in charge of all the parks and also had the world's fair. We put scooters in Central Park. They were very successful. We got the first ones on loan. Then, Jackie Kennedy came with her little son, Jon Jon, to have a ride on a scooter. That generated some nice publicity. Then we added Prospect Park and then put the scooters in all the parks across the whole city.

Then we patrolled all New York City streets because captains in all 79 precincts liked them. We were written up in the *New York Times* and the *New Yorker Magazine*. The Police Commissioners, Mike Murphy and Vincent Broderick, liked them. In fact, Broderick changed his budget to order 700 more for street coverage. He wrote, "The scooter is the most effective police patrol technique which has been developed in recent years. It preserves the concept of the foot patrolman and yet provides mobility and responsiveness which the foot patrolman lacks."

Now, why did I leave the New York Police Department? One word. Politics. I haven't got the time to go into it.

As Police Commissioner in Detroit, I put the scooters there and they were very successful. But there were problems such as how to fund scooters. I got not one dollar from the Common Council of Detroit. I got my first 30 scooters from the Chamber of Commerce. My plea at a dinner at the Hilton with the Chamber of Commerce, Mayor Jerome Cavanaugh, and Baron Hilton was heard. It was a great day when I had 30 scooters lined up.

I then started a program called Buck Up Your Police. I went to the people. I said, "If you care about your police, send one dollar to us." The Jaycees picked it up and ran with it, and we made $50,000 for scooters and other needed things.

Why did I leave the Detroit Police Department? Politics. There was a change of mayors in New York and there was a change of mayors in Detroit. Then I went back to be a professor at the John Jay College of Criminal Justice in New York. I stayed in Michigan and flew weekly to New York for two years.

Then the Republicans and the Democrats both asked me to run for sheriff. I decided to run as a Democrat. The Republican Chairman, Arthur Elliott, said to me, "If you run as a Democrat, you will not be funded."

I said, "If I present my programs, and have data and statistics to back them up, I'm sure the commissioners will vote on their merits."

He said to me, "You are certainly naïve." And I guess I was at that time. I got very little help for 12 years. I was the only Democrat at the county level.

But how did I fund the scooters in the sheriff programs? We sold hot dogs and beer at the Pontiac Silverdome. Then we sold the most programs ($19,000 or 67,000 programs in one day) that had ever been sold at Superbowl 16 with 150 volunteers. We had help from volunteers in Explorer Scouts, Reserves, Shriners, and a program called ESCAPE (Enroll in Sheriff's Crime and Accident Prevention and Education). I even had jail inmates out in the streets planting flowers.

Why did I leave as sheriff after three terms? Politics. Well, I was 65. I figured now I could go on social security. That was many years ago.

I felt my scooter patrols in New York City, Detroit, and as Sheriff were very successful. We led the Michigan State Fair parade. My nickname was "Scooter Spreen" and I was riding a horse named "Scooter." She was a beauty of a horse but I lost her—because I married another girl.

I am giving you copies of my book, *American Law Enforcement Does Not Serve or Protect*. I suggest you read the last chapters, especially about Dual Policing. Police must work directly with the people they serve. You've got to reach the hearts and minds of people. Most people will help you. I had a slogan in the Police Department, "It takes a team—you and your police."

People have helped me in New York, Detroit, and as Sheriff. And people will help you. But you must provide a police officer that has a name, a face, and a smile. And you can't do that just inside of police cars. Police cars are the response—after the fact—after the crime. They don't protect and serve, they just respond later. We need to be proactive with scooters, bikes, or segways. We must have a presence if we are to protect and serve. You've got to be out there and talk to people—and, of course, that's how you get your information to learn who the bad guys are and what they're doing.

August Vollmer, police chief at Berkeley, made this comment a long time ago. "We now have the police car, we have the radio. Foot patrol is obsolete." Most police departments now use only cars and that's just not enough.

It's been my pleasure to be with you today. I will leave you with my definition of police, which I put on the back of police cars in Detroit when I was commissioner. I say that POLICE stands for Protectors Of Liberty for Individuals, Community, and Everyone Equally.

A Detroit Police car with the slogan on the trunk "Protectors of Liberty."
I established this design change while serving
as Detroit's Police Commissioner.

# PART I
## Before Being Sheriff

# Before Being Sheriff

My mother and father brought me to America in 1923 when I was four years old. We settled in Brooklyn. I went to school and learned to speak proper English.

When I was 18, a friend, Freddy Bogens Berger, suggested that we study to become police officers. I agreed and then I passed the exam but Freddy didn't.

I became a police officer in the New York City Police Department (NYPD) at age 21. After two years as a cop, World War II arrived and I chose to enlist as an aviation cadet in the U.S. Army Air Corps. I became a lieutenant bombardier, and then an instructor (then in B-29s). Remember the Enola Gay? That B-29 plane dropped the bomb on Hiroshima. If the Enola Gay had failed or if the war had not ended after August 6$^{th}$ where might I be? I was lead bombardier for our group. Would I have had to drop the atom bomb? I'm glad I didn't have to face that.

We defeated Germany—our enemy then. What if my mother and father had remained in Germany? Things would have been quite different for me. I remember the Olympics in 1936. They were held in Berlin, Germany, and Hitler was there. I was 17 then. Probably I would have been forced into the Hitler Youth (like our new Pope Benedict), marching and shouting "Heil Hitler." Then I probably would have been a soldier in the German Army, goose-stepping in parades. Or maybe I would have been an S.S. officer—Achtung! Or Hitler's bodyguard—or worse!

Thankfully, after the war I went back to policing in 1946. I studied and went up in the ranks. I finally started college at age 35. After 12 years, I achieved a bachelor's degree, then a master's, and did considerable work on my doctorate—all but my dissertation.

I retired from the NYPD in 1966. I became a professor at John Jay College in New York. Then I was asked to come to Detroit to be their Police Commissioner in 1968. I saw it both as a challenge and an opportunity.

After serving as Police Commissioner, I was briefly a consultant to the Oakland County Prosecuting Attorney which led me into examining the needs of the county. That convinced me to run for Sheriff of Oakland County in Michigan and I served there for 12 years.

I ended all this in 1985 but still keep abreast of the law enforcement (policing) field as a concerned citizen. After a lifetime in law enforcement, I've seen and learned a lot and formed many opinions about policing and about the law enforcement profession which I love.

I have kept file cabinets full of information, letters, reports, news articles, and documents which scream to be shared with the public. Therefore, it is not just my memory but also my files that enable me to report so accurately on my 12 years as sheriff.

Southern Police Institute graduates around 1956.
I was the first lieutenant from the New York City Police Department to attend this three-month course. I am on the upper row, farthest on the right.

My wife, Elinor, and my daughter Betty in my New York City Police Department
uniform about 1961 upon promotion to Captain.

## Why I Left as Police Commissioner

Dear Jay,

Early in my tenure as Detroit Police Commissioner, I suggested a "love-in" on St. Valentine's Day. In that uptight city, I thought a smile would help everybody. I think it bought us some time after the deadly four-day riot of 1967. Now, I hoped that a new police administration plus two cool summers would help the people of Detroit and their police to move forward as a team. This team could make Detroit the kind of city we could all live in and be proud of, without fear.

I initiated a "Love In" on Valentine's Day to run for 100 days. Bob Talbert of the *Detroit Free Press* wrote on February 21, 1969, "Spreen's Love-In: Here's Why We Can't Afford Not to Join."

> On July 22, Spreen took office, inheriting a department's troubled past, and an immediate riot anniversary confrontation the next day ...
>
> So Big John Spreen has now asked us for love ...
>
> So what is this love that Johannes Spreen is talking about? He says:
>
> "It's caring about your neighbor so you report an assault you witness upon him or his home. It's caring about your city so that you don't want to see it suffer. It's doing your thing well within the law and within the bounds of propriety. It's putting your personal desires and politics second to your concern for your city.
>
> "It's helping to professionalize your police rather than policing your police. It's your never getting tired of asking what can we do to help. It's wanting to change things with calm, cool reason and considered judgments, not with destructive 'to hell with it' attitudes. It's having faith in people and police officers and the hope we can all live together in a better Detroit ...
>
> Spreen has laid it on the line. You and I can't afford not to join his "Love-In."

## City Council Members Had Their Own Agendas

Dear Jay,

I tried to improve things but I found it very frustrating to deal with city council members in Detroit. Little did I know then that these politicians would be nothing compared to what I would find later as Sheriff.

David Cooper, a reporter for the *Detroit Free Press,* captured some of my frustration in a 1969 article entitled "When the Council Turns on the Heat." I was appearing before Detroit's Common Council, making a presentation about needed improvements to the city's police department.

Spreen had a prepared text. He had barely begun, however, before he was interrupted by Councilman Billy Rogell. Soon, other councilmen were jumping into the middle of Spreen's careful presentation.

At one point during a later discussion, Rogell told the commissioner, "Don't give me that stuff!"

Rogell's comment sounded more like something the former Tiger player might have shouted at an umpire whose call he did not like than what a councilman would say to a commissioner.

Councilwoman Mary Beck was chairing the meeting, and kept relatively quiet until a TV cameraman placed a microphone by her side. After that, she was off and running.

Earlier last week, police department officials went before councilmen on a minor request. The proposal was comparatively simple, but most councilmen did not seem to understand it. One of their problems may have been that various councilmen kept interrupting police officials during the explanations.

At times, one of the city's new councilmen, Robert Tindal, speaks so often and interrupts so frequently that he seems to be trying to become the council's male Mary Beck …

When the Common Council learns to listen, it may begin to fulfill its constitutional duty as a legislative body.

## Council Decisions Were Not Made Publicly

Dear Jay,

I'll summarize an article from another reporter, Mark Beltaire, who wrote an article called, "Our Secret Council" for the *Detroit Free Press*. He was quite critical of the decision-making method used by those planning the welfare of the City of Detroit. In instances like this, the press is serving the public well to reveal operational flaws in those they have elected.

If Detroit's Common Council feels itself misunderstood, it can thank its own methods of operation for leading to that condition.

All the hastily assembled press conferences in the world cannot make up for the fact that the council operates in secret. The real budget decisions were not made as David Cooper of our city-county bureau has noted, in those 22 votes of 9-to-0 to override the mayor's veto.

They were made by the council in informal sessions, away from the glare of public attention. Surely, in those sessions, there were shadings of opinion that the people ought to know about. Some individual differences were brushed aside in the drive for a show of unity.

Still a third article on this subject was by John Griffith, for the *Detroit Free Press*. He quoted me when I said, "We must solve the crime and community tensions now—today. And there is only one way, the right way. The choice is there: the tax collector or the mugger, the burglar, the robber or worse. If the police are shortchanged, so is every Detroiter."

There were more tensions as Detroit had become a hot spot for various black nationalist groups. Meetings and conferences were constantly being held, many of which fired up people against the Vietnam War and the white control of the inner city of Detroit. It often fell to law enforcement officers to fight a losing battle to control crime and violence.

## Results of "Studies" of the Detroit Police Department

Dear Jay,

You know how politicians like to delay decisions while a "study" takes place. We had studies out the kazoo!

As if Detroit didn't have enough problems, I was trying to reform problems within the police department. I had outside advisors studying the department and they had concluded that we were short by at least 1,000 men. I was so upset about the off-handed refusal to add manpower that I nearly quit, but instead decided to stay on. Another newspaper story by the editor of the *Free Press* was "Spreen's Decision to Stay Offers Council Reprieve." Here are a few of the comments in this article, referring to ex-Mayor Miriani's comments about me:

> Louis Miriani ... produced the inane quote of the week when he said, "I thought we had a pretty good Police Department for many, many years. I don't know what he has done with the Police Department since he's been here."
> 
> The answer is obvious if Miriani or the other council members would look. During his first months on the job, Spreen conducted the most effective recruiting program in the department's history. He introduced the scooter patrol, despite a great deal of ridicule, and the scooters have proved popular and effective. He's gotten more men on the streets, and is currently having an efficiency study made of the entire department, from his office on down.
> 
> And he's been on the chicken and peas circuit, drumming up popular support for a dispirited department, meanwhile fending off the long knives wielded by Common Council and trying to make do with one of the most undermanned forces in the country on a per capita basis.

I also had problems with micromanagement by city councilmen. An example was in still another newspaper article entitled "Council Interferes with Spreen." This article referred to Philip, the son of former Detroit Mayor Eugene Van Antwerp.

> In a week marked by more than its quota of silliness, one of the silliest statements was Councilman Philip Van Antwerp's hint that if Police Commissioner Spreen doesn't promote more detectives Common Council may charge him with "malfeasance or misfeasance" in office ... It is precisely because of this sort of interference and restriction that the job of police commissioner in Detroit is so difficult. How does the council know that 70 percent of the detectives deserve promotion to sergeant?
>
> The police commissioner ought to have some latitude over promotions, and he ought not to be given a quota by the Common Council or by the detectives association. To impose this kind of restriction on him is to undermine his ability to do his job ...
>
> If there is misfeasance in office, it may instead be in the council, which bartered away the commissioner's power to decide how many detectives deserve promotions.

## Praise for the Scooter Program

Dear Jay,

There had been lots of criticisms of the scooter program I introduced. Then Will Muller wrote an article for the *Detroit News* called "Jeers Switch to Cheers for the Scooter." This reporter recognized the problems that faced me as Jerome Cavanagh decided not to run for mayor and what that might do to my position in an administration that did not select me. However, the article may have hurt me by being so flattering that mayoral candidates saw me as a rival or someone having my own following.

> There is, of course, the recent *Detroit News* poll which showed 55 percent of all Detroiters crediting Spreen's department with fair enforcement....
>
> Last week, six women, led by an officer of the National Association for the Advancement of Colored People, went to the department and offered their best help ... In the absence of leadership elsewhere, many people are looking to Spreen.
>
> Every count was against Johannes Spreen when he took the job. He was an outsider police officer, a former operations director in the New York department, certain to be resented within the Detroit department. He came at the call of a mayor in deep political trouble who had been hunting for months for

a police commissioner to take over a city deep in racial trouble. Spreen has been here less than one year. It's something for Detroiters to say in a public opinion poll, in street discussions and by their actions that they have more empathy for him than for their own councilmen.

Governor William Milliken toured the Detroit Police Department on March 20, 1969, and tried out a scooter.
I had introduced scooters when I was Police Commissioner of Detroit.

Detroit youth and police on July 22, 1969, when we opened a building for the PAYS Program.
We initiated the Police and Youth in Sports (PAYS) program when I was Police Commissioner of Detroit.

Showing Detroit police sergeants public literature to be displayed in all precincts.

# Media Problems as Police Commissioner

Dear Jay,

I often had trouble with the press who rushed to publish "news" without checking the facts. On November 12, 1969, I tried to correct that with this letter to the editor of the *Detroit News*:

> To the Editor:
>
> On November 1, 1969, the *Detroit News* published a letter to the Editor signed "Detroit Parents" which accused the Detroit Police Department of gross neglect of duty in a very serious incident. May I, on behalf of the officers of our Department, attempt to set the record straight.
>
> The parents' letter indicated that while their 18-year-old son was on a date with his girlfriend, the girl had been forced at gunpoint to accompany an unidentified male and was subsequently raped by him. It was further alleged that the boy ran to a nearby street, stopped a police car, and told the officers what had happened. The officers reportedly told the youth to go home and go to bed. It was stated that, as a result of police inaction, the girl was brutalized and required hospitalization.
>
> The investigation conducted by ranking officers of the Department reveals that these allegations are far from the truth. Ten days before the parents' letter was published in the *News*, all parties concerned had been questioned by our Women's Division in the presence of the father of the alleged victim. During that investigation, the girl insisted that she was not sexually molested on the night in question—either forcibly or otherwise. It was also learned that a considerable amount of beer had been consumed by all persons in the girl's company at the time the alleged incident occurred.
>
> We have been unable to determine why the youth made the allegations. To our knowledge, no crime has been established; and the complaining youth now states that if he did talk to police officers, he is unable to remember the conversation.
>
> As Police Commissioner, it saddens me that a letter such as the one from "Detroit Parents" was given enough credence by your editorial staff to be published. It saddens me, too, that many thousands of your readers probably found it credible since it appeared in a paper which has such an outstanding record for objectivity and fairness. It saddens me that every member of our fine Department bears the punishment each time the Department is pronounced guilty without a chance to have our side heard.

> I appreciate the opportunity you have given me for "equal time." I still have faith in both the people and the police of our community—that we are all on the side of equal justice under fair law in an orderly society and that this applies to the Police Department's treatment of the community and the community's treatment of the Police Department.
> Sincerely yours,
> Commissioner Johannes F. Spreen

Jay, I'll just add a little more on this subject. I felt that the media was rushing to judgment and taking with it the public. *The Detroit News* was not the only newspaper guilty of sensationalism. In fact, I told Lee Hills, publisher of the *Detroit Free Press* (at the Italian Ambassador's Ball in 1969), "Mr. Hills, if your paper keeps printing this way about events and policing, you won't have a rag left to publish." I was quite incensed at the *Free Press* coverage which was usually more one-sided than the other papers.

This was happening at the same time that the public was getting ready to vote out Jerome Cavanagh and vote in Roman Gribbs.

Then I had a decision to make. Should I resign or stay as police commissioner under a new mayor? Unfortunately, I may have made that decision too rashly because of a thirty-minute meeting with Mayor-elect Roman Gribbs. That meeting left me with a very bad, even bitter, taste in my mouth. I essentially told him that I wanted to complete some important programs and stay on at least six months. However, I quickly realized he was just picking my brain to see what he could learn so he could carry on without me. He was not a sincere man, or at least not with me.

Right after our talk, a reporter asked Gribbs if he would keep me. He put the reporter off for about three weeks, leaving me in a kind of limbo. This feeling lingered and I was left up in the air. I had postponed vacations with my family since I had come to Detroit, and felt I didn't know which way to move.

When I came home from talking with Gribbs, my wife Elinor asked what the Mayor-elect said. When I told her, she asked if we were going to be able to go on a Florida vacation that we had planned or even go to New York for Christmas. That is when the frustrations piled up inside me. The commitment to my community took second place to my commitment to my wife and daughter. Elinor, in her obligation to her husband, had packed up, left the home in Lynbrook, New York, and come to Detroit to follow me despite many reservations and urgings by her friends not to do so.

I decided to tell the press that they and pressure groups had been a problem. My exact words were:

I have felt that a few news people now and then were more concerned about titillating an audience or generating a sensational headline that they were about calming community tensions.

I have felt that some of the spokesmen for the New Detroit Committee, that prestigious group to which we all look with hope, have tended to undo with injudicious comments some of the good their funds were being spent to accomplish....

The Mayor-Elect has not asked me to remain ... so I can only presume he has someone else in mind. Also, I understand that in some quarters, I am no longer considered acceptable because of my color.

Having considered all this, I feel that I have met my original commitment to Mayor Cavanagh and the people of Detroit, and I am consequently asking Mayor-Elect Gribbs to remove my name from consideration as the next Police Commissioner.

Heather Thompson wrote *Whose Detroit?* She stated that Gribbs was a "leader in law enforcement who played continuously on white fears of black 'criminality' and 'dependency'." Indeed, Gribbs promised an "all out fight against crime in the streets."

She continued, "When Gribbs suggested the creation of 'small units of police' with crime-fighting responsibility assigned to certain neighborhoods, city liberals, both black and white, feared that this would only increase hostility between police and inner-city residents" (Thompson, 79-80).

Gribbs ran on a law and order program saying he would use all necessary policing to crack down on crime. He won a very narrow victory over Richard Austin, 257,312 to 250,020. It was the closest political contest in Detroit history. He didn't have a clear mandate from the people so his victory did not ease the tensions; in fact, it exacerbated them.

Thompson wrote that Gribbs' victory did not quiet the radical critics in the African American community. She charged that Gribbs' pro-law enforcement platforms and Austin's defeat not only led poor and working class blacks to become even more politically active, but made them far more radical than Austin had ever been.

Richard Austin died in 2001, after serving as Michigan's Secretary of State, re-elected five times to that position. He reshaped the office and changed it from a political patronage office to a more service-oriented operation. I always felt we missed a great opportunity when he lost the mayoral election. What a pity that the city was not ready for this man who could have united races and created a better Detroit.

## Was It Time to Get Out of Dodge?

Dear Jay,

After Gribbs took office, whites should have felt more secure. However, as Thompson pointed out, black and white revolutionary sentiment became more popular and powerful. Thompson said that caused many whites to begin embracing politics far to the right as the only way to combat the perceived threat.

When I withdrew my name from consideration for Police Commissioner, I received a copy of the following letter to Mayor Elect Gribbs on December 5, 1969, from the 12$^{th}$ Precinct Community Relations Committee.

> Dear Mayor-Elect Gribbs,
> We realize that you must presently be very busy formulating plans before you assume your office in January. In spite of this fact, we write now because we also know that once in office, your schedule will be an even busier one.
> As concerned and involved citizens of Detroit (and we do consider ourselves as such) we desire that you know and understand our feelings regarding Police Commissioner Johannes Spreen. We would like to see him retained in his position.
> During the past two years, we have cooperated with the Police Department of the 12$^{th}$ Precinct through an organization we jointly formed, whose name this letterhead bears. This relationship was begun with the belief that this would help Detroit remain a good place to live, work and raise our families. Our close association with our police of the 12$^{th}$ Precinct and the other members of the Police Department in our city convinces us that we are on the right road.
> On numerous occasions, we have collectively and individually received encouragement to continue, from Commissioner Spreen. He has, as a result of personal interest, encouraged and instructed the police to help us. It has, we feel, been a fruitful effort for both sides.
> Our group is composed of members of all neighborhood organizations in the 12$^{th}$ Precinct, as well as interested citizens and businessmen. This area, as you may know, is comprised of approximately 120,000 people. We urge you to retain, with confidence in our support, Johannes Spreen as Police Commissioner.
> Should you desire further elaboration on our position, we would be most willing to discuss this with you at your convenience.
> Sincerely yours,
> N. R. Litt, chairman
> 12$^{th}$ Precinct, Community Relations Committee

# Leveling with City Councilmen and Citizens

Dear Jay,

I gave a press conference on December 9, 1969, in Detroit, only16 months after accepting the position of Police Commissioner of Detroit. I explained to the press that three studies had been conducted of the police department. Highlights of a study by the International Association of Chiefs of Police were that the Department suffered from a shortage of supervisory personnel and uniformed sergeants for field supervision. They suggested that the department needed reorganization with fewer sergeants in the detective bureau. This was the opposite of what Van Antwerp on the Common Council had suggested.

Two other reports commended our personnel and recruiting operations, but agreed that the police staff needed the help of trained labor relations experts to negotiate with employee organizations. They agreed that recruit training was good but more in-service training was needed after graduation from the police academy. I certainly agreed and had instituted the Seven Minute Training videos as well as some other training, but more was definitely needed. It was like expecting a doctor to practice medicine after graduating from medical school without any additional training or reading.

The reports expressed particular interest in the community-oriented scooter patrol innovation and suggested that it be given a full opportunity to prove itself. They suggested further study of scout car operations, and a more effective utilization of available equipment and personnel. One report stated that the basic neighborhood patrol officer should be a well-rounded "generalist," which is exactly what we wanted our scooter cops to be.

The reports stated that the department needed at least an additional 1,000 police, as well as additional radios, cars, cameras and tape recorders. Our women's division was highly complimented by the Arthur Little researchers for their preventive work with youth and good rapport with the community.

I told the press that it was unprecedented that a police department should be so forthright about self-improvement and so confident in community understanding that it would lay the results on the table. We had nothing to hide. We considered these surveys to be tools to improve police performance.

Lawrence Carino, General Manager of the WJBR-TV2 station, delivered these comments on his television station following a December 9th interview.

Johannes Spreen's withdrawal from consideration as Police Commissioner in the new city administration was not entirely unexpected. Nevertheless, the reasons behind his decision should seriously concern all Detroiters.

There has been, as he said, a disturbing tendency in some quarters to assume that police officers are guilty of some abuse of authority until they are proven innocent.

There has been the negative attitude Spreen has so often encountered in his dealings with Common Council, with his constructive proposals for the Police Department too often lost in the endless bickering between Council and the Mayor's Office.

There has been the frustration of having to spend too much time reacting to problems of the past, and too little in developing programs for the future.

There has been the necessity of delaying needed improvements in the department until some outside agency completed yet another police study.

More personally, Spreen has had to endure the pain of being told by his daughter that he is commonly referred to by their classmates as the "head pig."

And now, presumably, Spreen will have the final disappointment of leaving the job just as many of the promising programs he put in motion are beginning to show results. And Detroit, in turn, will be losing a police administrator of uncommon vision and ability.

When the burden of the Commissioner's office passes to someone else—as now appears definite—TV2 hopes it is a man who can serve the community as effectively as Johannes Spreen.

## I Was a Quitter!

Dear Jay,

Earlier I wrote a book called *"Who Killed Detroit?"* I feel responsible to this day! Coming out of New York, I came to love the City of Detroit and its people. I wrote that the 17 months I served as Police Commissioner were much more satisfying to me than the twelve years I served as Oakland County Sheriff. You will soon understand why.

I feel that many decision-makers on the Common Council, New Detroit, Detroit Police Department, FBI, and other government groups played a part in the decline of Detroit. Yes, they were usually good-hearted and tried to do the best they could. But they could have done better. The police have been blamed too long and too often without others taking their share of the heat.

Certainly, the hate groups played a large part and often operated through violence. However, so did the criminals, both organized and unorganized and La Cosa Nostra in particular. The drug users, hippies who promoted a selfish lifestyle and loudmouths who appeared before groups requesting money played a part.

The people who fled Detroit are as responsible as the businesses that moved away and left huge employment gaps. The real estate industry that made a shambles of housing for blacks, segregating them totally from whites, played a major role.

Yes, when I took the job as Police Commissioner I thought I could help. I sincerely feel I did. I wish I had stayed because that job was important, challenging, and serious. Nevertheless, I removed myself from that important position when I became frustrated. Therefore, I must shoulder some of the blame.

Why did I leave? Because of politics—damned politics! A man, if he is caring and concerned, has obligations. Obligations to the community he lives in, to his family and to himself. In the month of December, 1969, they all came into play. But I made my decision after the meeting with Gribbs due to his cavalier attitude. I thought we were friends. He was Sheriff of Wayne County with an office across the street from police headquarters. We had met several times. Again, like New York, a change of mayors meant a change of police commissioners.

All in all, I decided it was time to get out of Dodge, even though I'd never been to Dodge City, Kansas, and didn't know why the sheriff left.

I am sad about the condition of the city where I came to do a job. Detroit's citizens and the police were responding, but I was disappointed when Mayor Cavanagh, who had told me he would run again, did not.

In addition, he did me a disservice. He put me in two polls which included his name along with Richard Austin and Roman Gribbs for mayor. (Ed Robinson, a former top aide to Cavanagh, told me this later.) I led both polls for mayor but I did not want to be a mayor. I feel that "competition" soured the former friendly relationship I had with the Sheriff of Wayne County, Roman Gribbs. He became mayor by one half a percent (.05%) of the total vote. Gribbs' opponent Richard Austin had named me as Police Commissioner. There probably was no way that Gribbs would have appointed me even if I had not withdrawn my name.

In retrospect, I often wish that when reporters asked if I would remain as Police Commissioner with Richard Austin, I would have given a different reply. I would like to have continued with many programs such as the Community-Oriented Police Scooter Program. After the shabby treatment by Mayor-Elect Gribbs, I chose with sadness not to be "evaluated" by him for Police Commissioner. However, as John Greenleaf Whittier said, "For of all sad tales of tongue and pen, the saddest are these: It might have been."

Gribbs brought in Patrick V. Murphy as police commissioner. He stayed only eight months. Murphy had 25 years experience as a New York police officer, just as I did, and served under me when he was a sergeant. He went from captain to deputy inspector before he left to become a police chief in Syracuse, New York, even while he was still employed by the New York City Police Department. Murphy was tapped for New York City police commissioner in October 1970, a post he held until 1973. That fine man went on to become Executive Director of Drug Policy Foundation and has an excellent reputation.

In Detroit, John Nichols followed Commissioner Murphy. Nichols was my former police department superintendent. Nichols served as police commissioner until he ran for mayor and was defeated in 1973.

Gribbs' most publicized accomplishment was the creation of STRESS (Stop The Robberies, Enjoy Safe Streets), composed of 100 mostly white police officers working in high crime areas (mostly black neighborhoods). STRESS engaged in surveillance and decoy operations.

Twenty-two Detroit citizens (mostly black) were killed by the STRESS officers, mostly shot in the back. It came to be known as a "killer squad." There is no danger to an officer when the suspect is running away from him! To do it properly, officers should be at both ends of a street where the decoy officer was. If an assailant runs at an officer, after commanding him to stop, he could legally shoot if he did not stop. Then he would be shooting him in the front—not the back.

Tension between the city blacks and the Detroit police was increasing rapidly. Black militants and black radicals made their voices ring in rebellion. STRESS became a rallying point for black militants. Many pages are devoted to it in the book by Dan Georgakas and Marvin Surkin. That book, *Detroit: I Do Mind Dying*, refers to me (page 56) when the Black United Front states that "public opinion was being misled by Governor Milliken, Police Commissioner Johannes Spreen, Mayor Cavanagh, Prosecutor Cahalan, the DPOA and *The Detroit News*, all of whom were guilty of racism."

That book made no mention of the many positive programs put into place following the riot of 1967. It devoted many pages to tearing down the police and the government of the city. STRESS was a bad concept badly executed.

The STRESS program was ended by the next mayor, Coleman Young. However, there was lots of pushing by Sheila Murphy Cockrel. I was aware of her because she formed an Ad Hoc Action Group to monitor police activities after the 1967 riot. She became a lawyer and married Detroit attorney, activist and leader Kenneth Cockrel in 1978. She served two terms on the Detroit City Council, and may still be serving on the City Council. She's a life member of the

NAACP and in 1968 was nominated by anthropologist Margaret Mead to receive the Mademoiselle Award honoring 26 young women who carved niches for themselves beyond traditional areas.

After being Police Commissioner, I resumed teaching at John Jay College. Having made my home in Michigan, I flew into New York weekly to handle a full teaching load of 12 semester hours and was also Director of the Law Enforcement and Protection Program at Mercy College of Detroit.

I brought in some Detroiters to be guest lecturers in my police administration courses. One course called "The Impact of Media on the Administration of Criminal Justice," I developed with the author of the well-known book *Sybil*, Flora Rheta Schreiber. She was a colleague and English teacher at John Jay.

Jay, I know you do some teaching and I hope this is helpful to you.

## Responses to Removing Myself as Detroit Police Commissioner

Dear Jay,

I received a thousand or more letters in response to the news that I wanted to remove my name as police commissioner from Mayor-elect Roman Gribbs, after he talked with me and indicated little interest in keeping me.

These letters, excerpted below, served as a guide to what citizens expected and valued from their police force. Since I did not expect to write a book, I obtained no permission from any of these people to use their quotations. I will not violate their privacy by revealing their exact identity.

Mrs. John Theodorou wrote after her policeman husband died in a Detroit shooting: "I am the widow of the late John Theodorou who lost his life from one of the shootings Friday November 22$^{nd}$, 1969.... I doubt if you remember but you met John and his little old brown dog in DeSantis's Parking lot when you paid your respect to another policeman who lost his life, Paul Begin. John was very impressed by you and told me he hoped you were going to stay on in your present position. I now add my hopes to his that you will not want or have to desert our bullet shattered, blood spattered, body strewn aching and tired city." I did remember her husband well and wrote her about my memories of her husband.

Mrs. Hazel F. wrote: "Last week I saw two young patrolmen walking the beat on Whittier and Kelly. It gave me a wonderful feeling and I told them so....

These two officers seemed very pleased and wished that more people would tell them how they felt about them. The fact that they were there is another credit to you. How long will they be around when you are gone?"

A black officer I met on the night we stopped the riot, patrolman Crear M., wrote: "Coach, the city had a great season under your leadership … It was great being on the same team with you."

A resident of Windsor, Canada, wrote: "As a former Detroit resident, I am taking the liberty of writing to voice my regrets on your resignation. I am 70 years young, retired, living in Windsor. I worked and lived in Detroit for 40 years. Fear drove me to reside in Windsor…. From one who appreciates the time and effort you gave so freely to make Detroit a better place to live."

Michael A. Y. wrote: "I think you have brought a warm heart to the leadership of the police department and thereby helped to humanize our idea of the police. There remains, it is true, a wide gap between our black citizens and our police, but I believe this gap has been reduced, at least among the moderate segments of the black community. Unquestionably, you have been the 'people's choice' in the white areas of our city."

Linda and Gary G. wrote: "I was very sorry to hear of your resignation. My husband and I feel that you have done a fantastic job in bucking up the Detroit Police Department. You have taken a badly beaten department and transformed it into something we both are proud of…. Now that you have made the Detroit Police Department something to be proud of, the job of Commissioner becomes a political plum."

Mr. and Mrs. George L. J. wrote: "My husband and I are two of many people in Detroit who are concerned for our children, our homes and our city. You gave us hope that the police can work in and with the community and perhaps there is hope and a reason for staying in Detroit. You made part of the news interesting and more exciting in that we knew something was being done to help us and our city."

A Redford High School student, Sherry W. wrote: "You are really 'with it' as shown by your groovy 'love-in,' in which Detroit gained some good favorable national publicity for a change. I am 15 and I think it is terrible that some of the other teens call the police 'pigs'. I feel that without police everyone would be pigs!"

James D. M. of Townline Realty wrote: "I am not or never have been a resident of Detroit but I know that what happens to Detroit directly affects us here in the suburbs and all of Michigan eventually. Thanks for a job well done."

John A. M., coordinator of the law enforcement program of the State of Connecticut, wrote: "I just read in the newspaper about Pat Murphy accepting your job. I'm sorry that you have lost out in the game of politics and hope that you have a suitable position to go to. If not, please contact me and I would see that you got hired on the September 1970 faculty vacancy on our law enforcement staff."

Every student of the fourth grade at Sumter School wrote me and a sample of one of their letters is from Bradley Scott D. "Mrs. Green's fourth grade class would like to tell you how much we appreciate your fine work. We are sad you are retiring. We wish you good luck in the future. We hope people stop calling you policemen bad names ..."

Attorney Walter S. N., whom I had seen many times in court, wrote: "More than 75% of our contact has been on the basis where I was advocating the position of a client or clients. This letter has nothing to do with advocacy. In my judgment, your stay in Detroit was all too short. You accomplished much to increase the possibility of the Detroit Police Department becoming a fully professional institution within the foreseeable future. You have been the primary salesman in the community for the concept that just law enforcement is the only means by which the rights of all citizens be they police officers or not, can be assured. Your constant seeking for recognition of the fact that with rights and power go equal and concomitant responsibilities has been inspiring."

Jay and Mary Lou L. wrote: "We need more people like you in leadership positions, who are not afraid to talk about love and bringing people together."

Harold G. D., who owned a bookkeeping and tax service, wrote: "I wish to express my personal thanks for your efforts to encourage law and order in Detroit. Also your constant reminders of the principles of 'love thy neighbor as thyself.' ... Your police program has directed attention to our social reform program."

Mrs. James K. P. wrote: "My family and I have enjoyed more trips downtown and into Detroit this past year than we had in the several previous years and I feel that it has a lot to do with our feeling that we had nothing to fear, thanks to the Detroit Police. If you haven't done anything else, it is so reassuring to see the policemen on duty either in patrol cars or on foot.... I liked your Buck Up the Police idea and contributed to it."

Brian P. C. wrote: "I am 19 years old and a student at Wayne State University ... It is so sad and yet somehow so sickeningly inevitable that you be victimized by that utterly detestable group of pseudo-political hot dogs that infest city hall ... For in a world of such hypocrisy and self-seeking public service, the sincerity, creativity, and fair-minded justice you have exhibited are truly an inspiration."

Pete K. wrote: "I am twenty years of age and a college student. I would like you to know that for the first time in almost two years I went downtown to see the auto show. You know what? It really felt safe down there for the first time."

Bonnie J. wrote: "I've never written a fan letter before, but I've been a fan of yours since you took office as Detroit's Police Commissioner.... You've brought a new vitality and enthusiasm to the Police Department. Your ideas have been refreshing and original. And you've helped give the police of this city a new, more humane image, which they really deserve."

Frank W. wrote: "Thank you for a job well done. You had style! You had flair! Your scooter program, the helicopter, the 'buck up your police', and the 100-day love-in were just great. I am truly glad you're staying in Detroit. History, later on, will bear testimony that you were right and the obstinate council, who had no guts, no vision, were wrong. The council couldn't turn the green light on. 'Hey, look about you' a saying my daughter told me about from Camp Dearborn last summer, reminded me of you. Soul is what it was. You made us all look up and around, and lifted our spirits high."

Physician Henry J. V., M.D., wrote: "I am certain you have laid a foundation for the development of a greatly improved department and respect for it by the people."

Mrs. Betty L. wrote: "One of the things I especially liked about you was the way you stood up for the men of your department. The police of Detroit have a very hard job and I think knowing you stood behind them boosted their morale and made them a better department. Another thing I like was the way you got out among the people letting them know you cared about them and about the community they lived in."

Judge John H. G. of the State of Michigan Court of Appeals wrote: "I am convinced that you have rendered a great service to the City of Detroit and have been one of the outstanding police commissioners Detroit has had over the past thirty years. The innovations that you have commenced with the Department are many. You have served during a most troublesome period and I think had there been a different commissioner, the racial tension would have been much greater."

A telegram from Dr. John F. B., the Wayne County Medical Examiner, read: "Your reasons for resignation are well-founded however I hope you will reconsider since the city needs you. You have done the best job yet."

President Rand H. of the Mayor's Committee "Keep Detroit Beautiful" wrote: "We had been so pleased with all you had accomplished for our city and were hoping you would continue with us."

Alison B. wrote: "I am a girl, fourteen to be exact, who is planning to be a policewoman. I read in the newspaper and saw on T.V. that you are leaving office. You will be a great loss to the police department. You're a very great man in my eyes. You have done so much to help combat crime in our streets. You have also proposed many good bills to make me wish I was of voting age to vote 'yes' on them.... Here is a copy of a poem I wrote that my mom wanted me to send along. Being a Policewoman is what I want to be very, very much.... Being a policewoman means helping not only those you love but helping all of mankind regardless of race, creed or religion."

Edward John "Jack" R., pastor of the Metropolitan Baptist Church, wrote: "Your contribution to Detroit will some day be equated to that of industry."

Joseph J. W. wrote: "I am the son of a Detroit police sergeant who retired several years ago, so perhaps I have more empathy for the kinds of situations you have had to deal with in your job. Both my wife and I are native Detroiters who love our home town, but who also moved to the suburbs before you took over. Although we can no longer vote in Detroit, my wife travels into town each day and I come in two evenings a week to study at Wayne. Therefore we both feel very grateful to you because you have done the best job possible to keep the streets of our home town safe."

Elaine H., secretary to Queen's Blue Collar Workers of America, wrote: "As a result of your efforts to promote a better understanding between the police-citizens and the inner city, many are recognizing the importance of the attempts to establish this line of communication."

Walter E. W., Service Director of the Marine Corps League, wrote: "May I commend you on a job well done and I am sure that had you stayed on as our Police Commissioner, this City would have become a safer one with less crime on our streets."

Thomas S. A. wrote: "I am a black man who has never written to a public official in all my 47 years. I feel impelled, however, to congratulate you for your efforts in regard to our police department and city as a whole. The best wishes of many thousands of blacks and whites go with you and your family regardless of destination."

Harrison E. B., Vice President and Treasurer of the Great Lakes Mutual Life Insurance Company, wrote: "I made several contributions to your 'Buck Up Your Cop' program with which to establish some of the equipment before denied you by the establishment. Detroit can hardly afford to lose men of your level regardless of capacity."

Mrs. Mamie M. wrote: "I only wish I could speak for the whole black race.... Whoever takes the job you are leaving whether his skin is black blue green white or grizzly would have to be a magician to deal with all the things I see going on in this world."

Annabelle L. wrote: "It is most refreshing to see my daughter return home from classes at Presentation Grade School and relate almost a one to one contact with the motor scooter patrolman who had a class conversation with these children and give the image of the policeman that I knew in my childhood.... I am black but live in a world of human beings who benefit based on merit and not color. We also marvel as a community that policemen are no longer in cars but are walking and talking and meeting people."

A twenty-year city employee who did not sign her name wrote: "I am so sad. I am black. I feel you have done and are doing a grand job and that you have a real interest in the City of Detroit. You care!"

Ann M. K. wrote: "It is policemen on scooters, policemen walking and talking and smiling policemen everywhere ... Actually life in Detroit has a new beginning."

Judith B. wrote: "It would be safe to assume that the bookmakers in 1967 would have given the Lord Jesus better odds in bringing back Lazarus from the dead than you had in breathing life back into the Detroit Police Department. The men in blue are finally beginning to enjoy more public support and respect, all of which must be attributed to your community-oriented programs."

Charles R. N., elevator starter, wrote: "You may recall me as the elevator starter at the Hotel Ponchartrain.... I believe I am one of the few who have moved from the suburbs back to Detroit to gain independence and enjoy the many things and places that Detroit has to offer ... Meeting the many guests and customers at my hotel, I extol the many virtues of our city in the way of museums, the fine Civic Center, theaters, parking and our fine zoo and shopping area and urge them to make use of them without fear ... In a recent visit to Cleveland to visit old friends, I was dismayed to hear from them that they refused to visit downtown because of the black problem.... My sixteen year old son has never had any trouble and remarks about the frequency of police patrols on foot and in cars and scooters."

An officer whom I knew, Jim K., wrote: "I am proud to have served the Department under your leadership and I am especially proud that you were the Commissioner that handed me my new badge on 11-21-69."

Mrs. L. R. C. wrote: "On Nov. 30, we drove our family downtown to see the lovely displays and decorations. I can say with all honesty we felt safe, we have always gone down before, but we never could get out of the car. We were just plain scared. This year was different. We saw policemen walking and two others on their scooters."

Of course, I had some letters from detractors. Mr. John G. B. wrote: "You certainly know how to blow your own horn, at least statistically. Have you ever been mugged or your children threatened if they didn't bring some money back to school with them after lunch? Guess not. Every time Spreen comes on my screen I could scream from pain in my spleen. This writer thinks Detroit will be better off without you and your grandiose ideas."

I wrote him, as I did the others, thanking him for his comments and explaining that my daughter went to a racially integrated school in the heart of Detroit.

I've got to tell you, Jay, that I'm quite embarrassed about all this. But I thought you might want to know some things that citizens appreciate so I sent them along.

## Leaving Detroit with Class

Dear Jay,

After I resigned as police commissioner, I decided to open the New Year of 1970 with good wishes to Detroiters. I thought I would return to teaching, write books and articles, do some consulting, rediscover my family, and get to see more of Michigan beyond the boundaries of Detroit.

Helen Fogel covered the story for the *Detroit Free Press* on January 1, 1970. The story, "A Wish for Detroit from the Spreens" came out with a picture of me and Elinor in front of our Christmas tree.

> The Johannes Spreens are wishing their adopted hometown a happy new year—and more than that …
> 
> "I hope," he said, that this is the year we reach an understanding that we are all people—the black community, the white community, the police community. I sometimes felt I was caught among the three …"
> 
> The Spreens came to Detroit 17 months ago where he took on one of the toughest—certainly, the most controversial job—in city government. During his tenure, he has worked intensely to maintain a high level of crime fighting, raise the level of police performance, especially in the area of "professionalism" and to stem the rift between police and the community and improve the relationship …
> 
> He explained how, on Moratorium Day, the scooter men had been mobilized when some 50 to 100 young people out of the thousands who took part became "troublesome."

"I shudder to think what might have happened if we had sent in armed, masked riot police," he said.

"The scooter cops pleaded, charmed, cajoled the kids," he said. "The kids have got their arms around the cop," he said. "That's the way it should be with the policeman—always there, helping, aiding, guiding, advising," said the retiring Commissioner.

"Happy New Year, Detroit."

The Detroit Scooter Patrol interacting with children on May 14, 1969, at St. Agnes School.

# My Newspaper Articles

Dear Jay,

I was asked to contribute articles to the *Detroit News* and I'm rather proud of one called "Can a 'pig' laugh?" printed on March 8, 1970.

> Police administrators and citizens recognize that in too many cases throughout the nation, police themselves have been part of today's problem of community tension and crime, instead part of the solution.
>
> What police are trying to do about it is to build complete and total "professionalism" into the practice of police work.
>
> The word "professionalism" is so much a part of the advanced police theory, training, and practice today that it is the most worn cliché in the police vocabulary.
>
> The substance behind the cliché is the principle upon which good, sincere, dedicated police officers must build in order to regain the citizen respect and community support police once had, but lost.
>
> The substance of what is meant by police "professionalism" is this:
>
> - Understanding the "what" and "why" of your professional role.
> - Knowing the "how" of police work thoroughly, and executing it proficiently.
> - Acting with firmness and impartiality to all people and in all circumstances.
> - Putting service before self.
> - Being better informed and alert to the sensitivities of particular individuals and groups.
> - Keeping one's "cool" always.
> - Performing so as not only to satisfy your own conscience, but also to stand scrutiny by the all-seeing public stare of the television camera.
>
> The true professional cop is color blind, except when it comes to traffic lights. He knows when to use a handshake instead of a handcuff. He recognizes the difference between a nuisance complaint and a genuine call for help.
>
> He knows how to laugh when he is called a "pig." He knows when to hold his fire, when that shadowy shape he's pursuing might be a boy, instead of a bandit.
>
> He understands when force is necessary, and he knows how to protect himself and the citizen who needs his help. However, he also knows when he is being baited and how to ignore the bait. In addition, he knows how to correct a dangerous traffic violation without making the violator resentful.

A professional who can do all these things has to be a paragon. But he can't get that way by accident, or through community neglect, or without sufficient education, training and incentive, or without a good mind, good body and firmness of character to begin with.

The making of a professional may start with the police ... but the process isn't complete until the total community has had a hand in the craftsmanship.

# British Police Training Conference

Dear Jay,

I was invited to a conference on Police Community Relations in England May 29-June 1, 1970. The Conference involved fifteen British and fifteen from the United States, including my replacement as Detroit Police Commissioner, Patrick V. Murphy.

By calling together an expert Anglo-American conference on police-community relations, a valuable interchange of experience and opinions from both sides of the Atlantic could occur.

In Britain, there is relative homogeneity whereas there is great diversity of the American population. In addition, there is disparity in size and population. I found that there was little in common between our two countries at that time. Police in the United States were fragmented into nearly 40,000 separate departments. In Britain (excluding Scotland and Northern Ireland), police forces numbered 47 in all, with centralized inspection and training and uniform pay structures. No such system for the application of common standards existed in the United States.

In Britain, civil service status and tenure are the rule, whereas in the United States often there was political patronage exercised over the appointment of police officers. It would be unthinkable in Britain to see the police involved in politics, whereas in the United States it appeared to be the exception when they were not.

As to police methods, there was a striking difference between the two countries in their attitude toward the use of firearms. British police officers went unarmed, unlike their American colleagues. (There have been some changes necessitated now in England.) Concern was expressed over the need for the development of non-lethal alternatives to police weaponry. The issue of firearms focused upon the extent to which the practice of carrying arms served to present a constant source of citizen fear and thus added to police isolation. (Today we have Tasers.)

They made a basic point that we live today in a doubting society in which authority is questioned and no longer wins automatic respect. Increases and movements in population, changes in its composition, technological innovations, new outlooks and, above all, a shifting of the basis of power confront the forces intended to maintain order.

The use of the motorcar and the ensuing multiplicity of traffic regulations were seen as significant sources of friction. Other social misdemeanors that burden the police, while demanding the exercise of their discretion, include drunkenness, prostitution, homosexuality, and gambling. A most serious discussion centered on the crimes committed by addicts in quest of money to buy drugs.

From American viewpoints, it appeared that the picture was somber and that the present state of police and community relations was "terrible and worsening." A phrase much used in the United States was the "war on crime," (now it is the "war on drugs") typified by military orientation, which had been taken over into the social sphere. The need for vigilance regarding community tensions underlined the importance of good police and community relations, which is the essence of the police officer's job.

The need to recruit more non-white officers on both sides of the Atlantic was recognized. However, attempts to recruit them ran into serious obstacles in both countries. Most blacks regard the police as "on the other side," and would shun any of their fellows who went in for police work. Many had not reached the educational standards to make them eligible to become recruits and those that had could often find better-paid jobs elsewhere.

There was general agreement that the police are only a part of two separate systems. The first was a system of criminal justice embracing the courts, prosecutors, corrections, as well as the police. (As an elected sheriff for 12 years, I have been involved in the entire criminal justice system.) Police-community relations are affected deeply by what other institutions in the system do, as much as what the police do themselves.

Secondly, the police are also part of a system of government rendering social services. If social services are weak or non-existent in some communities, a void is left, which police must fill if anyone is to do so. The public wants police officers to be visible, and to be in such a relationship with the citizens that the police officer is readily accessible. Consequently, the deployment of police personnel is of very great importance in police relations with the public.

The British policing system was discussed thoroughly. English police chiefs enjoy long tenures and therefore independence rarely found among American chiefs. Control over American police departments is to be found concentrated in mayors, committees of City Councils, political leaders, executives, newspaper owners, or in the chiefs themselves. The tenure of American police commissioners and police chiefs is generally short—usually less than two years. Police federations and unions also diminish whatever control the police chief executive has.

The issue of whether transferring responsibility for law and order to state or possibly federal authorities was discussed. Surprisingly, American representatives felt that state control would not be as effective as federal influence. Centralization seems inevitable and it was felt that positive gains can be had from the creation of metropolitan units. My views are somewhat different from this.

The group agreed that the handling of complaints against the police was a very important aspect in maintaining good relations between the police and the public. They agreed that methods of informing complainants of the results of investigations ought to be improved. They agreed that some complaints arose through misconceptions about police practice and the law.

There was widespread agreement that the appropriate responsibilities of the police include not only the prevention of crime and apprehension of suspects, but also additionally the provision of certain peacekeeping and social services. Such services can be justified where they maintain public order and develop responsible citizenship, and when other organizations cannot provide them equally well, e.g. the "cautioning" of youth offenders, handling of family disputes where they may lead to violence, etc.

When called to assist in crowd control, they sometimes use excessive force and they are at times used to provide a kind of "neighborhood control," stopping and searching members of the local community without (at times) sufficient cause. Street interrogation and search must be used with great care so as not to exacerbate police-community tensions and should be carried out by officers who are well trained in procedures and respected in the local community.

There was considerable concern expressed regarding problems of the press and broadcast coverage of police-related activities. They noted that the concern of most media organizations with making a profit led them to search for issues and incidents that attract an audience. Examples of violence receive far more coverage than general patterns of harmonious relationships. The result is that the media at times worsens relationships when a more balanced presentation would serve a better public service. At the same time, the press can bring to light important issues that hinder effective police-public relationships.

They felt that the most important problem of police-community relations exists between police and those who live in minority neighborhoods (Black, Latino, immigrant, etc.) As we have grown larger, more complicated, and more bureaucratic, all forms of accountability have drifted from our neighborhoods and communities to remote city halls, state capitals, and federal agencies.

The group conference emphasized that there are other changes needed if the quality of police-public relationship is to be improved significantly. Improvement is needed in the exposition of justice provided by the courts, and in the effectiveness of rehabilitative efforts, through prisons and partnership with community-based methods.

There was a bit of discussion about the rehabilitative methods used in Scotland for female inmates. In Stirling, the prisoners have a daily 4:00 p.m. tea with matrons to learn docile conversation and interaction. They keep a daily diary, which is read and discussed with them weekly. If pregnant when they are imprisoned, they may keep their baby. Thus, the prison includes prams and child-rearing activities, in which all inmates may participate if they wish. The recidivism rate of females is much lower then males. (I'll just add a note that in 2007, this prison made headlines by allowing women to bring in their small children and keep them until they are of school age—five years old.)

## Report to Prosecuting Attorney of Oakland County on Police Protection in Oakland County

Dear Jay,
I served for six months in 1970 as a consultant on Law Enforcement and Protection to Oakland County Prosecuting Attorney Thomas G. Plunkett. He asked for this report, which I submitted on October, 1970.

Pursuant to your request to provide counseling help to you in your capacity as Chief Law Enforcement Officer for Oakland County, this report is submitted.

The key to meeting most of the obvious needs of a criminal justice system that has no central administration, or no central authority even within the police segment of the system, is an organizational vehicle for liaison and cooperation.

What I propose is a "do it" group, which I have called a Law Enforcement and Justice Improvement Team for Oakland County, which would be the means of executing the most desirable and economically feasible recommendations of present and past research, many of which stopped after pointing to what ought to be done, without suggesting how it might be done.

Publicly, in Oakland County as well as America today, there is concern about crime in all its ramifications. There is particular concern about children being victimized by drugs and pornography.

There is also concern on the part of many citizens, especially young people, regarding the law enforcement and protection system and its processes. There is concern with the faulty functioning of our criminal justice system and a real desire on the part of most people to know more about it, because of increasing awareness that the criminal justice system can and does affect all individuals, directly or indirectly.

Finally, among the people of Oakland County, there is the anticipation of accelerated change in the future, and concern that this change should be intelligently directed, so that the county can remain a safe, pleasant and desirable place in which to live and work.

The principal areas of concern for county law enforcement authorities are: Will crimes continue to increase? How can they be controlled? How can community tensions be cooled? How can the criminal justice system function better? What needs to be done right now?

A variety of factors, including rising crime, have helped to stimulate a mass exodus to the suburbs during the last five years. Census figures now show more people in suburbs than in our cities for the first time. Believing that moving is the best solution, people are deserting our cities, yet this is only a postponement. Crimes are committed by people and wherever they go, the crime problem goes with them.

Oakland County has been fortunate to date—suburban, affluent, and not too densely populated. But change is coming, and the principal purveyors of change are our own children.

Nationally, violent crimes are up 131%, ten times the population increase. Fear has become part of the American way of life. Crime is spreading and probably will engulf the suburbs as well as the cities.

The drug problem is now universal. Oakland County is not without its tragic toll of youthful victims, and crimes inspired by the need of these victims to finance their costly indulgence. How sad that their future years of constructive contribution will be denied them—and us.

Uneasiness—the prelude to fear, seems to be a current fact of life in Oakland County. The crime stories of robberies and vandalism that once seemed so remote are getting close to home.

We are now quite aware of the social ills in our land, poverty pockets, poor housing, substandard education, and employment problems. There is a definite correlation between areas that embrace these factors and the spreading cancer of crime. As these tremendous social problems are solved, crime will lessen. However, affluence and education contribute to the spread of crime if moral principles have been eroded and law enforcement is cumbersome.

In Oakland County, some of our most troublesome and destructive young people are products of suburbia, not the ghetto. The youth culture confuses anarchy with freedom, and law with oppression. Therefore, crime is not confined by county boundaries.

Violent amateurs and seasoned criminals laugh at our fragmented and overlapping jurisdictions, at the difficulties of our prosecutors, at the delays and the decisions of our courts, and at the woeful shortcomings of our correctional institutions.

Our so-called "criminal justice system" is not a system—rather it is a "nonsystem." Its quality of justice is abysmal and its labored functioning is an invitation to continue with crime. When we finally get around to applying correction, we find that we have actually enhanced our subjects' criminal know-how. Frankly, that's criminal! Crime does pay and we pay for it!

In spite of the increasing attention being paid to police and the police function, in my opinion, people are not yet concerned enough with our police, the pivotal part of our criminal justice system. Courts and magistrates are of no avail without police to put into effect what people, laws and courts direct.

It also seems to me that a very vital portion of answers to crime control rest on developing awareness, cooperation and partnership with Mr. and Mrs. American Citizen as we respond to their needs and desires.

There is much room for improvement of our policing services. American police are fragmented into 40,000 individual departments. In Oakland County, there are 50 separate departments serving a population of almost a million. In all of Great Britain, which is not much larger geographically than our state, there are only 47 separate departments, serving 55 million people.

In Oakland County, the largest police agencies are the City of Pontiac Police Department with 150 officers, and the Sheriff's Department of approximately the same size. The entire county can muster about 1700 officers counting full and part time police and sheriff deputies.

Only four of the county's police agencies have more than 100 officers. Twenty have fewer than ten men. Many local jurisdictions are represented by a single officer; three of these are part time. Fifteen jurisdictions have no "local" police at all. Another is protected only by auxiliaries.

When agencies become too large, administrative problems hamper efficiency and increase costs. However, when they are too small, as is the case with most

Oakland County agencies, they are unable to provide the police services citizens increasingly demand and need.

Everything suffers—recruitment, training, police facilities, equipment, the ability to detect and arrest offenders, control disturbances and to provide the basic police services and adequate protection. Effective enforcement action against drug abuse and organized crime is at best limited.

This is a rapidly changing world with shifting populations. There is much to be done in the area of cooperative communication by our diverse police agencies. There is much room for working together in such areas of law enforcement as training, communication, records, photo and laboratory services, specialized investigation services, computerization, and the like.

If cooperation and coordination are not possible with and among our numerous police units, a possible but undesirable alternative could be national police. This is a concept alien to America. Better alternatives might be the regional policing concept applied in Toronto. There, policing and certain other government services are provided to 13 municipalities on a metropolitan area basis, while other functions remain the responsibility of the localities. Alternatively, consider Atlanta, where city police serve the entire county on a contract basis. Strengthened township forces or county-wide policing are other alternatives.

Oakland County, because of its relative affluence and continuing growth, is in a better position to attempt innovations that will more appropriately serve the needs of its population. Tiny local police forces, instituted to serve a widely scattered rural population with relative few and simple police protection needs, are anachronistic today.

I believe some form of consolidation of police services in Oakland County and adjacent populous counties will eventually better meet the needs of the people of the area most efficiently and economically.

However, Oakland County now needs collaboration between all county police and criminal justice agencies on more than the voluntary, informal basis that has existed so far.

For the intermediate range, consolidation and amalgamation of police agencies should be explored on a township or countywide basis. A future metropolitan-area police force is left to the political innovators of the future. Consolidation is essential to providing more effective police services at lower cost, with clear-cut jurisdictional responsibility and no more overlapping.

My general impression of the police agencies in Oakland County that I have personally inspected is that they are generally, but not uniformly, of good quality.

Personnel are generally good, some excellent. Some simply lack complete training and have insufficient manpower to even permit release time for training.

Presently, there is no single coordinating agency for the various criminal justice elements in the county. Oakland County urgently needs a criminal justice coordinating group to analyze trends, identify problems, establish goals, prepare solutions, state priorities, and win public understanding and support so the plans can be put to work.

With such an implementing and coordinating group, the county police structure can benefit from immediate steps in the key areas of training, communication, coordination, and citizen involvement.

The best programs and plans cannot work without the active support, understanding, and cooperation of citizens. Justice and democracy must be understood and lived. Institutions created in their names must be understood and supported. This requires a fifth party in the criminal justice relationship: the people—in addition to police, prosecutor, courts, and corrections.

As chief law enforcement officer, the county prosecutor has both the opportunity and a logical basis for exercising initiative in building a better county system of criminal justice.

I recommend that within Oakland County, a full-time paid group be established to keep up with what's going on, to effect harmony, liaison, and cooperation within the criminal justice system. They would disseminate information and experience within the criminal justice system to those burdened by day-to-day problems. They would also inform citizens and secure their involvement and support.

I suggest for this representative group the designation of Oakland County Law Enforcement and Justice Improvement Team (LEJIT). It should be made up of qualified representatives of policing and law enforcement, the prosecutorial function, the judiciary, and the processes of rehabilitation and correction.

This group should be carefully selected and should be capable of working together to serve the criminal justice units represented, but also serve the entire criminal justice system as a team. This team would be concerned about the present and actively prepare and implement proposals, seek grants both public and private, and assess promising developments occurring elsewhere.

A most important function would be to bring into the system the most important member—the citizen. They would be the "people's bridge" to understanding, appreciation, and active interest in local operation of the criminal justice system.

Such a team would fill the gaps that have been present since the start of the criminal justice system. In the past, the prosecutor, police, courts, and corrections have worked as individual entities with insufficient cooperation or communication. Effective liaison can open new lines of communication between the agencies and the public.

Through LEJIT, police agencies can have direct access to the prosecutor's office and the courts to voice their problems and views.

Training is the most neglected area in policing and is inadequate throughout the country. While time, money, and manpower are major obstacles, much can be done by professional cooperation. One important new method involves television. Videotape presentations on police procedures from the Detroit Police Department and other large departments can be used. The professional expertise developed by some departments can be passed on to other neighboring police departments. State Police Officers Training Councils also have some video training tapes available.

Videotapes and open-circuit television make possible not only instruction but communication within and between departments. Open-circuit TV presentations require the assistance and cooperation of a commercial or educational TV station. Closed-circuit TV training requires much planning and much funding, however. Training men in their own commands is less costly than sending them to some central location for such a purpose.

Information bulletins and training material can be assembled and digested by research and professional exchange, with the help of the county Police Academy and LEJIT. A monthly training pamphlet can be prepared and disseminated to all departments. It is difficult for small departments to keep abreast of vital information that is being made available daily. It is costly and time-consuming to read the many books, journals, periodicals, and reports in the burgeoning criminal justice field. Concise and palatable information can inform criminal justice people who can delve further for detailed information. Developments in criminal justice, research, planning, new programs and progress, new ideas, and innovations from all over the country can thus be made available to the various criminal justice officials in the county.

Oakland County needs a viable police academy that can fully service its law enforcement personnel. The current academy needs to be expanded and strengthened to provide recruits and others with quality training. It must augment 50 different agencies with a present strength of 1,700 full and part-time officers. It needs more space, more equipment, and more staff personnel to provide more and varied training for recruits, in-service, supervisory command, and executives.

Being part of the Oakland Community College offers recruits training in a civilian academic atmosphere. Additionally, curriculum emphasizing the practical realities of street law enforcement is more effective in liaison with the various chiefs' associations.

Supplemental on-the-job training is difficult due to a general shortage of personnel. Many departments can't send personnel to courses of a week or longer without weakening protective services. Consolidation of police services is the ultimate answer, but meanwhile brief training sessions at roll call and videotapes can help.

Training within the prosecutor's office could be expanded with seminars, videotapes, and the insights of others in the criminal justice system. Time, manpower, funds, and equipment are necessary to do this. This would enhance needed communication between the prosecutor and all law enforcement agencies in the county.

Police need to have a greater awareness of their relationship and responsibilities to the prosecutor's office. Police officers would benefit from briefings by prosecutor's office personnel such as the presentation of evidence and the encouragement and protection of witnesses.

These training mediums could take a police officer step-by-step through the proper procedures in a felony case from initial arrest to the final court presentation. They could introduce the needs of the prosecutor's office, including interview of the suspect by the prosecutor, evidence required, courtroom procedure, and delivery of testimony.

Training material, books, and videotapes should be kept by a county police library or academy available to all police departments. Beyond this, each police department should have a basic library of books in the field of law enforcement and justice.

Special training on narcotics is so important that no training techniques should be overlooked—films, videos, seminars, etc. Portable vans as classrooms would be useful to educate both police and citizens, and could be equipped with audiovisual aids and graphic displays. County departments of drug abuse control should inform the public about and provide treatment for drug addiction and abuse. Special attention should be given to educational efforts in the schools.

LEJIT could gather and disseminate information in bulletins and videotape presentations. LEJIT could be a source of information to the news media on county programs. Citizens should be informed on how to keep from becoming a victim, what assistance police can offer, and how citizens may assist their police and their county.

Schools provide an opportunity to instruct, guide, and advise the young. Many teachers in primary schools are not quite aware of the ramifications of the criminal justice system. LEJIT could provide team members to appear at schools regularly to inform and talk with students.

LEJIT members could be speakers presenting the story of county law enforcement to civic groups in town hall or other types of formats. It should generate new citizen involvement, interest, new ideas, and perhaps new solutions to some of our criminal justice problems. Such discussions could occur at a monthly "Open House" at various law enforcement departments or county facilities.

A LEJIT team could provide a liaison throughout the criminal justice system in the county on a daily basis. Coordination and liaison would allow for an exchange of research and cross-fertilization so conducive to new solutions.

The difficulties faced by many police departments can be made easier by coordination of effort, of services, and possible pooling of manpower and equipment. For emergency disaster-disorder control, mutual aid and assistance is necessary. LEJIT could improve the capacity for response and quickly coordinate police command of police to assemble other forces.

Citizens can be trained to realize that a police officer is a neighbor, a citizen paid to perform responsibilities delegated to him by his fellow citizens. Many citizens would like to help their department but they don't know how or whom to approach. LEJIT offers them an outlet and a vehicle. Charity work would be of tremendous assistance to the police, the prosecutor, and even corrections.

Currently "Light the Night" campaigns are very constructive. They are proven crime deterrents but they need a catalyst to turn on the lights of a community. In rehabilitative probation and community service sentences, volunteers could assume more responsibility to assist our sorely pressed correctional staffs.

## My Announcement to Run for Sheriff

Dear Jay,

On June 5, 1972, I announced that I had decided to run for sheriff. I made the following remarks at a press meeting at my house. This was two years after I had done the report for Tom Plunkett, who recommended that I should run for sheriff. I had studied and researched the sheriff's job and thought that I could do something worthwhile, so decided to run.

Welcome to Spreen Acres!

I hope that those of you who can, will stay long enough after our discussion to have some lunch with us before you head back to your chores. I thought we might enjoy a little German-style picnic together—a little bratwurst, a little beer, and what goes with it.

As I have indicated, I have had requests from a number of quarters to become a candidate in the 1972 political races.

Members of both parties have suggested that they would like to see me as a candidate for the office of sheriff of Oakland County on their party ticket.

I took the position that I would listen to whatever reasons they cared to advance, in favor of my running for office, but I warned that I already had a pretty strong list of reasons why I should run.

There is always an inherent appeal to a professional man when a fresh opportunity is present to be active in a leadership role in his chosen profession.

I guess that was my "Achilles' heel," whether my political friends realized it or not.

I know it's a cliché to call it this, but they were offering me what amounted to a brand new challenge. Moreover, challenges are what life is all about, in my opinion.

There is a problem of fragmentation of police agencies through the United States. There are some 40,000 different police departments, ranging in size from one man to New York's 30,000. There are all kinds of differences in selection standards, training, equipment, pay, and proficiency.

There is an urgent need for a new approach to coordination and cooperation among the multiplicity of small departments. The sheriff's role provides support for smaller departments. However, we do not want a "national police," for that is the road to "Big Brother" and the police state.

Nor do I think a single statewide police agency is the answer.

Present state police organizations provide certain valuable coordinating functions, but they are still too far removed from the local citizenry.

It seems to me that the best opportunity for helping coordination among the small local police agencies resides in the office of the county sheriff, who already provides police protection in his county, outside the jurisdictions of municipal agencies.

We know that effective law enforcement cannot stop at municipal boundaries.

America is looking at its police more carefully than ever before, and it is time to reaffirm in the office of sheriff the countywide assurance of uniform police protection and equal justice that it originally implied.

Because I see in the office of sheriff a challenge that includes an untapped opportunity for exploration, innovation, and service, I have decided to run for the office in Oakland County, and to enter my name in the Democratic primary.

As a career police professional, I have always kept my political party and voting preferences to myself. It is an unfamiliar role to be publicly adopting a party label.

I have chosen to enter the Democratic rather than the Republican primary after careful consideration. What ultimately decided the issue was that I had served as a law enforcement consult to Prosecutor Tom Plunkett for several months during 1970, and developed a great respect for his ability and integrity.

I do respect our two-party system, and the concerned and active members of both parties. I regret the need for party labels in connection with a law enforcement office. Law enforcement responsibility transcends party lines and partisanship. There can be no room for "politics" in the administration of police services. We are all entitled to equal protection from our official protectors in the police profession.

It has been suggested that I look upon election to the office of sheriff as a "four year contract with the people."

That is what I seek. For the police administrator, whether he is appointed to a municipal post, or elected to county office, owes his allegiance and his responsibility to the people. That's the way it should be, and that's the way I like it.

I do not propose to run a "political" campaign, because I am not and never will be a politician.

I propose to run based on my professional qualifications and experience, my educational preparation and development, and my continuing concern for the betterment of policing.

In addition, as I always have, I propose to campaign for aroused citizen interest, support and participation in the affairs of their local police agency. For only through citizen-police teamwork can any police agency be fully effective.

## Why I Decided to Run for Sheriff

Dear Jay,

After that June 5th meeting, reporters wrote about my announcement to run for sheriff. One was James S. Granelli, who currently writes for the *Los Angeles Times*. He wrote an article called "Spreen Calls Counties 'Hope of Policing'." His article had a picture of me and Elinor sitting on our patio in casual clothing. The article begins with a reference to my daughter who loved motor scooters.

> As soon as you saw the girl on the motor scooter, you knew you were approaching Lynhaven, the country home of Johannes Spreen.

Spreen, a former Detroit police commissioner and currently a teacher and lecturer, announced his candidacy Monday for the Democratic nomination for Oakland County sheriff.

Relaxed in a sport shirt open at the collar, Spreen contended that the county sheriff's department is "where it's at" in law enforcement.

"The hope of policing is in the counties," he said. "The cities are too big, too poor, and too political."

Spreen sees the sheriff's department as large enough to have "the technical and managerial know-how and the equipment and training resources" of larger police agencies but small enough to remain close to the people.

The sheriff's department has the best opportunity, he said, to help smaller police departments and to develop "better cooperation and coordination between police, prosecution, courts, and corrections."

Spreen, a 25-year veteran of the New York police force with a master's degree in public administration from New York University, worked for a few months in 1970 as a law enforcement consultant to Oakland County Prosecutor Thomas Plunkett.

It was Plunkett who suggested he run for sheriff, Spreen said. Therefore, after four months' deliberation, he "decided to team up with Tom Plunkett to assist better law enforcement."

Asked at the end of his announcement how long he has been a Democrat, Spreen said, "as of about two minutes ago." He said he had kept political party and voting preferences to himself.

"My own preference would be for a nonpartisan competition for such an office (as sheriff)," he said. "For law enforcement transcends party lines and partisanship. There can be no room for politics in that sense in the administration of police services."

What swayed him to run, he said, was that police were in trouble and the concept of policing had to change. The challenge and opportunity, he said, was to guide and direct that change and that the sheriff's four-year term would give him a chance to do that job.

"It all boils down to whether a man should teach his thing or do his thing. Should he be an analyst or a catalyst? I have come to believe it's more important to do his thing."

Friends such as Lyall Smith, the former sports reporter and now Detroit Lions publicist, and Birmingham Police Chief Rollin G. Tobin joined Spreen at his press conference.

Pressed to answer questions about his programs for the sheriff's department, Spreen said he would unveil specific proposals in the next few months before the August primary against Ruel McPherson, a District Court process server from Hazel Park.

He did hint in the interview that there might be a place for motor scooters in the county.

He was the man who put Detroit police officers on scooters so they could among other things maneuver through traffic jams when necessary.

Scooters used by the Detroit Police Department to patrol and train on Belle Isle.

Playing ping pong with Detroit youth in Buck Up Our Youth program.

## My First Venture into Politics

Dear Jay,

I had to design a political advertisement, and pay for it to run in the local newspapers. That was hard for me. It required that I blow my own horn. Don't let anybody kid you. The person who is running for office is the one who spends the most and has to come up with information for ads. Even though an ad says something like "Spreen Committee for Sheriff," you've got to design it all unless you pay someone big bucks. I had to learn so many things rapidly. This was my first ad and it ran in the *Detroit News* on June 28, 1972.

### Sheriff Who?

If you care who your next Sheriff will be, as we do, you will read this letter from our candidate ... and help us elect him!

Dear Concerned Citizen:

On June 5, after many requests from sincere, concerned people of both parties, I announced my candidacy for the office of Sheriff of Oakland County and entered my name as a Democratic candidate in the Primary Election to be held August 8.

Since then, people have asked me many questions. Particularly WHY am I running and HOW will I conduct my campaign. This letter enables me to give you my reasons for seeking the office of Sheriff and my hopes regarding the help and support of the concerned citizens of Oakland County.

### Why do I run?

Before becoming Police Commissioner of Detroit in July of 1968, we had never been in Michigan. We've found it a wonderful state with very fine people living here. We are proud to have made it our home. I have also found that the people of Oakland County are serious, concerned citizens who want better law enforcement and protection and if given the opportunity will help to improve our American system of policing and criminal justice.

### I like police.

Police are in trouble in America. Rising crime and community tensions are twin problems that must be solved. Presently, no city really seems to be "making it." We need people to help policing and their police departments. I believe that the Sheriff, because of his unique position as a countywide representative of the people, can carve a new role in American policing to serve the people directly, and provide an umbrella of support for local police agencies serving them by providing supportive and technical resources and assistance so they can serve their local people better.

**I can do the job—with your help.**

As Police Commissioner of Detroit, I felt that I had the people's support for what I was trying to do. If elected, I would have a firm 4 year "contract with the people," uninterrupted by politics. Personally, I would prefer that this were a non-partisan election. However, I also believe that the people, through the office of sheriff, can vote on a law enforcement basis, rather than on all other political considerations.

If elected, I will use my training, my education, and my entire 33 years of police background to provide the best law enforcement and protection possible for the people of Oakland County.

**How will I run?**

On my record and background which I will present to the people. I am not going to run as a "politician" because I am not one. As I stated to a reporter June 5, "we will conduct an amateur campaign in the best professional manner possible, with the help of my family, my neighbors, and my friends."

**You can help.**

When asked how we could finance our campaign—"Would there be a 'Buck Up Your Sheriff' type thing" I laughed and yet, thinking it over, it isn't a bad idea at all.

"Buck Up Your Police" money (almost half of which came from Oakland County citizens) did many things that remain to this day. It provided operational help (116 scooters), training assistance (videotape equipment in all commands), educational upgrading (bookcases and professional books in all precinct station houses) and so much more.

Yes, "Buck Up" confirmed my faith in the people. I still have that same faith and feel that if you think me best qualified, you will help me now.

If you believe as I do that the American sheriff can carve a new role and set new standards for protection of your homes and your communities, then please send what you can. Yes, any amount can help, and you can participate in the democratic process—you can Assist Better Law Enforcement!

Sincerely,
Johannes F. Spreen

Buck Up Your Police Department showing that we had raised $42,200 by that time.

# What's Wrong with the Sheriff's Department?

Dear Jay,

I soon realized that the public was not really aware of the differences between the county sheriff's offices, municipal police chiefs, state police, and various other law enforcement offices. I set out to educate and inform citizens about some of those differences. I also wanted to disperse information I had collected about the inadequacies of the current sheriff's department.

Only when people understand the responsibilities of those they elect will they participate effectively in the democratic processes. I issued this press release entitled "What's Wrong with the Sheriff's Department" in the summer of 1972. I hoped the newspapers would include much of it in their coverage, and some of them did.

> Ever since I became a candidate for sheriff, one of the most persistent questions asked of me has been "why?"
>
> Here's why I think the office of sheriff is important, and here's why I decided to give up teaching and writing, to get back into active police administration.
>
> If you look as what has been done to improve the practice of the police profession in recent years, you discover that most of the effort has been aimed at the large urban departments. However, as population increasingly spreads away from the large cities, bringing crime along with it, we discover that a variety of new problems is being dumped in the laps of smaller local police agencies.
>
> By themselves they simply do not have the resources or the capacity to deal with changed times and changing crime patterns. However, there is one police agency in every county that is in a special position to help local police and this is the sheriff's department.
>
> The role of the sheriff has not been too conspicuous lately. The sheriff's time has been taken up as a process server and a custodian of prisoners. He is supposed to be the chief police official of the county, yet his police role has often taken a back seat to courts and corrections services.
>
> The sheriff needs to take a fresh look at all of his responsibilities. The sheriff needs to upgrade the police protection aspect of his role. This is why I am running for Sheriff of Oakland County.
>
> I see the office of sheriff as an opportunity to help improve local police services. I see the sheriff as a catalyst to help local police units in Oakland County. He can help them in matters that require overall planning, cooperation, coordination of effort, and mutual assistance.

The sheriff is a key man in winning public support—an intermediary in securing greater teamwork between police, prosecution, courts and corrections.

Public support and teamwork are essential to giving the people of Oakland County the protection they need and deserve. Citizens are so used to inadequate service from the sheriff's department, they don't expect or get much.

One of the first criticisms I heard from police and citizens was that the southern part of the county subsidized the sheriff's department so the northern part of the county could get free protection. I recognized that this was an extreme viewpoint, expressed out of frustration. All taxpayers share the burden of the county services. However, neither the northern nor the southern parts of the county are getting the full range of needed services.

Rising crime in the county is introducing more problems than many small police departments can handle alone. Without the sheriff's participation, their commendable efforts at voluntary cooperation are rendered haphazard and ineffectual.

With the mobility of modern criminals, one small community police department can't track them all down. However, countywide burglary patrol and investigation teams, spearheaded by the sheriff's department, could do something to change this picture.

Currently, the sheriff's department doesn't keep records of where the various crimes are committed. Without such basic record keeping, investigators can't concentrate their efforts. Furthermore, a basic manual of procedures and standard operating rules for every professional police officer is needed. This is the leadership's fault. Deputies tell me about that deficiency in the current sheriff's operations. Conscientious police officers want to achieve. They want to do a worthy job. They want your respect, and they know they have to earn it.

Another deficiency that bothers them is insufficient basic police training and no training for supervision and command. Another is the lack of encouragement from leadership to advance oneself professionally. Although there is a target range for shooting practice, there is little instruction in how and when to shoot. There is little training in first aid, a serious omission for those who make a large number of traffic accident runs. There is no training in the use of department forms and accurate report writing, which affects court cases. There is no training in radio dispatch or the haphazard assignment of patrol areas.

Finally, there is no supervision of deputies on patrol to make sure they are doing what they should, no background check for deputy job applicants, and no exchange of information between incoming and outgoing shifts.

# Civilian Groups Can Help Law Enforcement

Dear Jay,

I addressed the Farmington Jaycees on September 22, 1972. Obviously, I was campaigning but I tried to tell them how valuable their organization could be to law enforcement as well.

> Thank you for the kind introduction and thank you for inviting me.
>
> I've had a soft spot in my heart for the Jaycees ever since I was police commissioner in Detroit. The local Jaycee chapter there provided me with one of the brightest memories of my term of office.
>
> The Detroit Jaycees found out how pinched for money the Detroit Police Department was. They also were convinced that I could accomplish a great deal of good with a relatively small amount of unbudgeted extra funds—money the police commissioner could use as he saw fit, in the right places.
>
> So the Jaycees pitched in on a citizen donation campaign. The campaign not only helped to raise money, but it also raised police morale.
>
> We called the project "Buck Up Your Police."
>
> It eventually raised about $50,000, all from individual donors, one buck at a time.
>
> The money was put to good use. In addition, the campaign really did "buck up" the Detroit police. It helped to prove to Detroit police officers that people believed in them, respected them, and wanted to help them do a better job.
>
> The success of that drive and the enthusiastic support of the Jaycees sold me once and for all on your organization.
>
> The guiding spirit of the Jaycee movement, as I understand it, is citizen involvement. It's caring about your community, and doing something to make it a better place to live. I'd like to talk to you about the entire county as a kind of community. As population continues to grow in Oakland County, the quality of life and the quality of police protection is going to depend more and more on the role of the sheriff—and whether the man in that office has the imagination and professional skill to anticipate and overcome the challenges of the present and the future.
>
> The title of sheriff is the oldest in the history of policing in the English-speaking world. We have more than 40,000 police agencies in the United States. We have national police agencies of various types, including the FBI, and the Secret Service of the Treasury Department. We have many large urban departments. We have state police, or state highway patrols. We have local police in cities, towns, villages, and townships and, of course, we have county police—the sheriff and his deputies.

We want our police to be close to the people they serve. We want our police to know and be known by members of their communities. Rapport between the police officer and the citizen is one of our chief defenses in curbing and preventing crime. It is a great advantage to keep police patrol services in the localities they serve, under local control. But there are great disadvantages when local police agencies are too small and too fragmented.

There are problems in recruiting, training, administrative expertise, purchasing, having and maintaining the right facilities and equipment, sophisticated communications and control, and important backup services like scientific labs and special investigators.

The sheriff provides those services to small police departments and remote areas with no local police. In Oakland County, the sheriff operates a $3 million a year public safety operation. He has a multi-million dollar jail to manage, and the welfare and rehabilitation of hundreds of prisoners. He has 230 police and civilian personnel on his payroll. He has 100 or so pieces of motorized equipment in his care, including cars, trucks, vans, boats, trailers, and a helicopter.

He covers a citizen population of nearly a million people. Within his county there are 40 municipal or other local agencies employing more than 1,200 police personnel. These agencies need the backup support of his department.

In addition, the sheriff is paid about $24,000 a year for his work. That's an executive salary, by any measure, and the people of this county ought to get what they're paying for.

As a professional law enforcement practitioner, I know that if we stamp crime out in one area, it moves to another. Crime in Oakland County is rising faster than crime in Detroit.

Most sheriff's departments have become underachievers, and citizens don't care. Underrating and under-manning the office of sheriff is chronic all over the United States. It is time for the sheriff's department to realize its opportunity and its full responsibility. The sheriff must provide the citizens and local police agencies with an umbrella of support, backup services, and effective countywide liaison that will help the criminal justice system serve our people better.

To professionalize the sheriff's department, you must start at the top, with a professional.

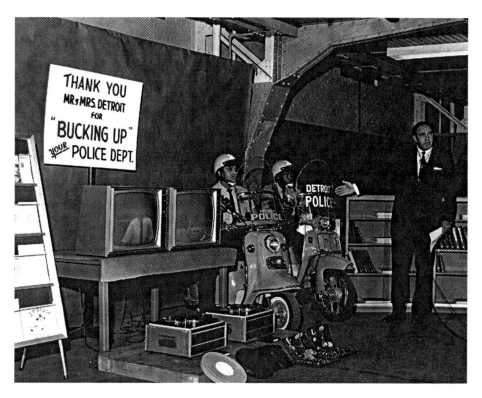

Buck Up Your Police project results.

At the office in the spring of 1979, running for third term.

# Spreen Campaign Headquarters

Dear Jay,

A bulletin went out on October 10, 1972, before the election on November 7. At the top, it said "Assist Better Law Enforcement. Spreen for Sheriff. Oakland County." Here is what the rest of the bulletin said. It must have worked because I was elected.

What does a political candidate do in the middle of a vigorous campaign, when his audience doesn't want to hear a "political" speech?

If he's a candidate for sheriff, he keeps his "cool" and talks about the "cool professionalism" that must be the trademark of tomorrow's police.

This was the approach of Johannes F. Spreen today, as the candidate for sheriff of Oakland County addressed the Southfield Rotary Club. Spreen said he was asked to keep the talk light and "non-political."

He said, "I can't talk about my experiences with crime because that is too serious." He couldn't satisfy the requirement to be light and humorous without talking politics, but he said that provided him with some of the most humorous experiences of his career.

Spreen instead chose to talk about the future, and how the police of tomorrow must cultivate "cool" rather than "cold" professionalism in order to both do their jobs more effectively and earn public support.

"As police emphasis has shifted toward allegedly more efficient and impersonal enforcement of laws and ordinances," Spreen said, "psychologically and tactically police have moved from a preventive agency to a punitive one."

"In other words, police have been trending toward 'cold' professionalism when they should be moving toward 'cool' professionalism." It's kind of like the old Dragnet television series where Jack Webb constantly told citizens, "Just the facts, ma'am."

"If police methods are genuinely efficient, they should not alienate anybody. If police methods are universally effective, then they should help those who need help most. Good police performance is the cornerstone of professional policing, as it is the cornerstone of any profession. And it has to rest on a spirit of emphasis on service to the individual citizen, protecting him against becoming a victim of crime."

# Part II
## Being Sheriff

# *1973*

World Trade Center opened
Watergate hearings televised; Mark Felt ("Deep Throat") resigned from F.B.I.
U.S. Drug Enforcement Administration was founded
Yom Kippur War: Egyptian/Syrian forces attacked Israel

## Changing the Sheriff's Program

Dear Jay,

I really enjoyed my first year. I was learning a lot about the differences between the county sheriff and the municipal police chief. I tried to pass some things over from the police world to the sheriff's office. One program hit the local television stations on June 20, 1973. WJBK-TV2 news director Carl Cederberg delivered the news and sent me a copy of what he said as they showed some pictures of my new SCAT program.

> While controversy galore has surrounded the Detroit Police STRESS program, we doubt that any similar hassle will develop over the SCAT plan announced by Oakland County Sheriff Johannes Spreen.
> In this age of acronyms, SCAT stands for Sheriff's Criminal Annoyance Team. And, Spreen says, SCAT will be in the specific business of annoying burglars—the kind of criminal accounting for two-thirds of all crime in largely suburban Oakland County.
> STRESS in Detroit is largely an undercover-type operation utilizing decoys. SCAT, in contrast, is a wide-open crime-fighting approach specializing in high visibility. In addition to his customary road patrols, Sheriff Spreen is deploying uniformed SCAT teams in distinctively marked cars that will do their best to attract attention.
> Instead of the usual after-the-fact report-writing and detective work in connection with burglaries, SCAT will concentrate on scaring burglars away or, better yet, catching them in the act. Spreen hopes that SCAT will help reverse a trend that has seen the burglary and larceny rate in Oakland County increasing faster than Detroit's over the past five years.
> Under the SCAT concept, the always imaginative sheriff and former Detroit police commissioner believes that burglars will be discouraged because "they know we're going to be there."
> TV2 believes that SCAT, like Spreen's famous scooter patrol in Detroit, may just work.

## An Early Lesson in Party Politics

Dear Jay,

*The Oakland Press* reporter Ralph Kingzett wrote an article called "Spreen Finds Sheriff's Post a Lesson in Party Politics." The article, printed July 26, 1973, pinned down what was beginning to happen between County Prosecutor Brooks Patterson and me. I thought the two of us would work as a team fighting crime. Then I found out he had been setting up a Strike Force to fight organized crime, which he would run. He was doing this without letting me know or working with me. I gradually realized he was politically ambitious, and I later learned that he wanted to be *president of the United States.*

> ... Spreen has been nonpolitical, but last fall the Democrats wooed him into running as their candidate for sheriff ... He was the only Democrat to win a countywide post in the Republican landslide ... He kept on Undersheriff Leo Hazen, the handpicked choice of retired Sheriff Frank Irons to succeed him and the GOP candidate who ran against Spreen ...
> Spreen has scored some successes in other areas. Perhaps the most publicized of them is SCAT—the Sheriff's Criminal Annoyance Team. SCAT members infiltrated a luxury-car theft ring and provided information, which led to a recent massive raid and arrests.
> Spreen also had people prepare policies and procedure manuals, because he found nothing on paper spelling out how a deputy functions ...
> The sheriff also cracked down on what he considers a widespread abuse of special deputy cars.... Spreen more than doubled the amount of detective manpower available, without hiring any new men.... He's also had basic law-enforcement seminars for deputies, some of whom have never had any formal training on policing.
> The sheriff has had a less than harmonious relationship with County Prosecutor L. Brooks Patterson. Spreen found that Patterson has gone to the county board with proposals that could affect his department without Spreen's being consulted beforehand. One involved a request for sophisticated laboratory equipment for testing suspected drugs. Another involved an organized crime task force. But Patterson does not have the authority to give those investigators police powers.

Jay, I'll just mention that I learned recently that sheriff's deputies stopped Brooks Patterson in June 2003 while driving. He was charged with reckless driving, admitted responsibility to a civil infraction (careless driving), and was sentenced to six months probation. The officers who failed to give him a Breathalyzer test (which might have been the basis of more serious charges) were suspended. This guy ought to be watched!

## There Were No Rules of Conduct

Dear Jay,

I did install the first rules of conduct and performance for the Sheriff's Department because I found that there were no printed rules and regulations. This was a cooperative result, even though some credited me alone. When I issued the 150 rules and regulations on August 1, 1973, I accompanied the document with this letter.

> The success of a criminal justice agency depends primarily upon the dedication of the individuals in that agency.
> Law enforcement today is a complex and exacting task. The same citizen on one day will call for, and welcome, your aid and assistance, yet another day this same citizen may strenuously resent an intrusion upon what he views as his rights and liberties.
> Providing the service of law enforcement and protection for the individual and the community firmly but fairly without regard for race, color, creed is most important. It is at times difficult, but it can be a most satisfying endeavor.
> The daily contacts with the people we serve are most important and will reflect how our Department will be judged. The officer who is working daily in the community is the most important representative of the Department. Upon his efforts individually, and upon his and his fellow officers' efforts collectively rest not only how the entire department will be perceived, but actually how the state of law enforcement and protection will be determined. The weak, unprofessional, unethical officer can damage severely the reputation of a criminal justice agency—and of those serving in it.
> It is most pleasing to me that a committee of members of the Department set down these rules of conduct and performance in a consensus agreement with input being able to be provided by any and all members. A profession sets its own standards to which members of the profession adhere. My congratulations to you for setting your own high standards!
> With a firm foundation of good men and women serving to the best of their abilities, our goals of crime prevention, peacekeeping and the protection of life and property can best be met and the people and the law enforcement profession will best be served.

## What Ever Happened to Teamwork?

Dear Jay,

*The Oakland Press* covered a controversy called "Does Oakland County need an organized crime task force?" The newspaper asked Brooks Patterson and me to send in our views and printed this story on September 26, 1973. It began with the reporter's explanation that neither was shown the other's paper. However, Patterson seemed to know my key points and argued them, so I can't help but wonder if he was shown my comments before he composed his own.

Since Oakland County Prosecuting Attorney L. Brooks Patterson announced plans last May for a prosecutor-controlled strike force against organized crime, the need for such an organization has been debated by officials and the public. In August, Patterson modified his plan to include other law enforcement groups in the control of the task force and to conform with ideas from the Lansing Office of Criminal Justice Programs, which has control of the $1.3 million in federal anticrime funds Patterson was seeking. Then this month, Patterson withdrew the application for funds and shelved his program because of what he called political opposition. Here is synopsis of our two views.

**Sheriff's view:**
... Organized crime poses a serious problem in our nation. I believe the county's many professional chiefs and their departments have been alert and vigilant to its spread in Oakland County.

With a background of almost 35 years of police knowledge and experience, I will rest on my public statements of past years that the better way to really attack organized crime is through a proper task force—a strike force composed of local law enforcement agencies in cooperation with each other, combined with state police, and with federal agencies concerned ...

Only through manpower, information, and resources can we ever succeed. In fact, in the narcotic trade, international cooperative action is most essential to dam the supply of narcotics ...

The Sheriff is a constitutional officer elected by the people to serve as their guardian of public safety. In such capacity, he is the chief police officer of the county and as such carries a responsibility to preserve the peace and prevent crime. Therefore, I submit the following questions for consideration:

- What are the priorities? Is organized crime our No. 1 problem?
- How extensive is the existence of organized crime in this county?
- Should the county duplicate a function being performed by State Police intelligence?
- Will the proposed unit overlap and duplicate efforts such as those of NET (Oakland County's Narcotic Enforcement Team) or SCAT (Sheriffs Criminal Annoyance Team)?
- Should another county police force be originated?

**Prosecutor's view:**
... The organized level of crime that was going to be the target of the task force was not just "the Mafia," for to chase the dons in and out of Oakland County would have been an exercise in futility and a fraud on the public.

The Organized Crime Task Force was more particularly designed to hit the managerial level of crime: crime in which there is a structured operation of criminal endeavor ... For instance, if an arrest of a particular person were made and the next day that person were replaced by somebody else who would carry on the arrested person's criminal activities; a criminal "organization" would exist. Such organized crime in Oakland County includes most importantly trafficking in narcotics. It also includes major theft rings, burglary rings, gambling, prostitution, numbers, and white-collar frauds ...

The proposed task force would not have diminished the constant attack of law enforcement against street crime, nor would it have shifted the emphasis of local enforcement ...

The task force, though proposed by the prosecutor's office and under the operational control of the prosecutor, would have had a board of directors made up of the police chiefs of the county and the sheriff. The board would have been involved in case development, target selection, and manpower assistance ...

When I saw a void in the war against organized crime, I ordered my staff to prepare a proposal for a federally funded grant. I told them to move quickly because the funds were available and every day's delay gave the enemy a head start ... I intend to reintroduce the task force application later. I urge the sheriff to change his mind and recognize that support for the task force is a vote for improved total law enforcement.

# *1974*

**Nixon resigns when tied to Watergate
Gerald Ford pardons Nixon
Patricia Hearst is abducted by the SLA
Freedom of Information Act is passed over Ford's veto**

## The Sheriff Don't Get No Respect!

Dear Jay,

It's tough when you're the only Democrat and those you must ask for funds are mostly Republicans. A kind editor of a local paper wrote an editorial opinion in early April called: "County Republicans Ought to Let Spreen Be Sheriff." He said, "Although Johannes Spreen is a Democrat, which still seems to bug some Republicans, he is the only sheriff we've got, and the office does deserve some respect."

He described how I was blasted for having a certain door at the jail unlocked and accused of not keeping a secure jail. Commissioner Donald C. Quinn, R-Troy, accused me of not doing my "primary job, that of keeping a safe, secure jail," The editor said "It is nonsense to say keeping the jail is his prime job. True, the sheriff is responsible for the jail, but his duties are a lot more extensive than walking the halls ... The sheriff's main job, whether or not the Republicans want it that way, is fighting crime on the street. In fact, the sheriff gets 30,000 to 40,000 road patrol calls yearly. They are from citizens—mostly in North Oakland—seeking a policeman.

The editor said "It's time the Republicans let the sheriff do the job he was elected to do and hold the potshots for the next campaign ... Now it seems time for some Republicans to forget the party and work to get the job done."

## Commissioners Didn't Listen

Dear Jay,

Maryanne Conheim, a *Detroit Free Press* reporter, wrote about my frustration on April 4, 1974. She called her article "Showman Spreen Fights Frustration as Oakland Sheriff."

> She said "Spreen, who is the Oakland County sheriff, can't even open his mouth ... Spreen was actually denied permission to speak to the commissioners at that meeting.
>
> Such are the frustrations of the job that followed 17 months at the helm of Detroit's police force. He found himself out of a job when his boss, Mayor Jerome Cavanagh, decided not to run for re-election in 1968 ...
>
> By the time he got his masters in public administration, he was an ardent believer in "training, training, training." That's one of his sore points with the Oakland County Commission ... His critics on the commission accuse Spreen of trying to stretch his statutory powers ...

"Some of his proposals smack of countywide police agencies headed by John Spreen," said Commissioner Paul Kasper, R-Bloomfield Hills. "I don't think this is appropriate unless the cities and communities request it."

## Being Popular Doesn't Always Help

Dear Jay,

*The Oakland Press* published the article "Spreen-Patterson poll to aid Dems in county exec race" on July 18, 1974. It gave the statistic of a poll about the popularity of Prosecutor L. Brooks Patterson and Sheriff Johannes Spreen to guide county executive election strategy.

> ... Spreen remains strongest in the populous south end of the county, where urban areas are less involved with the Republican tradition of the sheriff's department and recognize Spreen's name.
>
> Patterson got his best rating in the northern section above a line drawn through the south side of Pontiac.
>
> Although Spreen's popularity among all occupational groups was greater than Patterson's in the poll, Spreen scored the widest margins with business and professional groups.

Jay, here's a summary of those poll results:

Almost 1/3 of voters said they didn't recognize Patterson's name but 83.8% said they recognized Spreen's. Asked whether their impression was favorable, voters say yes for Spreen by 54.2% and for Patterson by 37.2%. Patterson's name impression was unfavorable with 5.9%; Spreen's with 4.3%. In the southeast corner of the county, Patterson's favorable rating was 29.4%; Spreen's 58.7%. In the southwestern corner of the county, Patterson's favorite rating was 14.8% behind Spreen's. Spreen's favorable impression was 20% ahead of Patterson's with persons aged 18 to 34. Blue-collar workers had favorable impression of Patterson of 43.1% and Spreen 47.1%.

## Trouble with a Rotten Apple

Dear Jay,

I had a situation where one of my lieutenants (Donald Kratt) was found to be using the term "nigger" often and I feared what he or someone else might do in a racially mixed situation. I told him to remove that from his "lexicon." I wrote to the Oakland County Civil Counsel and the Michigan Sheriff's Association about my options with this employee. The replies surprised me. First, you will see excerpts of my letter of August 28, 1974. Second, you will see excerpts of the Oakland County Civil Council of September 3, 1974. Third, you will see excerpts of the letter from the Michigan Sheriff's Association.

> Gentlemen,
> A situation has occurred in Oakland County in which I have been asked to supply Special Deputization for the expansion of the County Security Unit ... It is my understanding that with the appointment of the Sheriff's Department's former lieutenant, Donald Kratt, as Chief of this unit, the County Security Unit will be attempting to expand to cover the county parks, the Pontiac Airport, and miscellaneous other areas ...
> May I obtain an opinion ... as to my legal responsibilities for such deputization, the proper extent of their duties, the jurisdictional questions involved, the question of issuing them firearms, and any miscellaneous legal ramifications which may occur ...

> Dear Sheriff Spreen:
> ... Please be advised that the Oakland County Sheriff is not responsible for the acts, defaults and misconduct in office of any deputy sheriff ... In view of the foregoing, assuming that the security officers are deputized by you, you would not be responsible for their acts, defaults or misconduct in office.

> Dear Sheriff Spreen:
> Your letter directed to the Board of Directors of the Michigan Sheriff's Association was discussed at length September 11, 1974. The following is a motion adopted unanimously by the Board of Directors:
> "Sheriff O'Brien moved that the Board support the position that in deputizing men for that purpose Sheriff Spreen is setting a dangerous precedent and abdicating his responsibilities as sheriff, and that the letter should be referred to the Corporation Counsel of Oakland County for an answer...."
> Please note that you could be in criminal violation to fail to perform your functions in the preservation of peace and the detention of criminals ...
> Again, the Michigan Sheriff's Association requests you do not relinquish your statutory responsibilities.

## Replacing My Undersheriff

Dear Jay,
On October 15, 1974, the *Detroit News* carried an article by Robert E. Roach about my new undersheriff called "Spreen's Move Puts Pressure on GOP."

> ... Democrat Spreen's appointment of a new undersheriff—the only post filled solely at his own discretion—places in the unwilling hands of the GOP-dominated county Board of Commissioners the fate of current Undersheriff Leo Hazen ... Deputies—with whom Hazen is popular—were incensed after Spreen announced the moves.

## Acceptance of My New Undersheriff

Dear Jay,

A month later, on November 16, 1974, Ralph Kingzett of *The Oakland Press* wrote an article, "Sheriff's Dept. Quieting Down as Support for Nichols Builds."

> After a hectic week, things are quieting down at the Oakland County Sheriff's Department and the men seem to be uniting in support of Undersheriff John Nichols ...
>
> The union representing sheriff's department employees had Hazen as its guest at a meeting that night. Also on hand were Murphy, County Prosecutor L. Brooks Patterson, and Spreen's county commissioner, Patrick Nowak ... Murphy promised that he [Hazen] would be taken care of with another county job ...
>
> Hazen gets a job where he will be in a position to review Spreen's requests for money, men, and equipment.. And Nichols has been creating some respect among the deputies, who regard him as a cop's cop, and morale in the department is improving.

# *1975*

Saigon falls to communism
Jimmy Hoffa disappears
Ford assassination attempts by Lynette "Squeaky" Fromme and Sara Jane Moore
Federal government bails out New York City

# Longer Sentences for Crimes Using Guns

Dear Jay,

My statement at the Senate Judiciary Committee on Senate Bill #127 on February 15, 1975, started the ball rolling for criminals to get a tougher (enhanced) sentence if they committed a crime with a weapon. The editor of the *Oklahoma Journal* called my comments to the attention of Oklahoma sheriffs and wrote an article (3/12/75) urging citizens to back such a law in Oklahoma. I was asked to submit that speech to the sheriff's journal. The June-July 1975 issue of *The National Sheriff* contained my article, "Can Crime Be Conquered?" See my note at the end of the article about sentence enhancements for committing a crime with a gun.

> In 1938, J. Edgar Hoover spoke to the Detroit Economic Club. His subject was "Lawlessness as a National Menace." A few days ago, Clarence Kelley, the current director of the FBI, addressed the same body on that very same topic, asking the question, "Can Crime Be Conquered?" Sad, isn't it, that after 37 years the problem still exists, but to an even greater degree? Something *must* be done, and *now*, so that 37 years from now in the year 2012, we will not be asking, "Can crime be conquered?"
>
> I write these words not only as a county sheriff but as a police educator, with 37 years of police study and experience, having opened my first police textbooks the same year J. Edgar Hoover was in Detroit.
>
> Citizens are being murdered daily in their own homes and businesses and on the streets and police who respond to aid them are laying their lives on the line constantly.
>
> I have seen the distressing toll in robberies, burglaries, rapes ... citizens frightened and killed ... policemen hurt and shot. I have had the heart-breaking experience over and over again of attending their funerals. In the past ten years alone a thousand law enforcement officers have been killed, and 70 percent by individuals using handguns. The fact is that policemen walk and work on the fingertips of death.
>
> There is no reason why this massacre—this uneven battle—should continue.
>
> *The time for action is now!*
>
> Four years ago in May 1971, I wrote a newspaper column calling for an additional jail sentence for the carrying of a gun when it is used in the commission of certain crimes. I recommended five years mandated by law with *no* probation, *no* parole, *no* early release, and *no* good time.
>
> I believe the judiciary of Michigan still should have discretion over punishment for the crime itself, but no discretion on the charge of using a gun to

commit it, if he is convicted by a jury of his peers. I believe these "peers" are sick and tired of this nonsense.

We must do something about handgun control, but there is a vital difference between gun control and gun prohibition. We do not want to make criminals out of people who buy or have guns out of fear to protect their loved ones, themselves, or their homes. We are not going to accomplish anything by trying to ban all handguns.

Some persons are supporting a drive to prohibit bullets. Their slogan, "You need a bullet like you need a hole in the head," is commendable, but naïve. I assure you that the potential killer, killer-burglar, killer-robber, killer-rapist will have his gun and get the bullets, too!

We know that police cannot protect every person in his own home. We do not have the money or the manpower. We are losing the battle in the streets. Yet, we must do something—something better than we have done in the past.

Let us start by getting at the *real* problem. Let us get at the *criminal* who brings and uses a gun when he commits a crime. This is gun control. Later, we can address the problem of too many handguns possessed by too many citizens. That problem may alleviate itself if we solve the other problem first.

We need to punish the criminal, not the law-abiding citizen. There is a difference between a person who buys a gun to protect his loved ones and someone who is out to commit a crime with an instrument of death.

Certainly, the bum who uses a gun should not be allowed to thumb his nose at society. Let us remove these potential killers from the scene. If a five-year sentence went into effect, they would go away to prison say on July 4, 1976, and know that they would not be out again until July 4, 1981. Maybe, then, our good citizens on our nation's 200th anniversary will have a little freedom to pursue *their* happiness in these United States of America.

And if these hoodlums are convicted a second time of using a gun in the commission of these crimes, the mandatory sentence should be doubled or tripled. The third time we should throw away the key!

Just recently, several state legislators have proposed a two-year mandatory sentence for the use of a gun in a felony. While I still would like to see a stiffer sentence (five years), I definitely support their proposal. It would be good for Michigan to lead the nation with such enlightened legislation. We should congratulate their efforts.

The criminals, no doubt, always will be able to get a gun, and of course, the bullets for it, but if this legislation is passed, they will think twice before bringing a loaded gun with them when they go out to rob, burgle, and rape.

Who do we have committing crimes today? About three-fourths are recidivists—a small core who are committing the majority of crimes over and over again. And half of all serious crimes are committed by kids. Far more than half are drug addicts who are hopped up. Most of all, these people use guns. A gun should not be in such hands—hands which represent people who couldn't care less, or are immature or are crazed, hopped up by drugs, and whose fingertips could snuff out the life of a citizen or policeman.

The smart criminal is one who is "jail smart." He wheels and deals, delaying and adjourning the trial, using and abusing our criminal justice system, while the victim lies in the hospital or the morgue.

Let's stop playing games! Or if we *must* play games, let's change some of the rules.

We citizens must get smart now, so that we leave our children a better day 37 years from now.

I would be remiss if I did not lend my voice in support of these good legislative proposals. Let's send out a strong message to the bums and punks, and potential killers everywhere, and put some fear into their hearts. Let us save our good citizens and save our police.

Let's do it *now, here* in Michigan!

I express these thoughts today for myself and also for the Oakland County Sheriff's Department. In addition, I have a letter of endorsement for the bill from the South Oakland Chiefs of Police and I believe that there is not a police chief or a sheriff in this country who would not agree that something must be done about the use of guns while committing a crime.

Let us leave a better legacy for the future. Let us show that the law can work for society. Let us show that society can work for the law. And Michigan can lead the way.

Let us leave the gun-carrying burglar, robber, and rapist to his "peers" on the jury. Let him know that "if he does the crime, he'll do the time."

Jay, I am happy to report on some research on deterrence because of such laws. It has been found that if a sentence enhancement is well publicized, it can have immediate effects in reducing crimes with a gun by 4% within a year. That was shown when California adopted Proposition 8 in 1982. A few years later, because these criminals were in jail longer (incapacitated from committing crimes with a gun) such crimes dropped by 8%. The effect continued to increase to a 20% drop in crimes committed with a gun by 5-7 years after passage of the law. This was shown by Daniel Kessler and Steven Levitt in "Using Sentence Enhancements to Distinguish between Deterrence and Incapacitation" published in *Journal of Law and Economics*, Vol. XLII (April 1999).

When Virginia enhanced sentences by prosecuting criminals who committed a crime with a gun under federal law, not only was an extra five years added to the regular sentence but the federal prison required that the criminal be located far from his or her area (Project Exile). This well-publicized law was passed in 1997 and within one year, there was a 40% drop in gun homicides and a 21% drop in violent crimes. Ten years later, there has been a 46% drop in gun homicides,

65% drop in crimes committed with guns, and 35% drop in violent crime. The National Rifle Association has endorsed Project Exile.

Unfortunately, even though many states have such a law, they do not publicize it well or they choose not to enforce it due to crowded jails.

## Improper Use of Deputies by Politicians

Dear Jay,

The *Oakland Press* did a story called "Oakland Dems Want Sheriff's Badges Lifted from Courthouse Security Men" on May 2, 1975. It wasn't enough to have the Republicans to deal with; I sometimes had trouble with the Democrats on the Oakland County Board of Commissioners. They objected to what seemed to be a private use of some deputies to help a Republican (Daniel T. Murphy) by escorting people like Ronald Reagan around to do fundraising for Murphy. I wanted to regain control of my own deputies and deny requests for them to be used by fundraising politicians.

> Democrats on the Oakland County Board of Commissioners Thursday called on Sheriff Johannes F. Spreen to revoke the "special deputy" status of county security officers involved in last weekend's fund-raising activities for County Executive Daniel T. Murphy …
>
> News of the security force activities surfaced when an officer, Gary L. Hall, was ticketed for reckless driving by Taylor police on the I-94 freeway Sunday morning while escorting former Gov. Ronald Reagan of California to Detroit Metropolitan Airport.
>
> Reagan was the featured speaker at a fundraiser that cleared up a $40,000 Murphy campaign debt from last November's election. It also was learned that about eight of the security officers acted as Reagan bodyguards during the event.
>
> William M. Spinelli, Murphy's chief deputy, said that all the officers volunteered their time, and the Friends of Dan Murphy Committee, which sponsored the fundraiser, will pay rental for the cars and radios used.
>
> He said no taxpayers' money was used.
>
> Democrats still called the security officers' actions "improper."
>
> If Spreen revokes the deputy sheriff status, the officers won't have the power to make arrests, or even write parking tickets, unless the Board of Commissioners specifically authorizes the latter activity.
>
> Spreen has promised to be objective in his decision on continuing deputization. It is known that he has opposed the security force since last August when a former sheriff's department lieutenant, Donald K. Kratt, was named chief … Kratt was a Republican candidate for sheriff in 1972 but was elimi-

nated in the party's primary by Leo R. Hazen, who lost to Spreen. Hazen, too, is now a Murphy aide.

Spreen has claimed that protecting county property should be a function of the sheriff's department ...

The resolution, which would give Spreen control of the force, introduced by Lennon, was referred to the Board's General Government Committee for study.

## No Local Support for Grants

Dear Jay,

I called a press conference on June 4 to try to bring attention to how my pleas for grants were being rebuffed. Billy Bowles of the *Detroit Free Press* wrote an article that same day entitled "Failure to Get Federal Grants Puzzles Spreen." However, he neglected to mention what I said at the press conference. I had explained that these grants are administered by the state and are based on decisions at the local level. Those planners were under Rhodes, an appointee of Murphy. I had also told reporters that Republican Party executives told me I would not get the funds I wanted for the department if I ran as a Democrat.

> ... Spreen said he has made nine applications for five projects since becoming sheriff on Jan. 1, 1973. If approved, the applications would have brought the county about $900,000 in federal funds, with the county putting up only about $50,000 [in matching funds], Spreen said ...
> 
> Spreen said the county declined to put up the necessary share of funds for two of the projects—a crime prevention program involving citizen participation and an expanded traffic force to assist Oakland County municipalities ... Spreen said he plans to ask Gov. Milliken, the Michigan Legislature and the Oakland County congressional delegation to look in the LEAA funding to see if Oakland County is being treated unfairly.

## I Was Investigated for "Gathering Intelligence"

Dear Jay,

The day after that press conference and article, the Chairman of the Oakland County Board of Commissioners, Daniel T. Murphy, made charges against me. My department and I were accused of abusing power by probing private lives and gathering intelligence on innocent citizens. *Oakland Tribune* reporter William L. Willoughby wrote about how I invited the state police to investigate our files and offices to disprove these allegations. The article "Sheriff Asks State Probe of His Department's Files" ran June 11, 1975.

The person we were accused of gathering intelligence about was the former county health director, a physician and U.S. Air Force colonel, who had recently left Michigan for California. Later, he became health director for Kansas in 1976 and even later went on to be health director of New Hampshire. As an aside, he was awarded the Legion of Merit in 2004.

> Sheriff Johannes F. Spreen of Oakland County said today that he has asked the Michigan State Police to investigate his department to prove that it has never conducted a politically motivated probe into private lives of individuals.
>
> But, Spreen said, this doesn't necessarily mean he won't cooperate—at least in part—with a planned investigation by a committee of the Oakland County Board of Commissioners into the same subject.
>
> Commissioner Paul E. Kasper (R-Bloomfield Township), one of the Democratic sheriff's most outspoken critics, last Thursday called for a broad investigation into "possible abuse of police power."
>
> On Friday, the board's Personnel Committee, which Kasper heads, voted to conduct a full investigation into allegations made by "more than one person" that Sheriff's Department officials investigated the private life of at least one county employee.
>
> Lt. Carl G. Matheny, one of Spreen's top aides, confirmed that he made "a casual inquiry" into an allegation that the county's former health director, Dr. Lowell M. Wiese, M.D., used marijuana.
>
> But Matheny said that the inquiry was not a formal investigation and that nothing was uncovered. Possession of marijuana is a misdemeanor.
>
> Dr. Wiese resigned his $40,000-a-year position with the County within a month of the "casual inquiry," but county sources said Dr. Wiese told them he wasn't aware of the inquiry at the time he decided to resign …
>
> Spreen said he will turn over all of his files to the State Police because "I'd rather have the investigation done by a professional police agency. I'm not going to have a bunch of self-serving politicians do it …"
>
> Spreen denied that he has a file on Dr. Wiese or on any other county employee or official. He said he never ordered any political investigations.

## I Asked the State to Investigate Me

Dear Jay,

Ralph Kingzett wrote an article, "Showdown: How Will Spreen Respond to County Board Subpoenas?" which was published in *The Oakland Press* on June 18, 1975. I had been subpoenaed to appear before the County Board of Commissioners with all records about 55 elected or appointed county officials.

The board has a 15-12 Republican majority. Its Republicans are bent on investigating whether Spreen's department conducted political probes of county officials.

Spreen and his aides deny that they have done so. But they do admit to making a few "discreet inquiries" regarding statements that County Health Director Dr. Lowell M. Wiese, who since has resigned and moved to California, said he smoked marijuana.

The statements came from Kay Riley, a Pontiac School District employee who works in the adult-education program at Oakland County Jail.

Ms. Riley, who said she had dated Wiese, said he told her of using marijuana. She said she made this public because she was angry at the doctor's opposition to a grant request that would fund a prisoner-rehabilitation program at the jail ...

In addition to all 27 county commissioners, the subpoenas demand any and all records Spreen's office might have on a host of other elected and appointed county officials.

That list includes County Executive Daniel T. Murphy, County Prosecutor L. Brooks Patterson, County Treasurer C. Hugh Dohany, County Clerk Lynn D. Allen, Drain Commissioner George Kuhn, Civil Counsel Robert P. Allen, Murphy aide Leo Hazen and Security Department Chief Donald Kratt.

Both Hazen and Kratt once were high-ranking members of Spreen's department.

Spreen says his department never has conducted a political probe and never will.

He accuses Kasper of demanding the board investigation as a political smokescreen to take the heat off Kratt.

Democrats on the board had demanded an investigation into Kratt's reported use of county men, walkie-talkies, and cars to provide security for former California Gov. Ronald Reagan when Reagan spoke at a fund-raiser last month for Murphy.

Kratt said the men used from his department volunteered their time and administration spokesmen say Murphy's fund-raising committee will pay a mileage rate for the use of the cars.

But in May, Deputy County Executive William M. Spinelli told a committee of the board of commissioners he could not recall whether the Republicans agreed to pay for the cars before or after embarrassing publicity surfaced ...

In any event, if the board follows its routine procedures, the probe will be referred to committee. But no board committees will be meeting next week because nine county commissioners, including Houghten and Kasper and Murphy and two aides will be in Hawaii for the annual National Association of Counties convention during that period.

# I Answered the Charge Against Me

Dear Jay,

On June 19, 1975, I appeared before the Oakland County Board of Commissioners. I took this prepared statement, which I read.

> Honorable Commissioners,
>
> I appear voluntarily as Sheriff of Oakland County. I have long respected the theory of the founding fathers in the division of powers doctrine. While by law, there is enormous power vested in the Oakland County Board of Commissioners as a legislative body, I do not believe it includes the "discovery" of all records and files amassed by the Sheriff's Department in accordance with appropriate laws of the state, nor the authority to conduct such unwarranted incursions into the executive branch of government.
>
> As there is no legal aide assigned to the Sheriff's office and as Civil Counsel for the County has already been committed as advisor to the Board of Commissioners, I respectfully request I be provided adequate funds for provision of competent legal counsel for necessary advice and consultation.
>
> I shall not dignify the allegations—replete with insinuations and inferences directed to subtle assassination of character attending to the service of these subpoenas. The reputations of my staff and myself for professional conduct are well above that.
>
> To reassure this honorable body, and other elected and appointed public officials as well as the citizens of Oakland County, let me state that the Sheriff's Department has not now nor did it ever investigate personal lives except when a criminal allegation was made—and then only according to the law!
>
> As a law enforcement officer of some 34 years experience, I have always stood ready to execute orders of courts and those bodies properly authorized to issue such writs. I feel that, unless judicial resolution is sought, that this will be the first in a new series of desultory tactics to impede, embarrass, and emasculate the office of the Sheriff of Oakland County. I have no desire to become a docile party to the establishment of precedence, which may well impact not only Oakland County, but the entire state of Michigan, perhaps the nation.
>
> I now present to this Board sworn affidavits from the Undersheriff, from the commanders of various sections, including Chief of Detectives, and the lieutenant in charge of records, categorically denying improprieties in investigation or preparation and maintenance of records. I submit these now as evidence of my good faith.
>
> I do not intend to bring criminal files, personnel files, or jail records to this body unless so ordered by a court of proper jurisdiction. Included in such files, necessarily, may be items of embarrassment to some of the 55 named and only serve to further exacerbate an already inflamed situation.
>
> It would seem to me that instead of this travesty, it would be better if we would use all this energy and time to fight in a common alliance against the

perpetrators of crime instead of a fight against each other. Today's shocking national rise in crime (and Oakland County's is even higher) calls for the utmost cooperation and coordination among federal, state, and local law enforcement agencies, and it should extend to cooperation among branches of government. Cooperation (which begins with communication) should be the order of the day—it may well be the only thing that can save the day!

Thank you for your first invitation for me to speak before the Board in the 2½ years I have been sheriff.

Sincerely and respectfully,
Johannes F. Spreen, Sheriff

## I Finally Got My First Grant

Dear Jay,

Amazingly, during this investigation I was notified that we were awarded a grant. The *Spinal Column* weekly for west Oakland County did a story on it July 2, 1975, called "Sheriff's Unit Gets Funding for Inmate Rehabilitation: First Since Spreen's Election."

> The Oakland County Sheriff's department has been awarded a grant of $146,700 from the office of criminal justice programs for an inmate rehabilitation program at the county jail ...
>
> According to Lieutenant Harry Jones, supervisor of corrective services, the grant will be used to hire new personnel and provide improved counseling, education, and vocational training for jail inmates.
>
> Jones said the funds will facilitate the hiring of nine new personnel at the jail, including two detention officers, three coordinators, three caseworkers and a secretary-typist.
>
> A screening program will be established which will enable corrections officials to gear the educational program offered at the jail to the inmates on a more individual basis, according to Jones.
>
> The prisoners will be more thoroughly tested for physical problems as well as educational and intelligence levels, Jones said ...
>
> Oakland County and the state will each contribute $8,000 toward the rehabilitation program, Jones said ...
>
> The typical inmate is ill equipped to alter his behavior without the availability of a rehabilitation program, the grant application states.
>
> A statistical analysis reveals that 77% of the inmates had been in the jail on a previous occasion, 13.4% had been arrested 10 or more times, 32% had a serious substance abuse problem, 45% lacked a high school diploma or equivalent, 50% were unemployed when arrested, 24% were either divorced or separated, and 55% had dependent children.

# Press Urges End of Probe

Dear Jay,

An editorial opinion written by Neil Munro in *The Oakland Press* ran on August 21, 1975. It was entitled "It's Time to End Probe of Sheriff."

> The County Board of Commissioners' committee probe of alleged use of the Sheriff's Department for political purposes has withered to the point of focusing on six-month-old cocktail party quips.
>
> Two members of the department supposedly told a Road Commission attorney at a Lansing party that they were "out to get" somebody.
>
> Republican Commissioner Paul Kasper of Bloomfield Hills claims he was told that the policemen in question went to Lansing to more or less "spy" on Road Commission executive John Grubba.
>
> Unfortunately for Kasper, who is leading the inquiry, none of the participants in the conversation remembers hearing or mentioning Grubba's name.
>
> This kind of nickel-dime foraging for "sinister" off-hand remarks can go on forever.
>
> After all, lots of people who work for the county, including the Sheriff's Department, presumably have said lots of things to lots of other people. And a lot of their conversation probably has dealt with people they work for or with or otherwise know.
>
> A tape recording of all the gossip, meaningless threats, griping and second-hand information would no doubt go around the world.
>
> And virtually none of it would be of any consequence to any taxpayer.
>
> Kasper says he's willing to end the hearings. He obviously is reluctant to call any witnesses who might gore Republican, as opposed to Democratic, oxen.
>
> It would be sporting of him to call them and there are at least two, Sheriff Johannes Spreen and department Lt. Charles Whitlock, who have something to say. Spreen, at least, is clamoring to say it.
>
> But it would be a good idea for the committee to take Kasper up on his offer to call it a day. If anybody else has anything constructive to say, they can call a press conference or tell it to the prosecutor.
>
> Kasper can retire with his slim volume of "revelations" and the committee and the rest of the board can try some legislating.
>
> There has been little of that so far this year.

# The Investigation Cleared the Department and Me

Dear Jay,

I asked to appear again before the Oakland County Board of Commissioners on August 28, 1975. I took this written statement to the Board, which I read.

Honorable Committee:

I appear, again voluntarily, as Sheriff of Oakland County—this time at my request.

On June 5, certain charges were made by the chair of this committee against the Sheriff's Department and me.

I categorically denied those charges then, and requested that the State Police, whose reputation for integrity and professionalism is well established, minutely examine all our files, query all our personnel, and ascertain whether there had been any wrongdoing by myself or my department. They have done so, and we stand vindicated!

I said I would stand on that evaluation then, and I stand on it now. I stood behind my department then, and I stand behind them now.

After an extensive and expensive investigation—after 12 weeks—almost a quarter of a year—after great cost to the taxpayers, we come to this moment.

The allegations made by your chairman in his statement of purpose have all been discredited.

These allegations were made on spurious grounds—on events and incidents that any reasonable person could have straightened out by open, direct communication.

What has been shown after 12 weeks is nothing! This confirms the State Police findings.

There have been no bombshells. Whatever fires have been ignited have come from the "source of the gasoline itself."

What evidence has been adduced seems to indicate political activity—but on the opposite side of the fence. It seems the accusers and not the accusee should have the spotlight of scrutiny placed on them.

No testimony has been brought out to substantiate these charges. Not one scintilla of evidence has been produced.

The taxpayers have suffered a tremendous cost in dollars.

Commissioners on both sides of the aisle have discussed these "hearings" with me—they were embarrassed—they had no faith in the charges; they offered me their sympathy.

When some members of this committee were looking for justification for what they had embarked upon, the words of Undersheriff John Nichols put it, I believe, into perspective. He charged this committee with taking a small incident and blowing it out of proportion, "like looking at the dew on a rose and envisioning the damn Pacific Ocean."

I repeat, not a scintilla of evidence was adduced to support these irresponsible charges. Rather the pathetic performance of a couple of boorish megalomaniacs seem to have come close to revealing a conspiracy of politics on county time—but by the other side—and I was the target.

It seems to indicate a sinister cabal here in Oakland County. I know it is a crime to interfere with a law enforcement officer in the performance of his function. I ask: what is it when a group of people interferes wrongly with an entire law enforcement agency?

This is the first time such an investigation has been held in Oakland County. This was a political witch hunt—a Kangaroo Court—which almost degenerated into a true Star Chamber proceeding, but the concerned citizens who showed up each night prevented that and for that, my heartfelt thanks to them.

In order to ensure that this ill-defined power granted by the legislature is NOT misused again, we intend to seek legislative redress. The transcript of this hearing will provide prima facie evidence of the need to curtail this raw power.

My thanks also go to the members of the press who covered these hearings and put the spotlight of public scrutiny on this charade.

Law enforcement could be destroyed in America without the interest of concerned citizens, and without the fair and impartial monitoring by a free and independent press.

This mess, started by two irresponsible, self-serving politicians, has hurt a lot of people and caused much ill feeling and a great deal of harm. But ironically, we have had in all this evil the piercing rays of truth prevail—and the department and its Sheriff stand vindicated—both by the State Police and this "inquisition" and for that I am grateful. My thanks go to other commissioners of this committee.

I now demand the resignation of those commissioners responsible for this farce, and I demand that they make reimbursement to the county for misuse and waste of public funds.

I challenge their integrity and their motivation.

I have taken the issue to court—to a proper tribunal where the issue of the committee's authority will be resolved.

Thank you for your time.

## Commissioners Should Investigate Their Own

Dear Jay,

Alan Lenhoff wrote an article called "County GOP: Much to Answer For" which ran in *The Oakland Press* on September 2, 1975. Lenhoff, an excellent writer and prestigious man, is now the Strategic Director of Detroit Newspapers and on the Board of Directors for the University of Michigan campus newspaper.

In the article he said he thought it "will be interesting to see whether the Republican county commissioners who were so quick to call for an investigation of the Democratic county sheriff will be as eager to probe the recent charges of political spying by aides of Republican County Executive Daniel Murphy."

He described how in testimony before the committee investigating my alleged political intelligence gathering revealed charges of political spying and tricks by Murphy's Special Projects Director Leo Hazen and county Security Chief

Donald Kratt. Hazen admitted that he asked one of my top aides to keep a log of the sheriff's attendance, but denied it was politically motivated. He also denied being involved in a movement to recall me as sheriff.

He said, "Kratt, sheriff's officials say, has been keeping political files on sheriff's employees since Murphy transferred him from the sheriff's department to his security unit job after Kratt angered Spreen by apparently leaking departmental information to Murphy. Kratt refused to answer the charges under oath."

He pointed out that the probe of my office was spearheaded by Paul Kasper, Patrick Nowak, and Fred Houghten, because they said "public allegations" had been made about Spreen's activities.

He wrote "Those public allegations turned out to be largely rumors that reporters were investigating. In contrast, many of the charges against Kratt and Hazen were made under oath. But few seriously think that Kratt and Hazen will be investigated. The Republicans have been embarrassed enough by their failure to prove their case against the sheriff. And the minority Democrats say they are sick of the political fighting that they can't win and would like to get back to business as usual."

He concluded by saying

> Meanwhile, the probe has probably wasted about $10,000 in tax dollars for legal fees, court reporters, overtime pay, and related expenses. And instead of attending to the business of government and law enforcement, your 27 commissioners and the sheriff have been running into each other around the political bush, perhaps waiting for each other to collapse of exhaustion.
>
> The county commissioners have been astoundingly unproductive this year. They have fought back and forth on a slew of partisan battles, accomplishing little more since January than fine tuning the county's growing bureaucracy, traveling to conventions and rising up like zombies every few months to accept boxcars full of federal emergency hiring dollars for the recession-plagued county.
>
> It's time to turn things around.

# Media Urged County to Stop Wasting Tax Dollars

Dear Jay,

A few days later, on September 8 and 9, 1975, Channel WXYZ-TV had a little comment about the probe by Jim Osborn who said the following to TV viewers.

Fortunately for Oakland County citizens, the inquisition of Sheriff Johannes Spreen is about over. The charges and counter charges about Spreen's alleged political spying have produced no solid results. The investigation of Sheriff Spreen fell considerably short of its promise. It was a waster of the public's time and we're glad it's over. If the County Commissioners who organized this attack on the Sheriff pursued legitimate county business with the same enthusiasm, real progress might be seen. The end of this charade must wait for the conclusion of a couple of lawsuits, but the sooner it's over the better for Oakland County.

# *1976*

Legionnaire's disease strikes 182, kills 29
Tall ships celebration in New York Harbor
Courts allow removal of life support for Karen Ann Quinlan
Mao Tse-tung died

## Contract Policing Was Increasing

Dear Jay,

I ran for a second term in 1976 and won. One of our biggest activities was contract policing for small communities. I prepared this paper for those who wanted to know more about it and called it "The Facts About Contract Policing."

What are the facts about contract policing? To answer this question, we need to have a complete definition for this relatively new concept of policing in rural/suburban population areas; determine its goals and objectives; and finally, gauge how well these goals and objectives are met by contract policing.

Contract policing is the term used by county sheriffs' departments for the law enforcement services provided by the sheriffs' department through agreements with local agencies of government, e.g., townships, in exchange for a pre-established annual fee.

The objectives of this arrangement are to provide policing where costs for policing are prohibitive or taxing for the local government unit to finance its own force, yet provide all necessary and effective services. This contractual arrangement still allows the local governmental unit to maintain control of the contracted force through its control of funds, and moreover, the local unit can cancel the agreement any month, even though the contract is written for a year, and this can be done with or without cause.

All residents of the county already have the protection of the sheriff's department, if called, by state statute and funded through county taxation, but these services usually only include indirect technical assistance, jail services, and supportive services due to the existence of local police units in many areas and the manpower budget of the county force.

But through contract policing, the local governmental unit receives not only the above-mentioned services of the sheriff's department, but regularly assigned deputies to work directly within the local jurisdiction, often out of a local substation or set-up headquarters in the township, village, etc. The contract provides the necessary funds to hire qualified and trained deputies for the local jurisdiction. This is at a cost savings to the contracted area, since recruitment, testing, training, and equipment are provided for by the sheriff's department, plus often enough, supportive forces including dispatchers and an established and technical communications system.

On the other hand, where local units of government have or decide to have their own police force, it varies in size and quality of operations. To begin a force, it is first necessary to plan and execute a budget allotment. Then, hire a chief or director (it is usually a local leader in the community), who in turn finds 4-6 subordinates for patrol. Later, perhaps, a radio dispatcher will be found. Training, qualifications, and technical services are dependent upon subsequent budget allowances by the local governmental unit. The power of the chief or director allowed varies from community to community, depending upon political and governmental factors.

If contract policing is agreed upon, however, the community or township could experience a real cost savings, a great potentiality for professionalism in its policing, backup forces, and the elimination of duplication in services.

The local governing unit should contact the sheriff's department to start the process. Hearings are customary, and legal counsel is contacted for review of existing ordinances within the local area before a resolution for the agreement is made and voted upon, and the contract can be established. But this process is not as lengthy as the items may suggest. A month or two is average.

In Oakland County, Michigan, where contract policing is operating effectively, there are nine townships out of 25 with contracts with the Sheriff's Department. Two more are expected soon.

But the county also has some 42 local police and public safety units, particularly in the heavily populated south end, supported by local jurisdictions. However, in more suburban/rural areas of the north and west, the concept of contract policing has steadily grown in popularity. The existing local agencies of law enforcement have long been in existence. But population shifts to the northern and western sections are progressing, making contract policing an efficient and effective solution to the need for more quality in law enforcement.

Crime prevention and control demand teamwork, coordination, and expertise. Contract policing accentuates these qualities.

## The Pros and Cons of Contract Policing

Dear Jay,

There were so many questions about contract policing that Don Kubit of *The Oakland Press* ran a series of three articles exploring the advantages and disadvantages of contracting for law enforcement services with our Department. Here are excerpts from his last article, which ran February 25, 1976.

> Oakland County Sheriff Johannes Spreen calls police contracting "the wave of the future."
>
> "It is the best method of getting professionalism into police services," Spreen added.
>
> He said the "greatest virtue of contracting" was that it removed police from the influence of politics.
>
> "The officer knows the only reason he has a job is because people are buying his service. That job is on the line if he does not perform professionally," Spreen said.

Undersheriff John Nichols agreed with that assessment. "Police contracting is as close as you can get to a divorce of police and politics. The police are able to function in a political vacuum and are responsible to the people, not the politics of the township," Nichols said.

Spreen added that one of the strengths of the contract system is that the sheriff is the only elected law enforcement officer in the county. "If the people don't like what I'm doing, they can remove me from office," Spreen said. "But what can they do about an appointed police chief?"

... A continual criticism of the contract system is that in the event of an emergency, a contracted deputy may be called out of his assigned area, thereby leaving it unprotected. "There is no way of telling how many times a deputy is pulled out of his area. It may happen two times a week or twice a year," said Lt. Carl Matheny. "But the reverse also applies. If there is trouble in an area, we send in other men regardless of how many the township has contracted for."

## Open House at the Sheriff's Department

Dear Jay,

I wanted people to be more familiar with the Oakland County Sheriff's Department and issued this news release on March 17 inviting people to visit us.

Oakland County Sheriff Johannes F. Spreen will actively promote a renewed "open door" policy at the jail by inviting groups to see their jail in action.

"I believe that the people are our real bosses, and so they should be able to see what they are getting for their tax dollar," said Spreen.

The first groups to accept the Sheriff's invitation are the Birmingham Optimist Club, who will be hosted today, and the American Business Women's Association, tomorrow.

"Members of the staff are donating their off-duty time to the program," said Spreen, "and I'm providing the coffee and donuts for the first day."

"We hope more and more groups will accept our invitation to tour the jail," said Spreen.

Tours can be arranged by calling 858-5000.

## Does the Sheriff's Office Have What?

Dear Jay,

I issued a news release on April 9 about a new program to beautify the area with trusty labor under the direction of a woman named Helena Sexauer. Her name was pronounced "Sex Hour." When someone asked a deputy if we had a Sex Hour in the Sheriff's Office, he said, "Hell, we don't even get a coffee break!"

I learned that when Mrs. Sexauer died in 2002, county commissioners honored her for her lifelong devotion to maintaining natural environmental beauty.

> Oakland County Sheriff Johannes F. Spreen today announced "Project Beautification."
> 
> In a pilot program in 1975, it was observed that inmates enjoyed working on outdoor community projects. Under the direction of Mrs. Helena Sexauer, the new Administrative Reservist for Environmental Concerns, flowerbeds will be created and planted by trusty labor.
> 
> This year it is hoped that this program will take in all major intersections along Telegraph Road between 8 Mile Road and 12 Mile Road. Four such beds, under Mrs. Sexauer's guidance, were created last year by trusty labor. The labor to be used will be volunteers from the Oakland County Trusty Camp under the direction of Lt. Harry H. Jones.
> 
> "By this involvement, they will be beautifying our County and making a positive contribution to the community," said Sheriff Spreen.
> 
> This year in honor of our Country's 200th birthday, red, white, and blue petunias will be planted. "This will be a truly American way of all working together to say 'Happy Birthday America' from one of its most beautiful counties," said Sheriff Spreen.

## Trying to Be Non-Political

Dear Jay,

During my campaign for re-election, William Willoughby of the *Daily Tribune* wrote an article published on April 12, 1976, entitled "Sheriff's Non-Political Re-election Campaign Could Create Some Political Turmoil in Oakland."

Willoughby explained that I had decided not to seek a U.S. Senate seat or run against Dan Murphy as county executive. He wrote:

> Democrats must now turn elsewhere for a standard bearer to oppose Murphy.... Mrs. Elizabeth P. Howe, chairman of the county Democratic Party, said [Eugene W.] Kuthy has decided on his political future, but wouldn't say what Kuthy's decision is ... To date, no opposition has materialized on the Republican side, and Mrs. Howe said she doesn't expect a "serious" candidate [for sheriff] to run. She said she considers Spreen "unbeatable."

## My Announcement to Run for a Second Term

Dear Jay,

The community newspaper with the amusing name *Spinal Column* published an article April 14 called "Spreen Announces He'll Run for Reelection as Sheriff."

> Casting aside speculation that he would run for some other political office, Oakland County sheriff Johannes F. Spreen announced Saturday, April 10, that he will seek reelection to another 4-year term.
>
> "My real abiding interest and concern is, and always will be, law enforcement. And now, as a resident of Oakland County for over 5 years, I have a deep concern and interest for law enforcement in Oakland County. As sheriff of this county, I felt I should do something to keep this a safe and pleasant county in which to live," the Democrat said.
>
> Spreen's candidacy announcement also contained a statement of confidence in his undersheriff, John Nichols ...
>
> This culminated last summer in a board of commissioners' committee investigation into alleged political activity in the sheriff's department. Spreen's department was cleared of those charges by a state police investigation.
>
> Since that time, the political alignment of the board of commissioners has shifted from Republican control to a 14-13 alignment in favor of the Democrats.
>
> "There is greater potential for cooperation and open mindedness on the part of those actively involved in the county's government than ever before," the sheriff stated.

## Plans to Contain Three Sources of Crime

Dear Jay,

I presented a handout of our plans to the Oakland County Board of Commissioners on May 5, 1976. I made a 30-minute presentation to them excerpted here. (I referred to Governor William Milliken, who was the longest running governor of Michigan—14 years. In 2004, he broke party ranks to back John Kerry against George W. Bush.)

> This presentation is not all mine. The credit goes to the men and women of the Oakland County Sheriff's Department who thought, planned, worked, and contributed in a teamwork relationship to make this presentation possible.
>
> I had the pleasure of being invited by Governor Milliken to engage in a crime prevention conference yesterday. The polls taken by the Office of Criminal Justice Programs show two-thirds of the people in our state rank crime as

the number one concern, that 1 in 4 families were affected last year by crime, and that is a rise from the previous poll of 1 in 5 families.

Crime and the fear of crime makes, as you all know, for a community image and a state of mind. A bad image is bad for business, bad for community growth, and bad for community pride. People despair and move to areas where they feel safer, and as a result, we all suffer.

What can we do? We must do something about the recidivist criminal, that small core who causes us the largest cost, who commits the majority of the crime over and over again. We must do something about the young people who commit half of all our serious crimes. It's shocking that the age of the most serious offenders is 16, exceeded only by 17 year olds. We must do something about the drug pushers who create addicts, who in turn commit so many crimes in order to sustain their habits. These three categories cause the most crime and the most problems and shame America today.

Thank God, we now have a mandatory sentencing law for the use of a gun in a felony in the State of Michigan, and other states are following our lead. It must become a nationwide concept. Let the word go out "You will be punished for using a gun to commit a crime."

Let's take a quick look at the cost of crime. The National Crime Commission recently estimated that crime totally costs us between $20 and $30 billion a year. It costs over $1 billion in Michigan. It costs Oakland County over $100 million a year.

The FBI says that burglary results in an average loss to the victim of $310. In Oakland County, we have over 15,000 burglaries a year. That's almost $5,000,000. The arson crimes average nearly $3,000 and in Oakland County with 400 arsons a year, that's $1,200,000. Each auto theft produces an average loss of $948 and with Oakland County's 800 car thefts a year, which means $758,400.

The FBI has even tried to put a price tag on murder. Their guess is a social cost of $100,000. Last year there were 66 murders in Oakland County—$6,600,000.

It is only natural that the men and women in the Sheriff's Department have one primary concern—that of better, more efficient, professional law enforcement.

We will be passing out something to you today, which will represent the composite thinking of the men and women in the Department. Our purpose in presenting this to you is to keep you informed and aware of what our plans and thoughts are, not just for the immediate future, but on a long-range basis.

We are also passing out some of the accomplishments of the Sheriff's Department during the past three years.

As a public servant, I have an obligation to keep the people informed concerning the state of law enforcement in this County.

You have the power to order priorities, and the extent of your interest and involvement in law enforcement will be a great factor in determining the destiny of our own communities.

Let's continue to be tough on the criminal. Let's continue our efforts to prevent a crime before it occurs. Let's continue to educate the public in possible ways to protect themselves from the murderers, burglars and all criminals who prey on our society.

Please accept our invitation to visit us at anytime or call us. Our doors are open to each of you, and the Undersheriff and I welcome your questions and suggestions.

## Expansion Plans

Dear Jay,

The newspapers covered that presentation. I will excerpt one such article by Alan Lenhoff of *The Oakland Press* on May 7, entitled "Spreen Tells Plans to Combat Crime."

> Oakland County Sheriff Johannes F. Spreen Thursday urged the public and officials to support his plans to fight rising crime by instituting new programs in the sheriff's department.
>
> In a speech to county commissioners, Spreen listed 63 long-range goals for the department, ranging from improving training for patrolmen to expanding the county jail ...
>
> Expansion of the jail is under study by both the county administration and the County Board of Commissioners.
>
> Many of Spreen's proposals would create specialized police services that the sheriff's department would provide to local police agencies. They include:
>
> - An intelligence bureau that would keep tabs on suspected criminals.
>
> - A "major crimes" division that would specialize in investigating murders, rapes, and kidnappings.
>
> - Buying specialized equipment including covert listening devices, infrared nighttime surveillance gear, and a surveillance van.
>
> Spreen also asked for an improved radio communications center, more crime lab technicians, new programs for rehabilitating jail inmates, a room for reporters, and programs to educate the public on how to protect themselves against being crime victims.

# The Umbrella Concept of Police Services

Dear Jay,

Another article described my concept of the "umbrella" concept of police services. This came about because we had a series of child killings (three in the first four months of 1976 in different towns in Oakland County) and needed better investigation services and collaboration between agencies. This article (excerpted) was published in the *Daily Tribune* on May 6, 1976, called "Spreen Wants Oakland to Fund Police 'Umbrella'."

> Sheriff Johannes F. Spreen of Oakland County today proposed that the County pay for increased training of all city and township law enforcement personnel and centralize police functions such as dispatching and detective work.
>
> He called his proposals "an umbrella of protective support" and said each police department would remain responsible for its own local patrol.
>
> Spreen released a three-page list of proposals to increase cooperation among departments and innovations to "bring law enforcement in step with the rest of society."
>
> Spreen estimated that his proposals if implemented would trim approximately $1 million per year in the losses of county victims of crime.
>
> Specifically, he proposed that the County build a training facility, which would be used to educate all police officers in the County.
>
> The balance of Spreen's proposals deal with services, which he said are most efficiently handled by a countywide agency rather than by each department.
>
> Spreen also said dispatching can be handled more efficiently on a countywide level than each department handling its own communications. He said, "Just in the Royal Oak Township area, there are nine police agencies, each with its own dispatcher."
>
> Spreen said not only would centralized dispatching be more efficient, it would allow quicker access to countywide crime records.

# Stopping Big Shots from Obstructing Justice

Dear Jay,

Whenever we found that people were obstructing justice, I thought we needed to take a strong stand. Sometimes it made news like this *Daily Tribune* article of May 10, 1976, entitled "Sheriff Takes Badges in OCC Ticket Probe."

Oakland Community College public safety officers refused to wear their uniforms or patrol campuses today following the lifting of their county deputy status, a move that left them without arrest or ticket-writing powers.

The Oakland County Sheriff's Department removed the deputy status at midnight because of alleged attempts by the college's administration to keep a traffic ticket issued to faculty members and administrators out of court.

The county prosecutor's office is investigating to determine if members of the administration should be charged with obstructing justice, Chief Assistant Prosecutor Richard Thompson confirmed.

Thompson said, "The investigation involves the alleged interference by members of the college administration with public safety officers and the performance of their duty."

College officials declined comment.

According to Undersheriff John Nichols, the lifting of the deputy status is no reflection on the deputies themselves but came about because of the alleged actions by the administration. Nichols refused to call it ticket fixing, but said there were attempts to have at least one ticket resolved in some other way than taking it to court.

The 11-member public safety department patrols the college campuses, according to Sgt. Willie Hall of the OCC public safety department.

"We're just plain citizens today. We're just answering the telephone and we're not patrolling," Hall said.

"It's sort of a sickening feeling, because we can't do anything. If we saw a felony committed there is nothing we could do about it except call the police."

# Giving Publicity for Individual Anti-Crime Efforts

Dear Jay,

I was always trying to involve the people in crime prevention and sought to publicize their efforts. I was delighted to be in a picture with a little boy wearing a large cowboy hat and sheriff's badge we gave him. (Although he did not become a law enforcement officer, I noticed his name just the other day on a page of grateful citizens for officers who lost their lives in the line of duty.)

The caption in *The Oakland Press* on May 15 read as follows:

Avon boy earns badge of courage. Young Paul Ayotte has some time to grow into that sheriff's hat and badge, but he's already filled the role as far as Oakland County Sheriff Johannes Spreen is concerned. Spreen awarded a citizen's citation to the 7-year-old Avon Township boy for his "unusual display of bravery and citizenship." Earlier this year, Paul witnessed and reported an attempted theft of his neighbor's car. He gave enough information to deputies to lead to the arrest and conviction of a suspect. "This is the type of youngster who continues to give us hope for the future," Spreen said Friday before taking Paul on a private tour of the jail complex and to lunch. "His family and school can be proud of him."

## Asking the Public to Support a K-9 Corps

Dear Jay,

On June 26, 1976, I issued a news release asking for public contributions for a K-9 Corps. Here is the gist of the release, which I hoped would create good feelings.

> Sheriff Johannes F. Spreen requests public assistance in the funding of a vitally needed tracking dog program for Oakland County. "Up to this point," Sheriff Spreen said, "Deputy Stanley Clark and Edward Stout have trained and maintained their tracking dogs at their own expense for the Department's use.
> 
> "There is no greater pleasure that an officer feels than when he can return a lost child, safe and sound, to his parents, or track a felon to his lair," the Sheriff said. He then noted with tongue-in-cheek, "The use of tracking dogs, you know, proves once again that just like we can't replace men with machines, we can't replace his best friend, either."

Jay, I'm happy to say that in 2007, the Oakland County Sheriff's Department has two bomb dogs and 11 other canines for tracking, property recovery, narcotic detection, etc. Candidates for the canine unit are selected by the Sheriff. Each applicant must have at least three years seniority with the department, and at least one year in Patrol Services. Once the officer is selected, they enter an intensive five-week training academy with a dog that is pre-trained by the Oakland Police Academy. The team is provided a special vehicle and weekly training in order to maintain and reinforce their skills. The unit receives over one thousand calls per year.

## Joining a Prosecutor Candidate for Election

Dear Jay,

I issued a joint news release with a candidate for Oakland County Prosecutor on August 4, 1976. I might just add that Timothy E. Dinan still practices law and teaches law at the University of Detroit Mercy.

> Timothy E. Dinan and Johannes F. Spreen announced that they will run as a law enforcement team last night at the Ark Lanes West in Southfield.

Dinan and Spreen have as individual goals the initiation of more effective law enforcement in Oakland County. They have set as their joint goal the development of a "new kind of cooperation" with all law enforcement agencies in the county.

It is their intention to open lines of communication between the Prosecutor's Office and the Sheriff's Department, and then to extend that to all other levels of government with which they work.

They are confident that with the benefit of such improved communication they will be able to produce more creative solutions to the ever-growing problems of law enforcement in the county.

Spreen says, "Tim Dinan is a man of integrity. I am impressed by his dignity and decency, and know he is dedicated to professionalism based upon merit and high standards. Concerning the Prosecutor and the Sheriff of Oakland County, it is most important to have good teamwork."

Dinan echoes, "I strongly reinforce Sheriff Spreen's posture towards cooperation and I want to emphasize that, if elected, I will consider that tantamount to a four-year contract with the citizens of Oakland County. I am honored and privileged to have a man of Spreen's caliber as a teammate. Working with him will be an effective means of extending a positive influence in the promotion of effective law enforcement."

## Organizing Crime Watches and Patrols

Dear Jay,

We initiated a pilot program involving deputies and high-crime neighborhoods where watch groups were organized and patrolling was increased. After 74 days of operation, on October 21, Chief of the program Glen Watson reported a 53% reduction in crime in those vicinities. To my surprise and delight, he also sent me copies of 12 letters from individual watch groups, with numerous signatures on each one. The letters attested to the success of the program. An example is this one which had 16 signatures.

> Dear Sheriff Spreen:
> 
> We would like to say thank you for a job well done! We appreciate the trial program to prevent crime in our subdivision. It seems to have helped greatly. It has also reduced speeding through our subdivision, which is a great relief to the parents of small children.
> 
> Deputy Len Schell did an excellent job. He made himself known to both adults and children, and made everyone alert for suspicious happenings.
> 
> We would like to continue this program. Perhaps we could arrange to share our program with a neighboring subdivision in order to do so. We are

willing to continue cooperating with you, and would like to have this program arranged.

By the way, in 1991, it was Captain Glen Watson and a deputy who found two victims attached to a death machine of Dr. Jack Kevorkian in Pontiac.

## Opening a Reserve Program

Dear Jay,

On October 29, we opened our Reserve Program. Undersheriff John Nichols issued this announcement.

> The Sheriff takes pleasure in announcing the formation of an Oakland County Sheriff's Reserve Program. In order that the department contributes its full support to making the program functional, it is necessary that the full and complete understanding of the recruiting, policies, role, function, and uses of the Reserves be clearly understood.
> 
> The Reserve program will consist of two classifications.
> 
> Administrative Reserve will function in an advisory capacity to the Sheriff. These Reserves will not concern themselves with road or correction duties except possibly for familiarization in the "ride along" program. They will serve as resource persons, planners, and advisors. They will consist of business, industry, scientists, professors, medical people, and other individuals whose expertise may be needed in future programs and for day-to-day operation.
> 
> Operational Reserve will function as an augmentation to the Protective Services. It is to this section that most of our attention will be directed.
> 
> Reserve officers will not be substitutes for regularly sworn deputies. However, it is contemplated that they will augment the existing Road Patrol. They would not be used "instead of" but rather "in addition to" regular deputies.
> 
> Reservists may apply to the township deputy detail in which they reside or have their business. They will be screened, recommended, and under the control of the sergeant in charge of the local detachment. A comprehensive training program of 40 hours including full pistol qualifications has already begun. No reservist will be permitted to patrol until he has successfully completed this course and is fully pistol-qualified.
> 
> Each Reserve deputy is required to sign an affidavit in which he states that he understands that:
> 
> 1. No powers of enforcement are given unless under the supervision of a sworn member of the Oakland County Sheriff's Department and for a specific purpose.
> 
> 2. Use of the badge or identification for purposes other than specified will result in recall and dismissal.

3. They will wear a uniform and insignia only as directed by superior officers of the department.

4. They will abide by all rules, regulations, and orders for conduct and discipline in the Oakland County Sheriff's Office.

5. They understand that unless they possess a proper C.C.W. permit, their deputy status does not permit weapons to be carried off duty or out of uniform.

Application forms are submitted through the Sergeant in charge of the township detail. Upon his recommendation, limited background information surveys are conducted. No individual will be given reserve status who shows any background information that would be detrimental to the reputation of the department or would reflect discredit to the department. Should an individual fail to perform adequately or violate the rules of the department, he will be dismissed without recourse. The individual will enter a six-month's probationary period after training. During this time, road deputies who have participated in patrol with the reservist will be asked to evaluate his performance, demeanor, attitude, conduct, and dedication. Valid unsatisfactory fitness reports will be deemed suitable grounds for immediate dismissal of the reservist.

## We Led the Michigan State Fair

Dear Jay,

When the Detroit Police Department deactivated its Mounted Division, which traditionally led the Michigan State Fair, I volunteered the services of our 25-officer Sheriff's Posse. Undersheriff John Nichols and I led the Posse during the parade toward the Michigan Fair Grounds. A picture and article about us was published in the October-November 1976 issue of *The National Sheriff* journal. I was riding a horse named Scooter. The article said among other things, "By coincidence, Sheriff Spreen introduced scooters in the New York Police Department in 1963, the year Scooter was born."

Sheriff Spreen and Undersheriff Nichols led mounted posse to open Michigan State Fair in 1976.

## Swearing In Deputies Every Four Years

Dear Jay,

I issued a news release on December 30, 1976, intended to educate the public about deputization.

> One of law enforcement's most unique programs was held today in Oakland County. Sheriff Johannes F. Spreen and Undersheriff John F. Nichols presided over the quadrennial ceremony of redeputization.
>
> Most policemen are sworn in at the start of their career, and their authority is maintained until they are separated from their department. This is not true with a Deputy Sheriff. His authority expires every four years, so he must be re-sworn at the beginning of the elected Sheriff's term of office.
>
> In the old days, deputies gathered in the Sheriff's office and learned at that time if they would still have a job in police work. Their security was often tied to their politics, relationship, or contributions to the Sheriff.
>
> Today's deputies no longer fear the "swearing in" because of merit system protection and union contracts; however, they still must be sworn in before midnight of December 31$^{st}$ for a renewal of their professional contract for their particular function.
>
> Due to the large number of regular and special deputies (435), the program was held in the Court House Auditorium.
>
> Also officiating on behalf of the Oakland County Sheriff, Johannes F. Spreen, was County Clerk Lynn D. Allen.
>
> The Sheriff and Undersheriff briefly addressed the gathered deputies. They described the accomplishments of the department in the past four years and the hopes for an expanded professional law enforcement and criminal justice service role in the future. The Sheriff pointed out that increased professionalism, pride in the department, and respect by the community were due to the fine efforts of all members of the department.

# *1977*

Egyptian president Anwar al-Sadat visits Israel
Son of Sam murderer arrested
First Concorde SST leaves from New York City
Alaskan pipeline is completed
New York City blackout
Carter halts development of B-1 bomber

# Sheriff Patrols Welcomed

Dear Jay,

This was quite a year for me. In February, I sent deputies into South Oakland. Most chiefs approved. Past program SCAT (Sheriff's Criminal Annoyance Team) received much approval. This is the year I went to jail (got out too soon) on Saturday, the day before Mother's Day. I learned that hundreds of people were going to gather at Genesee County Jail to protest my imprisonment the following Monday. Bob White and a team of lawyers got me out in 23 hours, just when I was starting to enjoy it. They had a jailbreak the floor above me that night. I said if they had broken into my cell (a locked room) would I have been considered friend or foe.

But let me start at the beginning. We decided to send patrols into the cities in the south of Oakland County to cut down on crime. Two weeks after I began the program, the *Daily Tribune* covered it in an article of 2/28/77 called "Sheriff Patrols in SOC Okay with City Police Officials." By the way, one of the police chiefs quoted here, Tobin, had a daughter who joined our department by the end of 1977 and became the first female patrol officer in the Oakland County Sheriff's Department. I'm sorry to say that Tobin died in 1993 from contaminated blood during a hip replacement. His wife was still fighting the hospital in courts in 2003. I'm not sure how it all turned out. Here's the gist of the article.

> Sheriff Johannes F. Spreen's two-week-old program of sending deputies into South Oakland cities is receiving nods of approval from most area police administrators.
>
> It has given the average South Oakland resident a first look at the deputies, who devote most of their time to guarding the Oakland County Jail and patrolling the rural townships of North Oakland. For some who have been ticketed, it may be a little unpleasant but it could mean safer streets ...
>
> They have concentrated on monitoring high-accident intersections for traffic problems, but Spreen said they also have the freedom to patrol potential crime areas ...
>
> Spreen, who advocates using innovative police techniques to combat crime, has long argued that the sheriff's department should provide more police services to cities.
>
> Other firsts by his department include:
>
> - Transportation of prisoners from city jails to the county jail at county expense.
> - Serving of civil papers and subpoenas.

- An undercover interagency drug-fighting force, headed by the sheriff's department.

"I have given the sheriff's department an extended invitation to visit Birmingham," said Chief Rollin G. Tobin. "That brings two departments into the City. If you're a professional criminal and you think you have one agency figured out, it has to tear you apart if you find out that there's a second police agency in a city. When the sheriff's department worked here two weeks ago there were 17 cars patrolling in Birmingham. That's more cars than normally patrol downtown Detroit. We didn't have any major crime during that time."

Chief Donald Geary of Ferndale said he favors the program too. "The more police we can put on the road, the better. If Spreen can spare the men and still fulfill his commitments in the townships, he can put 50 deputies in here. I don't care who gets the credit as long as I have fewer victims."

Spreen said the program is part of his "umbrella plan" to offer support services to local police. Spreen said he would like to see his department offer specialized detective and patrol services, plus countywide emergency police dispatching and centralized record keeping—to free local police for more effective patrolling.

## Police Executives Must Set Examples Even If It Means Going to Jail

Dear Jay,

I am a little worried to tell you about this. On the other hand, you know how the men and women under a top cop "in trouble" must decide whether they should use him as a role model.

I went to jail when I felt I had to stand firm for my decision to not have a bad law enforcement officer on my force. I hoped, at the time, that my stand would be depicted by the media correctly so that the issues would be clear for the public and my officers to see. I especially wanted everyone to know that we don't want bad cops or bad deputies on the payroll, and that law enforcement executives should not and would not cover up their crimes. Here's what happened.

I was arrested and jailed for refusing to obey a court order to reinstate a sheriff's deputy whom I had fired the year before. You see, on March 11, 1976, I fired Detective Sergeant Keith Lester, 33, after he was charged with larceny by conversion for failing to turn over $200 a court gave him to pay a crime victim. He had pocketed $200 of a $750 restitution payment made by three youths in a larceny case in which they stole a trailer. The restitution was to be collected by Lester and given to the victims.

The charge against Lester was dismissed in February, however, and he sued for reinstatement of his job and back pay of $20,000. Judge Thorburn had dismissed the case because he said Lester should have been charged with embezzlement, not with larceny by conversion. Judge Beer granted the request to dismiss the case.

My view was that the charge against Lester had been improperly dismissed and that Lester was guilty. If I reinstated Lester, it would have lowered morale in the department. Besides that, Lester should have followed normal channels of appeal through the county employee appeal process to regain his job before he went to court.

Oakland County Circuit Judge William Beer ordered me to be jailed indefinitely on contempt charges. He said I would stay in jail until I changed my mind and intended to lodge me in my own county in a local jail. Sheriff John O'Brien of Genesee County heard the news and sent his administrative assistant to suggest to Judge Beer that I be taken to the Genesee County jail in Flint, Michigan. I was grateful.

The judge's order came late after a day of legal haggling. I had appeared at a press conference with a toothbrush in my pocket, saying that I was ready to be locked up for my principles. I told the reporters, "I never thought I would see such a day when I myself would be charged with a crime. But I'd rather be right than free." The Oakland County deputies later presented me with a plaque that contained those lines.

Judge Beer, 67, who had been a judge for 20 years, said that I had violated the separation of powers doctrine by refusing to obey his order. The judge told reporters, "Judges' orders, even if distasteful, must be obeyed."

Judge Beer denied my request to delay the jailing from Friday to Monday so that I could arrange for my wife, who was suffering with multiple sclerosis and curvature of the spine. She had undergone six operations during the last year and I wanted to spend Mother's Day with her instead of in jail.

When he denied the request, he said, "That has already been fully discussed."

Just before being sentenced by Judge Beer, there was a graduation ceremony in my jail for inmates who had attained their G.E.D. We had the Pontiac School system in our jail, teaching inmates so they could obtain jobs and pursue a better life. I had been scheduled to give the graduation address.

I had felt that a motivational type speech was in order. The inmates did not know that I was myself going to be jailed that very afternoon. I praised their efforts, told them they were started on a better road, and to keep going.

I then related the story of my life starting as a little immigrant lad from Germany who could not speak the English language. I wound up telling them about growing up in the Depression, gathering old newspapers to sell for a few cents, shoveling snow, and lugging boxes of wood to make a little money because we were so poor. I described how I helped my father make cigars by stripping tobacco, how my parents didn't speak English very well, and that I never went to college until I was 35 years old. I congratulated the ones getting their G.E.D.s and added, "If I can do it, you can do it."

I told them to keep on and said, "When you get out, I don't want to see you back. Go out. Be a success. You can do it."

At the conclusion of my remarks, I informed them that I would immediately become an inmate like them. I was very touched when they all stood and gave me applause that continued until I left the room.

Before going to the jail, I called my wife and told her that if she felt she needed me, I would acquiesce to Judge Beer's order.

She said very crisply, "Stick to your guns, Sheriff. We're all right." I'll never forget that remark. She really would be all right. A contingent of officers from the Sheriff's Office was already at our home to offer assistance to my wife and daughter.

I turned my gun over to my undersheriff, John Nichols, and was taken into custody by Kenneth McArdle, administrative assistant to the Genesee County Sheriff, John O'Brien. O'Brien, a fellow Democrat, arranged for an attorney for me. I wasn't handcuffed, but the Judge had cautioned McArdle that I was to be treated "just as any other prisoner in jail."

When I arrived at the jail, Sheriff O'Brien welcomed me and we chatted for fifteen minutes before I was taken to the booking area and fingerprinted.

A deputy checked my personal property, which included a wallet with $54, an uncashed paycheck, sheriff's badge, checkbook, tie, tiepin, and shoes. I said, "I never violated a court order before. To me, this is kind of like a comedy, but it's a tragedy. All I know is my 35 years in law enforcement seem to be going up in smoke."

My wife had packed clothes into a small suitcase, which I was not able to take along. My attorney, Robert White of Grand Rapids, began working on an emergency appeal of Beer's order. White told reporters that I might be released the next day if he could get the appellate judges to hear the case.

They let me keep my civilian clothes rather than wearing a prison uniform. I was placed in a cell apart from other prisoners, a 10-foot square room. The room had a bed, a desk, two barred windows, and was usually used for intake. I was in "solitary confinement for my own protection." The idea was that some of the 303 prisoners serving time for murder or robbery might like to show a sheriff or a policeman what jail is like.

Prisoners on the floor above me called officers with shotguns to control a disturbance during the 24 hours I served in jail. A group of inmates had overpowered a guard and stolen his keys. But they returned to their cells after they found that the guard's keys did not fit doors that would let them out. I was thinking, suppose they can't contain it? Suppose it gets down here? Would I be considered friend or foe?

I slept from about 1 a.m. to 4 a.m. and then decided that was no good way to spend time. So I got up and made some notes. Here's what I wrote at 4:00 a.m. on May 7$^{th}$, 1977.

> You do a lot of thinking in jail. You think about how long you may be in, how long you will stay behind bars. You realize the importance of freedom. You think of your loved ones, particularly when they are dependent upon you and you cannot be there to help.
>
> In my case, you think of why you are here. How can you as a sworn servant of the law possibly be in jail for violating that law? You wonder at the strange turn of events, this strange paradox that has led me down this particular road ending up behind bars. Have I really flouted the law of my country? I guess I have but that was never my intention. And I would not say I flouted, I respectfully differed.
>
> How strange, I hear the sounds of people and traffic passing by and yet I cannot leave and join it. Why?
>
> My thoughts were on the protection and service of the people, under the law of our land. To do so with the best possible service under my constitutional obligation as the chief peace officer of the county.
>
> Yet this has led me into a collision course where principle met principle head on. Where I as an officer of the court had to object to its ministrations. I felt for the public good and the people I serve.
>
> Yet I am sure those same motives were in the mind of the judge who put me here. How odd; we are both attempting to do our job. Is there a greater morality over the legal letter of the law?
>
> I do not feel I really violated a law violently. I wanted to pursue another road but that was apparently impossible. I do not feel unclean inside. I do not feel wrong. I did what I felt was right.
>
> It is unusual that my 35 years in law enforcement and my earnest belief in proper and professional law enforcement have led me tonight to a barred cell in the Genessee County jail.

I also kept thinking about my decision. It was the first time in my 35-year career as a policeman that I had not lived by the law. I thought, "Did I flout the law?" I guess I did but I only meant to respectfully disagree with it.

When Mayor LaGuardia gave me the oath of office in 1941, he said there would be rough times ahead. He said I'd be looking down the barrel of a gun. But he never said I'd be looking through cell bars as a prisoner.

Supporters and well-wishers sent some 30 telegrams and made 74 calls on my behalf while I was in jail. One telegram from my own department read, "We are proud of you. Hang in there. The department stands taller because of your action."

Another telegram sent by the administrator of the Criminal Justice Institute in Detroit said, "All professional law enforcement personnel salute you as an administrator and as a man." That was very gratifying. I put myself out there on a limb, and it could have been cut off.

I arrived after supper had been served so they got me a hamburger from a nearby Burger King. Saturday I ate the normal prisoner fare of cereal for breakfast and hot dogs and beans for lunch. I talked with several of the inmates at meals. One, who was in for non-payment of child-support, told me he would be perfectly willing to pay if his wife would use the money for the child and not for herself and her boyfriend. I thought it odd that we put a man in jail where he could not earn any money for child support. There has to be a better way.

Through the night, a 30-page appeal was delivered to a court clerk Saturday morning. By early afternoon, a three-judge panel of the state Court of Appeals freed me on personal bond. They met Saturday and granted my motion to postpone the Circuit Court order pending appeal after I served 23 ½ hours. The judges set no date for the appeal hearing.

I told a couple of the jail trustees who befriended me that they ought to continue their education. I said that if I could overcome hardship, so could they. The reporters who covered this said that I was often accused of being more of an educator than a police administrator.

I was 57 at the time but I did what I felt was important and necessary. I believed I had an obligation to law enforcement to try to upgrade the profession. I felt that Keith Lester had violated a trust and to restore him would be wrong. We would have no confidence in him. The public would have no trust in him.

I'll never forget that when I came home, my wife and daughter had draped yellow ribbons across the bushes and a large sign on the garage declaring "Way to go, Pa." I was able to spend Mothers' Day at home with them after all.

The brief tenure in jail sort of rounded out my education. I told some of those who greeted me that I hoped I never had to take advantage of Sheriff O'Brien's hospitality again, or reciprocate.

I was vindicated two months later by the Michigan Court of Appeals, which ruled that I should not have been jailed for refusing to rehire a fired deputy. At the press conference after the ruling, I told reporters that the judge made a number of mistakes but it sure was nice to be right and to be free. Especially when I learned that Deputy Lester was not only fighting his dismissal but was arrested on another criminal charge of willful neglect of duty.

Part of my fervor against rehiring Lester came from previous orders from the appeals board and the courts forcing me to rehire four other deputies. I couldn't have that because after awhile, half the department would be less than satisfactory.

Judge Beer, to his credit, later appeared at a party held in a restaurant for a fundraiser. He said to all that Johannes Spreen was a decent, honorable man, in effect that he had been wrong.

Much later, we found out a very interesting thing about the Judge who had sentenced me. Judge Beer was discovered to have had nine kids in all, three by his first wife and six by his secretary. He led a double life for years until it was discovered after one of his children died. One of his kids (by the secretary) wrote a kind of gossip column in the *Detroit News*. Jim Ellison wrote a book about Beer called *Judicial Indiscretion* that was made into an NBC movie of the week but with a different title and phony names.

My Undersheriff John Nichols, when I was placed in jail, wrote a letter to *The Oakland Press*. Here is an excerpt of that letter.

> In your editorial of May 10, 1977, you either failed to get the facts, failed to check the validity of those facts as you received them, or ignored the basic facts entirely. The unfortunate point is that the whole premise and tenor of your offering was based on this erroneous belief! That being that Sheriff Johannes Spreen ignored the law without availing himself of the proper channel of legitimate appeals. THIS IS NOT TRUE!! The Michigan Court of Appeals had been petitioned and the case accepted, Docket No. 77-1485, when the Sheriff was sentenced for contempt. The appeal which you described as made while "Spreen was in jail" was, in fact, the *second* appeal including a Petition for Release from that jail. Thus, Sheriff Spreen had quietly followed normal procedure.
>
> The Sheriff's contention was and is that his (Lester's) discharge was proper under the rules as they are written. The dismissal by the court was not a finding of innocence as attested to by the trial judge's statement quoted by you …

I shall not attempt to convince you that Sheriff Spreen did not "in effect, put himself in jail." I do point out that the judge had other options open to deal with the violation. Those same options he has exercised countless times in other cases before him, both civil and criminal. Fines, suspensions of sentence, probation, all were open to him. He chose jail. That was his right, his prerogative, but not his mandate. Yes, Mr. Munro, I do agree with you on one point. Courts are not perfect.

I shall mention, only in passing, the economic motivation for the Sheriff's "defiance" which you did not consider, apparently. Some $21,000 in County funds would have been spent to repay the defendant officer. The Sheriff protested not only in behalf of police professionalism but as a taxpayer, in the interest of the taxpayer, against premature if not improvident expenditure of these funds.

Jay, I hope you can appreciate what I was trying to do, and I surely hoped my people could appreciate it. I know my family did. Let us hope you never have to go through such an experience.

## My Toothbrush and Walter Cronkite

Dear Jay,

After my short stay in jail, Jim Fitzgerald wrote a very amusing article on May 18, 1977, in the *Detroit Free Press*. He entitled it "A Sheriff's Toothbrush Thwarts L. Brooks."

> The damnedest thing happened in Oakland County the other day. Prosecutor L. Brooks Patterson came to work wearing his sternest anti-parole frown, but he couldn't find one TV camera to put his righteousness on the 6 o'clock news.
>
> "Where are all the news people?" Patterson asked.
>
> "They are in Sheriff Spreen's office, looking at his toothbrush," he was told.
>
> Thus began a dismal few days for Patterson who, more than anyone, appreciates the power of publicity. He has become nationally famous by noting what makes people sick and then appearing on TV to proclaim that he is sicker about it than they are.
>
> If Brooks took the Pepsi test, he would vomit after sipping the Coke ...
>
> Patterson speaks eloquently, with high emotion and magnificent indignation. He has made men cry, and he has made them gnash their teeth. More important, he has prompted thousands of people to say: "That man should be governor."

In view of Patterson's popularity and ambition, it must have bugged him considerably when the entire nation, including Walter Cronkite, began talking about that gutsy man from Oakland County in Michigan—but they weren't talking about L. Brooks Patterson.

They were talking about Sheriff Johannes Spreen who got himself arrested and put in jail rather than compromise his principles.

How often does a sheriff get locked up? The media came running. Spreen got tanned from the TV lights. Dozens of microphones were stuck into his mouth. Reporters begged him for quotes ...

Spreen had fired a deputy for allegedly stealing some money. A judge ruled the deputy had been improperly charged and should be rehired. Spreen refused, thus breaking the law he is paid to enforce.

"I'd rather be right than free," the sheriff said after calling a press conference ...

There was much applause and praise for Spreen's brave stand against the dumb judge. And, inevitably, it was said: "That man should be governor."

## The Case of the Deputy I Fired

Dear Jay,

On May 18, 1977, the *Spinal Column* newspaper carried an article about the firing of Keith Lester. Let me just mention that Keith Lester's case became rather famous and was used as a precedent in other trials. The case was called *People vs. Keith Lester, 78 Mich App 661.*

The Oakland County personnel appeals board hearing on the firing of sheriff's detective sergeant Keith Lester has been postponed ...

Originally, Lester was charged with larceny by conversion for allegedly withholding $200 in restitution he was to have paid to a crime victim. Circuit judge James Thorburn dismissed the charges earlier this year, ruling that the deputy probably should have been charged with embezzlement rather than larceny. The Oakland County prosecutor's office is appealing Thorburn's ruling to the state court of appeals.

Following that ruling, Lester's attorney filed suit to have the former detective sergeant reinstated to the sheriff's department. Beer ruled in favor of the request last month, setting the stage for Spreen's refusal to comply with the order and the sheriff's one-night stay in the Genesee County jail.

Under the offer made last week to Undersheriff John Nichols, Spreen would have reinstated Lester, who would have collected some $20,000 in back pay and resigned from the department.

# The Day They Turned Crime Over to Public Relations

Dear Jay,

The *Detroit News* carried an article about our child kidnappings and murders on May 19, 1977. The article by Joel J. Smith was "Kidnap-Slayings Prompt Plan: Drive Set to Keep Kids Alert." My office and I were not included in the plan.

> A group of Southfield public relations professionals is working with the investigators of a series of Oakland County child murders in an effort to come up with a program to emphasize the dangers of children talking to strangers.
>
> Phil Meagher, executive director of the Southfield Chamber of Commerce and a member of the group, said the volunteers hope to come up with a plan that will be a constant reminder to children during the summer months to be cautious of all strangers.
>
> He said the first objective will be to aid the special task force set up to search for the suspected killer of four Oakland County children.
>
> Meagher said the group is leaning toward printing about three million placemats, emphasizing through cartoon characters various ways a child might be lured into a kidnapper's car.
>
> Meagher said other members of the group are public relations firms, the community affairs manager for Allstate Insurance, the public relations specialist for the Southfield police department and a Southfield city council member.

# Michigan Sheriffs' Association Commended Me

Dear Jay,

I was so proud to receive this letter from the Michigan Sheriff's Association on June 1, 1977, from their president, Bernard Grysen.

> Dear Sheriff Spreen:
>
> The Board of Directors of the Michigan Sheriffs' Association, on behalf of the membership, wishes to commend you for demonstrating the highest standards of integrity and courage for refusing to abandon the noble principles which have governed your law enforcement career.
>
> Your refusal to comply with Judge Beer's order to reinstate a person whom you believed had violated the public trust may ultimately be determined to constitute contempt of court. We offer no opinion as to the propriety of that act however we share with you a real concern that the high standards of professionalism of the law enforcement community would be seriously under-

mined if Sheriffs and other police administrators are required to reinvest persons who have abused the police power entrusted to them. We owe the public a higher standard of responsibility than to sit idly by and permit that to happen.

We sincerely hope that your position will be vindicated by the Appeals Court. You have our support.

## Unions and Lawyers

Dear Jay,

Having to deal with my objection to re-hiring a bad cop, I had to protect myself, which meant I had to use the services of lawyers. At that point in my career, I was very pessimistic that the judge who ruled against the unions and me and who supported a bad employee was undermining the purpose of law enforcement. I prepared the following position paper to use in my defense.

For more years than I choose to recall, I, like you, have listened to speeches proclaiming the need for a greater degree of professionalism in police work.

But as I stand before you today, I seldom have been more pessimistic about the prospects for establishing true professional standards for law enforcement. A good deal of my pessimism is due directly to the state of affairs in police labor relations today.

The crippling malady afflicting police management today is simply that management cannot effectively achieve its legitimate goals. In some departments, management has, by inaction and inattentiveness, allowed employees to virtually determine their own working conditions and level of services to be delivered to the public. Other agencies have failed to understand the nature of collective bargaining and surrendered, often without even a protest, basic management rights. Still others, which have attempted to fend off some of labor's illegitimate demands, find themselves manacled and shackled by either the courts or labor arbitrators.

Strikes in public employment in Michigan are illegal. But making a strike illegal does not mean that employees will not strike. The record shows that public employees, including police, will strike whenever they believe it is in their interest to do so.

So what happens in Michigan if an employer seeks to obtain an injunction against an admitted unlawful strike? Our Supreme Court has ruled that a public employer cannot obtain an injunction unless he proves exactly the same things needed to end a private employment strike—namely, violence and irreparable harm. The result is plain: no one is able to get an injunction.

In my department with nearly 400 employees, labor counsel has informed me that only three people are positively exempt from union representation: myself, my undersheriff and one confidential secretary. When we are brought before a court of law and asked to justify our actions, the high-priced and inventive legal counsel used by employee unions has outclassed our governmental attorneys. Too often, we have lost cases on minute procedural points despite having overwhelming evidence to support our positions.

We must, like the unions we face, organize ourselves, and use the best talent available. If that means hiring administrative assistance whose sole responsibility would be the administration of our labor agreements, then we should do so if possible. We need to use a labor attorney to negotiate our union agreements and try our cases, rather than using inexperienced government attorneys.

So that I am not misunderstood, I want to express some ambivalence about the role of attorneys in my suggestions. I agree with this observation by a dear man:

> The lawyer's nature is to make things more complicated. If you think it's simple, he will smile and show you it's complex. Admit it's complex and he will smile and show you it's incomprehensible.
>
> This complexity is largely the creation of lawyers who make, interpret, and enforce the laws. Even lawyers can't understand a lot of the laws. One lawyer says it means this, and one lawyer says it means that. And then the court, which is also lawyers, says lawyer A has it right. With the result that lawyer B appeals to another court, which is also lawyers, which says the first court had it wrong.
>
> So lawyer B appeals to the Supreme Court, which is also lawyers, and they divide on which understanding is correct, but agree to let the guess of the majority prevail. And then some new lawyers move into the Supreme Court, and everything is reversed once more.
>
> Meantime, years pass, parties to the original offense die, forget what they saw, go mad waiting for a conclusion that never comes, go bankrupt paying lawyers to keep up the good fight to decide the meaning of the law written by lawyers.

Despite such misgivings, I firmly believe sound legal counsel from an attorney specializing in labor relations matters is vital in today's litigation-mad society. But to cure the malady I spoke of earlier, we, as police administrators must re-examine our own roles. We must believe in and retain our right to manage while recognizing our fundamental accountability to the public we serve and the trust accorded our position. There is no need to segregate and compartmentalize professional responsibility into the stereotyped industrial model of union demands versus management rights. Our employees, I believe, desire to be accorded professional status and we must aid them in fulfilling that desire.

If these things are done, it will not be necessary for someone with 35 years in law enforcement to risk jail.

## Police Administrators and Unions

Dear Jay,

After I was released from jail, I gave an address to the National Sheriffs' Convention on June 20, 1977. What I told them then is just as true now. I began my address rather humorously.

> I don't know if I should speak to you today as Sheriff of Oakland County, Michigan, or as Prisoner #7702276, Genesee County Jail. This has much to do with labor unions and I will tell you about that. But first let me say that law enforcement does not work in these United States. It probably never has and it probably never will. The big cities and their police chief executives are embattled just as are the suburbs and their myriad of small independent departments.
>
> As Police Commissioner in Detroit, I watched and felt the rise in power and influence of the unions as they grew smarter, more powerful, more militant, and encroached upon some of the territorial imperatives of management. I was also saddened by the political polarization between the mayor and the unions, as gleefully reported in the Detroit press.
>
> Strikes in public employment are illegal, of course, but what does that really mean? Making a strike illegal doesn't mean that employees won't strike. So what happens if a law enforcement employer seeks to obtain an injunction against an admittedly unlawful strike? The Supreme Court has ruled that a *public* employer cannot obtain an injunction unless he proves exactly the same things needed to end a *private* employment strike; namely violence and irreparable harm. The result is that no one is able to get an injunction.
>
> What if a public employer really does decide to discharge his employees for striking? In one Michigan county, a sheriff has been restrained from disciplining anyone involved in a strike until it could be determined whether he had the lawful right to just *say* what action he intended to take.
>
> Judicial interference in labor matters has not been limited to strikes. Circuit courts in Michigan issued injunctions against two law enforcement agencies when one required a union steward to wear a police uniform while on duty and the other prevented a department from rotating the shifts of its ser-

geants to break up a "buddy" system that had resulted in sloppy supervision and bribe-taking.

When arbitrators are used, very few issues, large or small, escape their keen eye for detail. I was amused when a union asked an arbitrator to rule on whether washrooms in a county jail should be equipped with roll or napkin-type toilet paper. The arbitrator agreed with the sheriff that he should be allowed to determine which type of paper would be furnished. Once he made this decision, the arbitrator directed that the sheriff had a *contractual obligation to ensure* that the paper containers were *kept well filled.* Of course, the arbitrator's decision was based upon the labor contract's language governing "employee safety procedures."

Headlines in the press vividly display conflicts between the leaders of police unions and city mayors and councils. Who really controls law enforcement today? Is it law enforcement management? It's those who have money. We in management ain't got much and the union has! We in management don't have dues paying members but unions do. Members and money mean clout!

There is no doubt that we at the top must become better managers and be fair and square. Some cooperation between unions and management is most essential. We should be working together for each other in the people's interests.

But management needs rights too, and management needs professional help to allow us to respond to the unions on more equal terms. As Sheriff of Oakland County, Michigan, in our department of 400 employees, only the sheriff, the under sheriff and the secretary were not union members! But when I needed union support for a crime and prevention patrol after the murder of seven kids, where was the union as we lost funds on a close vote by the commissioners.

To cure these problems, we must re-examine our roles as police administrators. We must believe in and retain our right to manage while recognizing our fundamental accountability to the public we serve. Let us be the managers of our enterprise and be the main man in that seat with our hands firmly on the throttle. We can certainly ride together with unions on the same track that leads to professional status of law enforcement, but we must control the train. That is what we were hired to do!

## The Child Killer Investigation

Dear Jay,

I addressed the Southern Police Institute Alumni Association in Atlanta on July 29, 1977, about our Child Killer investigation. They had been dealing with three Atlanta "Lover's Lane" killings. Atlanta had asked me to address them because they knew about our Oakland Child Killer Task Force and wanted to learn what they could from us.

The first Atlanta killing occurred on January 16, 1977, when a killer shot La Brian Lovette and Veronica Hill. Lovette drove from the scene but crashed into a vehicle and also died. On February 12, a killer injured a couple and they described their assailant as a large black male. On March 12, a stalker approached another car and killed Dianne Collins and wounded her boyfriend. The killer or killers were never caught but at that time, they wanted to explore every avenue to solve their murders, and feared that they might have a serial killer,

I began by telling them about some other murders near my county and how they had been handled. I told them about the two-year Michigan investigation of seven Ann Arbor co-eds from 1967 to 1969. The investigation led to the arrest and successful conviction of John Norman Collins who is still in jail and even maintains a web site about his innocence.

Those murders began with Eastern Michigan accounting student Mary Flezar on July 10, 1967, when she went for a walk one night. Her body was found on August 7 with multiple stab wounds and her hands and feet were hacked off. Two days after her remains had been identified, a young man turned up at the mortuary, asking for permission to take snapshots of the body which was refused. Employees at the mortuary could not give a description of the man.

Almost one year later, on July 6, 1968, student Joan Schell was found dead in Ann Arbor and had been raped and stabbed 47 times. She had caught a ride with someone in front of the student union building. She had last been seen on July 1 with John Norman Collins, a student at Eastern Michigan University. Her miniskirt was wrapped around her neck. When questioned, Collins, a nice young fellow, claimed he was with his mother at the time. Police took him at his word.

In late March, 1969, Jane Mixer was found covered by a coat in a cemetery. A law student at the University of Michigan, she had been shot and strangled. Mixer had been strangled with a nylon stocking, and two bullets had been fired into her brain at point-blank range but there was no other brutality. Her jumper was pulled up and her pantyhose pulled off but she had not been sexually assaulted or stabbed.

That same month, on March 25, construction workers near the scene of Schell's murder had found another victim. A 16-year-old named Maralynn Skelton who had been hitchhiking was killed by crushing blows about the head. A garter belt had been twisted around her neck. A stick had been rammed into her vagina, and police reported evidence of flogging with a heavy strap or belt before she died.

About three weeks later, 13-year-old Dawn Basom was found half-naked in Superior Township, strangled with a black electric cord. The eighth grade student's body was slashed across the breasts and buttocks. A handkerchief was stuffed into her mouth and her blue stretch pants were missing. She had been reported missing by her mother on April 18, when she failed to return home from visiting a friend. She was last seen walking down the Penn Central Railroad tracks, which passed near her house. Her chest and stomach had over a dozen slash marks, made with a razor or a very sharp knife.

On June 9, 1969, some teenaged boys found Alice Kalom, graduate of EMU, in a vacant field near Ypsilanti. She had been raped and stabbed repeatedly, her throat slashed, with a bullet in her brain. The public outcry was increasing. A psychic was brought in, but proved to be of little help.

With this latest murder, Governor William Milliken stated that Col. Frederick Davids, commander of the State Police, was in charge of the Michigan State Police part of the investigation. Governor Milliken's 21-year-old daughter was a student at the University of Michigan. Officers investigating the killings discussed contacting an expert criminologist. Chief Krasny stated, "It's apparent we need a new, fresh look at the crimes. It's possible a trained, competent criminologist can, through his experience and training, give us a fresh approach. I'm certainly willing to try it."

The public continued to call in tips, but some were hoaxes. In one of them, a writer sent a letter to the *Detroit News*, stating he had information about the killer and was seeking a reward. The writer wanted the money to be turned over to the Detroit Catholic Churches cardinal. The writer stated that newscasters should mispronounce the name of a weathercaster on a date set by the writer. This was done, but no information was ever supplied by the writer.

Soon the police had another victim, 18-year-old freshman student Karen Sue Bieneman. She was declared missing on July 23, 1969, and was found a few days later, strangled and beaten to death, her breasts and stomach scalded with a caustic liquid. Her panties had been stuffed into her vagina with short, clipped hairs from someone other than the victim included.

While waiting for her on the day she disappeared, a shop manager had seen her companion on his motorcycle. She overheard Beineman say she had done two foolish things in her lifetime. One was buying a wig and the other was accepting a ride with a stranger on a motorcycle. She then exited the store and left with this unknown person on the motorcycle. The motorcycle was believed to be a Honda 450. Investigators obtained a list of all Honda 450s in the state and attempted to find the killer through this list.

He was John Collins, who was arrested but denied guilt. During the investigation police found that he had a history of sexual harassment. In a bizarre twist of events, State Police Corporal David Leik had returned to his home in Ypsilanti from a family vacation. He found a floor had been painted black and figured it was done by his wife's nephew, John Collins, who was taking care of the family dog while they were gone. Blood was found where the repainting had occurred. Collins was identified by the store manager, and tests showed that hairs found attached to Bieneman's underwear matched those found at the home of Collins' uncle where he was living at the time. Collins went to trial and, on August 19, 1970, was found guilty and sentenced to life in prison without parole.

Investigators found that Collins was a chronic thief who had violent rages, often toward females who had angered him. Dates had described him as brutal, into bondage, and he was repulsed by women in their menstrual cycle.

Sheriff Harvey was notified and ordered that only a few personnel respond to the scene. He had planned that when the next victim was found, a mannequin would be placed where the body was recovered. This was done because police thought the killer had returned to at least two other locations where he had left his victims. The County Prosecutor gave his approval to this plan.

Six detectives from the sheriff's department and the state police staked out the murder scene on Saturday, July 26. About midnight, a man walked down Riverside Drive. It was raining steadily so it seemed unusual for someone to be out walking. When he entered the ravine, the detectives felt they had their man. He was close to the mannequin but quickly discovered it was not Beineman's body. He ran away with the detectives in pursuit. The detectives were not able to locate him. When that information came out, the officers were criticized.

Sheriff Harvey and Prosecutor Delhey were castigated in the press and one editorial called them "Keystone Kops" looking for "glory." Sheriff Harvey responded badly to the criticism stating, "While the governor was up there in Lansing wringing his hands and invoking 1935 laws, we already had the prime suspect under a tight look for a week."

John Collins' preliminary exam was held during August of 1969 in front of Judge Edward Deake. Judge Deake found that a murder had been committed and there was probable cause to believe Collins committed the crime. The only murder Collins was being prosecuted for was that of Karen Sue Beineman. The murder trial of John Norman Collins turned out to be the longest trial in the history of Washtenaw County. On August 19, 1970, the jury found Collins guilty of the murder of Karen Sue Beineman, the only victim of the seven murders that Collins was convicted of killing.

Collins was sentenced to life in prison in August of 1970. When the sentence was announced Collins stated, "I never knew a girl named Karen Sue Beineman. I never took the life of Karen Sue Beineman." Those were the only words that he ever uttered publicly about the murder up to that time.

Interestingly, a movie called *Now I Lay Me Down to Sleep* about the murders was based on the book *The Michigan Murders* by Edward Keyes. Collins was interviewed in prison by William Treml. Collins told Treml he was dismayed by the movie project as he felt it could jeopardize his fight for freedom during the appeal process. Movie producer William Martin promised that he would stop production if Collins asked for and passed a lie detector test, which he never did.

During the years of 1967 to 1969, law enforcement officials expressed sympathy to those Southeastern Michigan agencies involved in the murders of seven coeds from Ann Arbor, and said, "It can't happen here." Collins, by the way, is still in prison.

During 1969, the gruesome nature of the Los Angeles Manson Murders caused police officials in Oakland County to say "It couldn't happen here."

Oakland County is one of the wealthiest counties in the U.S. It consists of small communities and rural farmland. Its population is composed of General Motors executives, business people, factory workers, farmers, and various professionals. The kidnapping of Jimmy Hoffa from a nice restaurant had made news but was not as personal and revolting as the murder of these children and young women.

But in the winters of 1976 and 1977, "It did happen here." Despite repeated warnings, most of the police community was not prepared. The distant problem had hit home. As I tell you about the problems we encountered, these events will sadden you as parents and infuriate you as professional police officers.

Law enforcement in Oakland County is extremely fragmented. There are 43 police agencies in the county ranging from five man departments to the City of Pontiac with 200 police officers. Coordination of the police effort is virtually impossible. One intersection in our county is policed by four jurisdictions, as well as served by the State Police and the Sheriff's Department. If an officer from each jurisdiction met there, they could only talk by getting out of their cars because they are all on different radio frequencies. This is not coordination! This is inane!

Each police agency jealously guards their bailiwick from encroachment by other agencies as a king would his kingdom. Efforts to coordinate law enforcement are met with suspicion and disfavor by many of the local chiefs and their political superiors.

This fragmentation became a horror story in the murder investigation as two sheriffs' departments, state police, the FBI, and eight local police departments were directly involved. In addition, two medical examiners' offices, three crime labs, and two prosecutors' offices worked on these crimes.

Oakland County had the misfortune of losing seven children to murder within a very short time. Four of these are believed to have been the work of the same person or persons.

On February 15, 1976, 12 year-old Mark Stebbins was reported missing. Four officers handled it as a runaway until the next day when circumstances made them suspect foul play. Four days later, his body was found next to a dumpster.

The state police and county crime labs were not called to process the scene. By the time the county medical examiner's office arrived, the body had been moved. It was taken to the police department rather than the county morgue. The police took clothes off the body and it arrived at the morgue nude. The killer had not tried to conceal the body. It did not immediately appear that Mark was sexually abused, but later post-mortem disclosed that he was. To this day, the crime is unsolved. No one knows what might have been found at the scene had proper crime scene procedures been followed and a crime lab involved.

On December 22, 1976, 12 year-old Jill Robinson left her home after arguing with her mother. It was believed that she rode her bike to her father's home a few miles away. When she did not arrive, she was reported missing by her mother. A friend saw her riding on a main corridor, according to the investigation. The day after Christmas, her body was found 200 yards from a police station.

She had died from a shotgun blast to the head. Again, no crime lab was called to process the scene. And again, there were no attempts to conceal the body and no apparent evidence that she was sexually abused. The head and face were blown off. The condition of her hands and body made it appear as if she had just walked out of her home and was murdered.

Noting the similarities of the two cases, it was suggested that a coordinated effort involving state police, sheriff and local authorities be implemented, but the offer was declined by the local agencies. I had welcomed the suggestion because coordination had always been my belief throughout my tenure in this office.

Less than a week passed before 10 year-old Kristine Mihelich left her home January 2, 1977, to go to the store three blocks away. She was reported missing after a short time. Fearing the worst, two detectives initiated a search. The news media broadcast similarities to the two previous murders and our office and the state police offered assistance but it was refused.

The body of the girl was deposited in a very small community with only a five-man department. Many problems in protecting the crime scene arose at the outset. Traffic, onlookers, response of many local departments, media, etc. created confusion. The chief of the tiny department, having no personal experience in homicide investigation, turned the matter over to the State Police who then requested assistance from area departments. That afternoon, 30 investigators committed themselves to finding the girl's murderer. The Oakland Task Force had been implemented.

The Sheriff's Department crime lab processed the girl's room for evidence that would hopefully be used later. Some 20 days after her disappearance, her body was found. She had been suffocated and gently placed next to a street. She was fully clothed and still wearing her backpack. Again, there was no positive evidence of sexual abuse.

Hundreds of leads came in but by the first of March, only 11 investigators were sifting through 800 tips and trying to solve the crime. It was discovered that one jurisdiction had virtually no report and in another jurisdiction, evidence had been misplaced and mishandled. Another agency was reluctant to submit their report to the Task Force.

The work of the Task Force was hampered from the start by each jurisdiction's different procedures. The press allowed a politically ambitious prosecutor to assume the role of coordinator and spokesman. He summoned a Canadian crime expert to handle fingerprints when our department could have handled that task. Our fingerprint investigator is just as qualified and is used by the City of Detroit for all their questionable homicides. I have some handouts of his published article on "The Iodine Silver Transfer for Obtaining Fingerprints from the Skin."

On March 16, 1977, 11 year-old Timothy King left his home to go to a corner drugstore. He was reported missing that evening. The next morning, Task Force members were sent to coordinate the investigation. The news media put the public into a state of fear saying that a maniac child killer was on the loose.

The Task Force recognized that they might have no longer than four days to find Timothy alive. That evening, 300 investigators converged to find Timmy. They stopped suspicious vehicles to search for the missing boy. A witness furnished a composite of a man she saw talking to a boy believed to be Timmy, as well as a suspected vehicle. This information was given to the media in hopes that a citizen might recognize the subject.

Six days after Timmy disappeared, his suffocated body was found along a main street in Wayne County. The killer had broken his pattern and dumped Timmy outside of the county.

The state police crime lab personnel processed the scene and the body apparently revealed no sexual abuse. An autopsy later revealed he had been molested.

Several concerned groups posted rewards totaling $70,000 for the arrest of the child killer. The Task Force was flooded with over 12,000 tips. Parents turned in sons, brothers turned in brothers, and church members turned in their pastors. Realizing the individual agencies could not bear the financial responsibilities of immense investigations, the Task Force was awarded $700,000 to fund and equip 21 investigators for six months to identify and capture the killer.

A computer system was installed to assist the Task Force. Before the computer, several tips concerning the same individual would be investigated by several investigators, results in a loss of time and duplication of effort. The computer system allowed names of suspects in any of the four homicides to be entered and checked. Working under the theory that the killer was not successful every time he attempted to abduct a child, the Task Force surveyed all area schools. What they found was startling. Over 1,100 cases of attempted abductions were never reported to the police or to the child's parents. The reason given by the child, "If Mom knew, she wouldn't let me play there any more."

Although admirable efforts were made at supervision of the 300 investigators, coordination was nearly impossible. It was a case of "too much, too late." Some departments were virtually using the Task Force as a training experience for their personnel. Chiefs were committing rookie detectives and patrol officers to investigate the homicides and were rotating their personnel periodically to allow everyone to participate in the investigation. Some of the officers never had a chance to become familiar with all of the cases, yet they were burdened with the responsibility of catching the killer. The mere fact that some of the investigators were inexperienced led to the improper elimination of some suspects.

Unfortunately, the notoriety of the investigation received nationwide coverage, and some investigators lost sight of their objectives and placed more emphasis on pleasing the media. They ignored the accepted practice of sometimes withholding information known only to the police and the responsible parties.

The Task Force solved several problems but could not act until called in by a local agency. It was formed hurriedly to meet a local emergency and was battling against all the individual and departmental quirks and jealousies that are symptoms of the chronic fragmentation of law enforcement.

I think that the problems encountered here exemplify problems in law enforcement in general. It is fragmented, uncoordinated, ineffective, and costly. What is the answer? One county police agency may be the answer. Crime knows no jurisdictional boundaries. I urged police administrators and political leaders to ignore political differences and to put an emphasis on service to the citizens.

What if the Sheriff's major crime unit consisting of Sheriff's investigators teamed up with the best investigators from local agencies within the county who had been trained and ready to be summoned to the crime scene? The investigation would have been under one command. With the expertise and talent available within the county, I sincerely doubt that experienced homicide detectives would have mishandled evidence. Lab technicians, trained in evidence rules, would have handled the crime scene. Reports would have been professionally written. One man would have properly coordinated press releases and the media would not be given confidential police information that could impede the investigation. Thirty investigators, who frequently work together, would have been better than 300.

I told them in Atlanta how the 1967 report of the President's Commission in Law Enforcement and Criminal Justice showed the fragmentation of urban police in the Detroit Metropolitan Region. This problem, pointed out a decade ago, is still with us and so is our unapprehended child killer and others like him.

These cases haunt me to this day. In 2002, the mothers of the four victims provided blood samples to compare DNA in hair found on or near the bodies. The purpose was to determine if samples found near the bodies belonged to the children or to a suspect. The killer was sometimes dubbed "Babysitter" because it appeared that the child was fed, bathed, clothed and cared for at least several days before each murder occurred. The murderer has never been caught.

Jay, that was the end of the talk but I am happy to tell you that in December, 2006, police arrested the first possible suspect in the Child Killer investigation. Sgt. Garry Gray is currently in charge of the Oakland Child Killer Task Force. The arrest of 65 year-old Theodore Lamborgine who now lives in Ohio was announced December 12th. Lamborgine and Richard Lawson, who is in prison for sexual and assault charges against children, were involved in a sex ring together, say reporters. Officials are not sure that Lamborgine is responsible for the murders of the four children in Oakland County but it is the first arrest in the case which began in 1976-77.

I can also tell you that another suspect was arrested and convicted of the murder of one of the girls in the Ann Arbor investigation. In July, 2006, a 62-year old male nurse was arrested and convicted of killing Jane Mixer. He was found by a DNA test matching his blood to that of the victim and will serve the rest of his life in prison. Law enforcement and other investigators had always felt that Jane Mixer's murder was different, not as violent, so she was one victim that Collins did not kill.

It pleases me to know that our fine officers never give up on investigations, especially those involving murder.

## Rebuttal to Criticisms by Prosecutor Patterson

Dear Jay,

On August 4, 1977, the following essay was published and distributed under the title "Sheriff Johannes F Spreen's Rebuttal to Criticisms Made by Prosecutor L. Brooks Patterson and Southfield Police Chief Milton Sackett."

> The following remarks were made by Sheriff Johannes F. Spreen in reference to Southfield Police Chief Milton Sackett's response to Spreen's speech in Atlanta recently, to wit: "It is obvious that Sheriff Spreen has not taken the time to be properly appraised of the facts surrounding this investigation. His criticism is unwarranted and is without basis and demonstrates a lack of personal knowledge of this investigation."
>
> Sheriff Spreen commented on Sackett's statement by quoting from his speech as follows: "the body had been moved from its original position." When the Medical Examiner's investigator arrived and took pictures, he did not know the body had been turned. The pathologist later could not figure out what had happened for over an hour because the pictures of the position of the body and the lividity of the body were not in agreement—the reasons being that the body had been turned over before the Medical Examiner's investigator arrived.
>
> Also, the Medical Examiner's Office ordered the body to be brought to the morgue. Unfortunately, instead it was taken to Southfield Police Department first, where the clothing was removed. The body was finally taken to the morgue where it arrived with the clothing off.
>
> What occurred was not only a violation of procedures, but possibly the Medical Examiner's law.

## Professionalism and Ethics

Dear Jay,

I was asked to give the commencement address to Grand Valley State College graduates in Allendale, Michigan, on August 18, 1977. They have since become

Grand Valley State University and now offer a Master's Degree in Law Enforcement as well as an Undergraduate Degree. I had just been appointed to the Standards-Ethics-Education Committee of the National Sheriffs' Association. Therefore, I entitled the address "Professionalism and Ethics."

Law enforcement has been a career in this country for well over 100 years; from the early beginnings with the uncertain steps of individual men scattered across a growing nation to today's massive, highly technical and machine-oriented police agencies.

But despite all of the advances in technology, science, and experimental methods, it is still the individual men and women who hold the key to the success of law enforcement.

The modern police officer must be a doctor, lawyer, sociologist, psychologist, philosopher, marksman, athlete, diplomat and, above all, a perfectionist—a perfectionist because he is given no second chances and any mistakes are magnified for public view and review.

His job is people—their lives, their welfare and their property. Most of the time he is an architect—picking up the pieces society has broken and trying to put them back together again. Everything he does affects somebody, somewhere, sometime. His influence, for good or bad, outlives him for generations because his actions are indelibly imprinted on the hearts of men.

He is on duty and on trial 24 hours each day and lives under a microscope and in a fishbowl for all the world to see and examine. And some of those he would die for want to destroy him.

Without him, there would be no society, but rather a jungle of disorder and anarchy. He can reduce crime but he alone cannot eliminate it because he has no control over the causes of crime, and he merely takes over where society has failed.

And society has failed in many areas by not being able to understand the causes of strife and discontent and then abdicating its responsibility so that law enforcement is left by itself to control and bring order out of chaos. Yet, while it demands order, society basically resents restraint and control and accordingly withholds complete faith and ultimate trust in law enforcement.

For modern police officers, the key to obtaining that faith and trust is professionalism, not only of each individual but collectively. The actions of an officer in Pocatello, Idaho, affect an officer in Grand Rapids, Michigan, and vice versa.

Police work has long been a vocation, yet until only recently has there been any effort to make it professional. Law enforcement has claimed for a long time that all police are professional law enforcement officers. Yet there are still many today who are quite unprofessional and who bring discredit to the badge and uniform. It is disgraceful that there remain officers who have no education, no training, and no motivation, carrying the authority and awesome responsibilities of the badge and uniform.

With the constantly increasing level of education of America's citizens and a large portion of them being youths who are attending colleges and universities, the need for higher educational qualifications of police officers is becoming more evident. Communication and understanding between the officer and the citizen, particularly the young citizen, are becoming increasingly vital in combating crime and lawlessness in today's modern society. Parity of educational attainments facilitates communication and understanding. It is naïve and incredulous to think that the police officer in today's changing social, economic, political and philosophical society can cope with its concomitant problems and challenges with an inferior education and without sophisticated training.

This is particularly true of the police officers who daily make split-second judgment decisions with which sociologists, psychologists, judges, and others have difficulty in retrospection.

But the problem of police in a democratic society is not merely a matter of recruiting persons who have to their credit more years of education, nor is it a matter of obtaining newer technological and scientific equipment.

The true measure of a professional has to be his conduct with and approach to the people he serves. His attitude and behavior are of major concern in determining professionalism.

In order to move towards the goal of professionalism within law enforcement, police officers must internalize attitudinal changes in their approach to the populace they serve.

The police professional must be concerned with how he can help the citizen. He must be interested in the causes of the problem as well as the problem itself and he should not be satisfied until an effective solution is found.

The true professional will become a problem-solver rather than just a technician responding to a specific incident. He will develop a concern for the total person (and his environment) as well as the specific complaint.

What now occurs is a significant alteration in the ideology of police, so that police professionalism rests on the values of a democratic legal order, rather than on technological proficiency. It is vital to recognize that order is not the ultimate end of government in a free society.

Properly understood, this end is perhaps best expressed in the phrase "law and justice in an orderly society." This statement emphasized the idea of the American dream for all people, implying equal protection of the law and respect for the rights of persons as persons. Every citizen in a free society is entitled to be treated as an individual and on the basis of his individual acts and not as a group.

The movement towards police professionalism is in keeping with these basic principles of democracy because professionalism implies that as a person, one may have his opinions, his beliefs, and even his prejudices. But as a professional, he will sublimate his personal preferences in favor of what is in the higher interests of impartial public service for the common good.

Professionalism in police work is measured by a number of gauges. The high levels of educational attainment which many recruits bring to police work is one indication and another is the number of officers who pursue college educations after they join the force. Professionalism includes firmness, fairness, and impartiality in the performance of police duties. It includes courtesy and consideration and even compassion in dealing with people. It also must include loyalty, integrity, and strict adherence to a code of ethics. Professionalism is also self-respect and pride in the uniform and badge of office.

Although police work is only just becoming a true profession, police officers can and must conduct themselves professionally and demonstrate professional traits. Complete professionalism can only be attained through professional conduct. Each citizen must receive fair and equal protection and must be treated with respect, dignity, and consideration.

The fair and just manner in which the police officer conducts himself is the best way he has of earning the respect of the community, and with this respect comes support. I think that police officers nationwide are learning that the community's respect no longer comes automatically when they don their uniform but that it must be earned. Fairness and impartiality in performance is one method of earning that respect. Another important method is through training; keeping a step ahead in competence and knowledge. New laws are enacted and old laws amended; the enforcement needs of a community change; new concepts of police technology and department police emerge; and rapid changes occur in social conditions and behavior patterns within the community. Police officers are affected by these changes and must be able to adapt constructively to them. Training is one answer, and it offers the opportunity to renew job interest and motivation so that the officer is not only a step ahead in competence and knowledge but also in enthusiasm.

Now that you are leaving the first training phase of your career, you take with you the first seeds of knowledge in law enforcement. Properly nurtured and cared for, they will help guide you as long as you wear the badge. However, most important is that you also take with you the highest standard of professionalism, the Law Enforcement Code of Ethics.

Police ethics cannot be separated from police professionalism, since the function of ethics is to serve as the collective conscience of a profession. The principles of police ethics have been derived from the nature of law enforcement as a profession.

The term profession, as it best applies to law enforcement, is defined as an occupation that:

1. Is dedicated to the service of others,

2. Requires specialized skills and knowledge,

3. Governs itself in relation to standards of admission, training, and performance,

4. Is guided by a code of ethics, and

5. Forms associations within itself to improve its competence and further its general objective of service to others.

Not all police departments in this country qualify as a profession under these characteristics, but it is evident that law enforcement does qualify as a profession, and that these features of a professional represent the ideals that law enforcement is trying to attain.

The whole concept of police ethics is contained in the first paragraph of the Law Enforcement Code of Ethics. Whatever will advance the ideal described here is ethical; whatever hinders it is unethical.

> As a law enforcement officer, my fundamental duty is to serve mankind; to safeguard lives and property; to protect the innocent against deception, the weak against oppression or intimidation, and the peaceful against violence or disorder; and to respect the Constitutional rights of all men to liberty, equality, and justice.

There are two ways to approach police ethics. The first is to consider them as a set of positive precepts; the second as a set of negative injunctions. Both approaches are necessary, since the concept of ethics requires that certain things be done and certain things be avoided. The second paragraph of the Code of Ethics stresses the positive side of police ethics.

> I will keep my private life unsullied as an example to all; maintain courageous calm in the face of danger, scorn, or ridicule; develop self-restraint; and be constantly mindful of the welfare of others. Honest in thought and deed in both my personal and official life, I will be exemplary in obeying the laws of the land and the regulations of my department.

This paragraph sets forth high but necessary ideals for the police officer. Together these ideals point to the kind of character a police officer must have. He must himself practice what his profession preaches. More important, he must actually be what his profession demands.

Whatever a policeman does in private life has an effect on his public life. In a sense, a police officer has no private life; he is always "on duty." But there are certain qualities that are particularly expected of him in his official capacity. High among those is courage. To be courageous is not to be ignorant of danger, but it is to fulfill one's duty despite danger. This is indispensable in a person whose sworn task is to protect others from unlawful violence or to protect property from thieves or vandals. Without physical courage, a policeman simply cannot fulfill his responsibilities.

Moral courage may sometimes be harder to maintain than physical courage, but it is just as necessary. Today it is more necessary than ever. Civil disorders, student protests, and an increasing general dislike for police often subject police officers to scorn and ridicule and to nearly intolerable verbal abuse. But the modern police officer must have the self-discipline and moral courage not to respond to such kinds of antagonism. Officers who cannot handle this kind of abuse can prove to be a danger not only to those who abuse them but also to their fellow officers and the general public as well. More than one "incident" has turned into a major riot because certain officers did not have the moral stamina to withstand verbal taunts and insults.

Certainly, the ethical police officers never use more force than is absolutely necessary or than is dictated by department policy. He must, above all, avoid anything that resembles brutality. This extends to verbal brutality as well as physical brutality.

Another area of ethics that is critical to the very foundation of law and society and the survival of law enforcement is police corruption and policy loyalty.

As a new police officer, you will develop a most compelling need to feel that you belong. You are a "rookie," a "boot," an ignorant, idealistic newcomer that to the disdain of older officers has been released by the training academy on an unsuspecting public. Senior officers will watch your every move and if you make a mistake, you will be ridiculed. However, your desire will not be dampened and you will survive to learn the "streets" with these older officers. You will work hard at learning the job and work hard at being accepted because no one wants to be left outside. Strong ties of loyalty will develop between you and these other officers. You will do your job diligently and try to live by the Code of Ethics because that is the way of the professional.

But soon will come the test; the true test of a professional. How will you meet it?

It used to start with a cup of coffee but now it's a meal and after dinner your partner gets up and walks out; there is no bill. The Code of Ethics flashed through your mind and you wonder what to do. Your partner tells you to hurry up, so you throw a dollar down on the table and leave. All night long, the Code goes through your mind but your partner tells you to forget it, everybody does it. And it happens again the next night and the night after.

One night your partner calls in sick and you are out there by yourself; you're excited. You see your first ticket; a car racing through a stop sign and you make your stop. The driver gets out and it's the owner of the restaurant. He reminds you of all the free food you've had and all the other cops he feeds. Now you're on a tightrope. Do you write him the ticket, ruin the free meals for the other guys, and become a loner; or do you just give him a warning and let him drive away. And as he drives away without the ticket, he smiles because he knows that part of your badge is missing and he's got that small tarnished portion in his back pocket.

Rationalization will ease your mind because you hear everybody on the department does it so it must be all right.

Now your partner is back, the calls are coming in hot and heavy, and you forget about the incident with the ticket as you race to a breaking and entering in progress call. You screech to a halt, jump out, and find an open door and the excitement rises. But all is secure and you contact the owner and wait for his arrival. After checking his stock, he advises you that he's missing two fur coats and takes you in to his office. You fill out the report and as you get ready to leave, he hands you a bag. Inside is a fur coat, and there is one for your partner. The owner tells you he likes the way you handled the call and that he's covered by insurance anyway so you take the coat. A nice present for your wife.

As you walk to your patrol car, the last paragraph of the Law Enforcement Code of Ethics goes through your mind:

> I recognize the badge of my office as a symbol of public faith and I accept it as a public trust to be held so long as I am true to the ethics of the Police Service. I will constantly strive to achieve these objectives and ideals, dedicating myself before God to my chosen profession ... law enforcement.

In panic, you look at your shirt and all that remains is a stain, the last remnants of a tarnished badge.

Of course, we who have studied and practiced law enforcement feel that society is partially to blame. It demands high standards of its new officers, yet it makes them face an almost insoluble dichotomy; society wants police officers who cannot be bribed but it also wants to bribe police officers. When the police officer fails in the eyes of the public, the agency is branded. The public demands that sanctions be taken against the miscreant, and society exacts its own brand of "justice" from his family and friends. This suggests the extent to which the public perceives police officer personnel as an organization, rather than as a profession.

The malfeasance of one officer is often quite sufficient to bring the entire department under suspicion. When this happens, police officers soon discover that the good name of the agency cannot be restored by simply punishing the offending officer. It is assumed by the public that, since individual malfeasance could only occur because of structural defects within the agency, a punished officer is merely a scapegoat so that others are protected. Thus, the criminal police officer not only brings shame and disgrace upon himself but he also discredits his department and fellow officers who strive each day to live by the Code of Ethics and faithfully serve their community.

The need for high standards of police ethics has never been greater than it is today. At a time when various social developments are bringing into question the very nature of law and order, it is imperative that the police, dedicated to the preservation and protection of those values, maintain in themselves an example that will elicit respect for the principles on which democracy rests.

Police officers must fulfill their sworn obligations in order to win the respect of the general public. Integrity alone can earn them that respect. Without it, they will sabotage their every effort. This fact is especially urgent at a time when the whole nation is undergoing a "crisis of confidence" in the police. Unless that confidence can be restored, the work of the police will be to no avail.

# Police Chiefs Thought I Was Taking Over

Dear Jay,

An article in the *Daily Tribune* on October 31, 1977, called "SOC Police Chiefs Rap Sheriff" was critical of my proposed Regional Service Study. Here is a good example of how the press inflames people and situations by giving minimal information to get reactions from authorities for their stories. Let me also tell you that Chief Cribb surprised me when I first met him by saying.—"You're from New York. We don't trust you. You're too flamboyant." I let him have a piece of my mind.

> Questioning the "sincerity of his motives," South Oakland Police Chiefs have requested a meeting with county Sheriff Johannes F. Spreen.
>
> "For the past five years, we have attempted to deal with the Sheriff in improving police services in Oakland County," said Chief Frank Cribb of Clawson, president of the SOC Police Chiefs' Assn …
>
> "This is a never-ending process," said Cribb of Spreen's airing of ideas to the press before other police chiefs hear of them.
>
> "We have cooperated a hell of a lot longer than he (Spreen) has been around and will go on cooperating after he's gone," said Cribb …
>
> At last week's press conference, Spreen singled out coverage by *The Daily Tribune* of a speech to the County Board of Commissioners where he called for a study on consolidating police services.
>
> Asked what he would leave to local police departments, he said street patrol and handling of citizens' complaints of poor or improper service. A long list of items he earlier suggested should be considered in the study for possible transfer to a central command included:
>
> - Centralized dispatch of all police officers,
> - Selection and training of personnel,
> - Possible law enforcement by contract teams,
> - Special investigation teams for dealing with local crime emergencies such as the slayings of seven youngsters being investigated in South Oakland,
> - Organized crime intelligence,
> - Data processing analysis of crime detection and forecasting,
> - Riot control,
> - Investigation of crime scenes and laboratory work,
> - Cooperation of auxiliary police,

- Funding for regional police investigative teams to work across city and township boundary lines and,

- Coordination of public relations and release of information on crime.

In today's response to Spreen by the South Oakland Police Chiefs, nine examples of current cooperation between forces were listed.

- Oakland County Narcotic Enforcement Team, in cooperation with the Michigan State Police, Oakland County Prosecutors Office, and the Sheriff's Department.

- The 18-community South Oakland County Mutual Aid Agreement.

- The CLEMIS (Court and Law Enforcement Management Information System), a countywide criminal justice records system through the Oakland County Data Processing Division.

- Area crime labs, provided by the Michigan State Police.

- The Natural Disaster Task Force.

- The Oakland Police Training Academy in cooperation with Oakland Community College, which was the first county-level police academy in Michigan.

- The South Oakland County Criminal Blockade Plan, which is part of the Michigan Blockade Plan.

- The Tactical Support Unit, a forty-man unit trained in coping with civil disorders.

- Oakland County Kidnap Task Force, in cooperation with eight South Oakland communities, the Michigan State Police, and the Sheriff's Department and the Oakland County Prosecutor's Office.

## My Proposal to Support Local Police

Dear Jay,

In October 1, I prepared "A Cost Effective Proposal to Provide for the Delivery of Quality Professional Support Services to the Various Local Police Agencies in the County of Oakland, State of Michigan." I presented it to the Oakland Board of Commissioners on October 20, 1977. After my presentation, I distributed a summary of the plan with a suggested timetable for accomplishing what was proposed. Here are some excerpts of that presentation:

I talk to you today, sincere in my belief that most of you are as concerned as I am and care as much as I do about a plan to deliver cost effective, quality professional support services to the various local police agencies in Oakland County.

This plan is a result of many years of having been out in the field and inside in administration with much consultation with concerned citizens, law enforcement experts and other professionals.

Ten years ago, the President's Commission chose Oakland County, Michigan, as the example of a community badly in need of such a cooperative effort. In spite of this focus of national attention, little, if anything, has been done to implement the sound proposal of the President's Commission, and of similar studies.

Since this attention was drawn to the Oakland County community, a number of serious interjurisdictional crimes have been perpetrated, with only minimal success in the apprehension of the criminal. The most recent and notorious offenses involve the enticement, kidnapping and murder of a number of very young children of the Oakland County community. The murderer has not yet been apprehended. Although an ad hoc community effort at cooperation did materialize—called the Oakland County Task Force—the duplication, fragmentation and, at times, half-hearted cooperation and misuse of the Force's resources may have prevented the realization of its full potential.

For those of us in law enforcement administration, the lack of a coordinated approach in dealing with increasing suburban crime has been a growing and crucial problem over the last decade. I have spoken about it on numerous occasions, most recently at the Southern Police Institute Alumni Association. Now, I have reached the point where I feel that lip service is no longer acceptable. I firmly believe it is time for action. That is why I am here today to present to you a proposal and a plan of action for bringing about a more coordinated, cost effective means of delivering quality police services in Oakland County.

Jay, I left with the Board of Commissioners this proposed plan of action:

- Seek the support of local public interest groups.
- Approach appropriate state and federal political leaders to obtain support.
- Inform all police and other appropriate governmental personnel of the existence of the project.
- Identify potential sources of funding at the state, national, and foundation level.
- Inform appropriate legislative committees.
- Develop grant proposals.

- Secure appropriate consulting firm after public bid.
- Establish monitoring and reporting techniques for accomplishing the objectives of the grant.
- Begin the project by January 1, 1978, and complete it by March 31, 1979.

## First Female Patrol Officer in Oakland County Sheriff's Department

Dear Jay,

I always encouraged women to enter law enforcement and was so happy to have our first woman patrol officer in the Oakland County Sheriff's Department. My own wife had been a New York City police officer. William L. Willoughby of the *Tribune* did a news story on her 12/27/77 entitled "Woman Deputy Wants No Special Treatment." Here are some excerpts from that article:

> ... Publicity is the last thing Miss Tobin wants at this time. But she is the first woman to become a road patrol officer for the Oakland County Sheriff's Department, and she is the daughter of a prominent South Oakland police chief.
>
> It's hard enough starting a difficult job like that, without incurring the possible resentment of her male colleagues, she says. "I don't want them to think I have an oversized head. I'm feeling enough tension without this."
>
> ... She thinks there are areas of police work that she might be able to handle better than a male officer. "I haven't been out there yet, so I can't tell. But I think a woman could be more effective dealing with juveniles, family fights, or sex crime victims. Women tend to be more open. They feel more. It's hard sometimes for a woman—like a rape victim—to discuss certain things with a man."
>
> ... Miss Tobin also will bring a college degree to the job. She holds a bachelor of business administration from Mercy College of Detroit, with a specialist's certificate in law enforcement, also from Mercy.
>
> Her boss, Sheriff Johannes F. Spreen, is the director of the law enforcement program at Mercy.
>
> Her paraprofessional job helped her get something else—a future husband. She plans to marry Dep. Donald McLellan of the Sheriff's Department next September.

Jay, I recently learned that her husband is now a captain in the Oakland County Sheriff's Department and has been working with the International Association of Chiefs of Police on the Weapons of Mass Destruction policies and plans. I am not sure whether Sue stayed with her career or not. She may have become a mother, of course.

# *1978*

Jonestown Massacre and suicide of 900 people
Camp David accords for Middle East peace meeting in Maryland
Love Canal in New York declared federal disaster
*Hustler* publisher Larry Flynt shot and paralyzed

## Asking Support from Sheriffs for Gubernatorial Run

Dear Jay,

I decided to run for Governor in this year. I had to get 18,000 signatures. Republican candidates only had to get 9,000. I lost out getting on the ballot by 108 signatures by the deadline. I wrote the letter below to 83 county sheriffs in Michigan. I needed their help in getting enough names on petitions to get on the ballot as a candidate for Michigan governor.

In the end, Republican Governor William Milliken was re-elected for a third term (ran 14 years altogether). I wish I had been able to run against him. Laws passed since then prevent a governor being re-elected for a third term. Milliken made news in 2004 when he broke party ranks to support John Kerry's presidential bid against George W. Bush.

> Dear Sheriff:
> I have always been dedicated to law enforcement, and in the last six years particularly to the very important role of the Sheriff. I see the Sheriff as the key and the hope for cooperative law enforcement in the future.
> I am running, as I hope you know, for Governor on the Democratic ticket. While you may have another commitment or preference at this time, I am especially asking you to help at least get me on the ballot.
> I promise to speak out for all Sheriffs' departments and for proper cooperative law enforcement in general, as a very important factor in the quality of life in Michigan. With a background of 37 years in law enforcement, mostly with city police departments in New York and Detroit, I have developed the greatest respect for the vital role of the office of Sheriff.
> Please give me the opportunity to at least speak out on issues important to you and to Michigan—and I would like to hear from you on these.
> Enclosed please find a number of petitions, and I would ask for at least 150 signatures through your good offices. If you can get 1,000—all the better. I need your help. Our deadline for petitions is June 6, therefore we would like to have them all in by June 1.
> Thank you.
> Sincerely, Johannes F. Spreen
> P.S. The results of a survey taken indicate that my name has more recognition in southeast Michigan than all other Democratic candidates combined. I can win the primary. Even if you like the present incumbent, you will have a choice between him and a candidate, who I believe will be more acceptable to you.

# I Was Sued for $2.25 Million

Dear Jay,

On May 16, 1978, I wrote Robert Allen, the Civil Counsel for the County of Oakland, concerning a lawsuit (Paul G. Valentino, Paul G. Valentino, J.D., P.C., and Janice Spitler v. County of Oakland and Johannes Spreen—Civil Action File No. 76 140161.)

This was a truly weird case. It was written up in *Time Magazine*, May 15, 1978. Peter Lazaros, a convicted perjurer and suspected bank swindler, was arrested on fraud charges and died in our jail during early May, 1978. While performing a routine autopsy on him, doctors found a ring he had stolen in 1977. He had stayed at the New York Pierre Hotel and asked the Bulgari jewel firm to bring an assortment of expensive gems to his room. He declined to buy them but the Bulgari officials later discovered that a $35,000 four-carat diamond and platinum ring were missing. When they questioned Lazaros about its disappearance, he threatened to sue. Lloyd's of London settled Bulgari's insurance claim for $17,000.

Police assume that Lazaros swallowed the ring when he was jailed and then died of undetermined causes.

The lawsuit against me, however, had nothing to do with that. It began when Lazaros failed to appear for a creditor's examination over some judgments of $850,000 against his trust. My department was obliged to arrest him. We did so but he became ill and had to be hospitalized to recover enough to appear in court. While in the hospital, he was to be guarded by our personnel.

On May 6, 1976, the guard was removed under the directions of Undersheriff John Nichols and the patient left the hospital. Nichols removed the guard because of a letter from Oakland County Prosecuting Attorney, L. Brooks Patterson, who wrote:

> Dear Judge Thorburn: I have advised Undersheriff John Nichols that it is not necessary for him to maintain an around the clock security guard over Peter Lazaros while the latter is confined to the hospital. I am further advised that my instructions to Undersheriff Nichols represents your thinking in this matter. The removal of the guards is solely my responsibility. If there are any questions regarding this recent action, please do not hesitate to contact me personally.

The case dragged on for years and the court order against me on December 2, 1982, stated;

It is further ordered and adjudged that the intentional act of the Oakland County Sheriff, Johannes Spreen, in refusing to re-arrest Peter Lazaros on the advice of counsel, after being informed by the head of security at St. Joseph Mercy Hospital that Peter Lazaros was discharging himself from the hospital on May 7, 1976, was without lawful excuse and contrary to the court's order for bench warrant, writ of superintending control, and the statutes of the State of Michigan. It is further ordered and adjudged that Oakland County Sheriff, Johannes Spreen, was negligent for his failure to levy or otherwise act upon the writ of execution issued and delivered to the Oakland County Sheriff on May 3, 1976.

The patient left the hospital and left the jurisdiction where his person and his property could no longer be assessed and confiscated. However, he was re-arrested and died in our jail a few days later, perhaps due to the ring he swallowed. The family was notified of his death. His brother came to the jail, was very emotional, and came running at me. My deputies thought he was going to hurt me. I waved them off because his brother had died in my jail. I walked toward him to offer my condolences. Instead of attacking me, he hugged me for that.

I wrote my lawyer when the case was filed against me and he sent this response. The case was finally settled in 1983.

Dear John:

In response to your inquiry of May 16, 1978, I will answer your questions in the order asked.

1. Yes, this office does represent you. Further, while the insurance company, at the moment, claims they have no responsibility to represent you or to pay any judgment, in the event a judgment is rendered, it will be paid by the County.

2. The defense, as far as this office is concerned, is the fact that you were acting and obeying an order of the prosecuting attorney.

3. As of this moment, the prosecutor is not a defendant to the lawsuit, and unless the plaintiffs hereto make him a party, I am not sure we will.

4. In view of the fact that this office does represent you and you were sued in your official capacity and the County will pay a judgment if any is rendered, I see absolutely no need for you to employ outside counsel.

## Poor Choice for My Defense

Dear Jay,

For my defense, I selected Circuit Judge William Beer who had put me in jail. Why? He had come to my wife's restaurant for a party after my election and regretted that he had wrongly sentenced me to jail.

That choice of defense turned out to be a mistake and I lost the appeal so that the plaintiffs were awarded $2,247,000.

Judge Beer was still involved with me by the time the appeal was decided on April 30, 1984, but I was shocked to learn in 1983 about the Judge's personal life, which I described earlier.

## The Sheriff's Role

Dear Jay,

I wrote the following letter to the *Detroit News* that was published June 26, 1978. It seemed to me and many other sheriffs that a "role definition bill 1517" had caused the Michigan State Police, local police, many local politicians and some of the media to attack the sheriffs in Michigan through misstatements and untruths.

This bill was based on the recommendations of two special committees appointed by the governor in order to end some of the confusion concerning the role of sheriffs' departments in patrolling secondary roads. The State Police budget had just been increased by $29 million dollars this year to a total of $130 million, yet people were accusing the Michigan sheriffs of wanting to build an empire. I have excerpted my letter to the editor here.

> The sheriffs of this state are not out to empire build, but are attempting to serve the citizens of their counties to the fullest extent. In 1976, the majority of fatal accidents occurred on the secondary roads in those areas patrolled by the sheriffs' departments and local police. The 83 sheriffs in Michigan are the only police officials in the entire state that are directly answerable to the citizens they serve. The sheriffs must place their record of performance in law enforcement on the line and in front of the voters every four years. Who do the State Police answer to?
>
> The politicians, local police chiefs and State Police officials and those in the media who oppose the sheriffs' departments and claim the money that will be allocated to the 83 sheriffs' departments is a waste of money must not regard very highly the lives of those citizens that they allegedly serve. This

money will be used to provide for increased patrols of all the secondary roads within the counties in order to prevent accidents and serve the citizens.

Opponents of the sheriffs' departments claim that this bill will further fragment law enforcement. To the contrary—this bill, for the first time, defines the roles of the State Police and the sheriffs' departments and gives the primary responsibility for patrol of the secondary county roads to the sheriffs' departments. It will eliminate duplication of effort and the waste of taxpayer's money for that duplication. Actually, it will alleviate some of the horrendous law enforcement problems caused by fragmentation.

Johannes F. Spreen, Sheriff Oakland County.

## Harmonizing Law Enforcement Efforts

Dear Jay,

Well, two days after that article, I addressed the Michigan Sheriffs Association in Flint, Michigan, on June 28, 1978. It was election year, so this talk and my comments got some news coverage. I began with how law enforcement doesn't work well in the cities because of politics and tenure. No chief or commissioner lasts long enough to provide proper direction and continuity to make police programs effective. So here's what I told the Michigan sheriffs.

> After finishing a 17½ month term as Commissioner of Detroit Police, and after some deliberation, I decided to run for sheriff in Oakland County. I didn't know much about sheriffs then, but I ran because some men in Oakland County Sheriff's Department said they wanted more professionalism. I asked if they were willing to work for it. When they agreed, I soon learned that I didn't know enough about county commissioners and county politics.
>
> Now, after 5½ years as sheriff in a county having the largest number of separate independent police departments, I have gained some meaningful insights (not without some scars and a brief sojourn in jail), and have some pretty definite ideas and opinions.
>
> It is my strong feeling that after so many years in law enforcement that the law enforcement system in these United States does not work. It really never has, effectively—and unfortunately, probably never will. While big city policing has its problems in facing up to its task, certainly the excessive fragmentation of smaller law enforcement agencies is impeding law enforcement effectiveness.
>
> I am particularly distressed by the law enforcement mess in Michigan created and exacerbated by Governor Milliken and Colonel Hough—those two Lansing politicians. It is one of the reasons that I ran for Governor. There are other issues that I am concerned about and I feel I can articulate them. However, as of this moment, now that the Governor has vetoed Senate Bill 1517,

we here are most concerned about the Governor's action in setting back harmonious law enforcement efforts.

Please allow me at this time to gratefully thank those sheriffs who got me qualified in their counties by getting me the necessary 100+ signatures. And my thanks to those sheriffs who intended to, but were unable to, because of the short period of time or for whatever reasons. My regret is that perhaps you and your concerns may not be represented at the top level of government by whoever is elected to the office of Governor.

May I point to the findings of the National Sheriffs Association's intensive survey of the needs and capabilities of the nation's Sheriffs' Departments recently released, to-wit: "By far the most pervasive problem facing county law enforcement agencies is the lack of adequate funds"—that the great difficulty is in convincing county commissioners of our needs.

Let's look at our problems. What are they?

- The law enforcement mess in Michigan.

- Law enforcement ineffectiveness.

- Police fragmentation problems (the child killer investigation in Oakland County is an example of fragmentation at its worst where State Police have not worked in equal, professional cooperation with the Sheriff of the County.)

- Law enforcement overlap and duplication.

- Law enforcement confusion and conflict.

- Law enforcement competition, hostility, yes, even "civil war" with verbal insults and disparaging remarks flung at sheriffs.

What are some of the solutions?

- Certainly role definition—defining who does what, when, and where.

- Financial support from the state.

- We must establish roles, responsibility, and rapport for and among law enforcement agencies in Michigan.

- The sheriff as the people's representative can be the pivot man between local law enforcement and the state police. He should be involved, not excluded.

- The sheriff should be a service agent serving the independent police departments and people of his county.

- Law enforcement must not be remote and removed or it becomes ineffective.

Colonel Hough's remarks to the Role Definition Committee were "Let the sheriff do the jail keeping and leave law enforcement to the state police." That smacks of takeover and is tantamount to a Big Brother approach. Is a police state beginning here in Michigan?

What happened to Governor Milliken after his state of the State message January 6, 1976, where he said, "I am concerned that State government is assuming responsibility and authority which might better be carried out by local governments, either independently or through joint efforts."

Our state budget has escalated tremendously in the last ten years. Our state police budget is going up 29% next year. Our governor has given $12,000,000 of state police service to Detroit City for its freeways. But, there is not one cent for the state's 83 counties to finally make law enforcement work in Michigan—to properly fit in the missing piece in the jigsaw puzzle that is Michigan law enforcement and clarify the picture. We know that people are fed up with politicians and promises; that people are fed up with our systems of politics and game-playing; that people are fed up with political corruption and lack of ethics. We read so much about this in the front pages nowadays.

Law enforcement needs streamlining. Law enforcement and justice should not take so long. Certainty of punishment should be our standard. Determinant sentences are a better deterrent and it keeps the criminal from ripping off people. And, certainly, we should put a stop to judge-shopping and other bad practices in the justice system.

In conclusion, we sheriffs are not united with one voice. You can make law enforcement work. It is not right to have a sheriff's car and a state police car respond to the same situation. It is not right for people to be unsure of whom to call for help. While the state police should never be relegated to the role of highway patrol, neither should the sheriffs' departments be relegated to jailers only, contrary to Colonel Hough's feelings. There is so much to be done to protect the citizens—and there is enough work for everyone.

The state police can be more effective in certain areas such as narcotics and drug abuse control, and in the fight against organized crime takeover. Sheriffs are limited by county boundaries. State police can provide great services in the area of central records, central lab services, law enforcement information network, etc.

The sheriff working as a bridge between small local departments in his county and the state police can be the key for better, more effective law enforcement. Yes, the sheriffs are ready to come into their own, to provide leadership in law enforcement, to represent the people, and to improve the quality of life in this great state—county by county by county.

## Cleared of Contempt

Dear Jay,

The *Detroit News* published an article by Graham Dower called "Court Reversal Clears Spreen of Contempt" on July 19, 1978. Boy, was I happy! He wrote "Michigan's Court of Appeals yesterday reversed a contempt of court citation issued against Oakland Sheriff Johannes F. Spreen.... Oakland Circuit Judge William J. Beer alleged that Spreen was in contempt for refusing to honor a court order to rehire a former detective sergeant. The officer, Keith Lester, had been fired in March 1976, after being charged with larceny for apparently failing to provide $200 in restitution to a mobile home owner, as ordered. Spreen spent a night in jail before being released in May 1976."

Dower added that since his dismissal, Lester had been charged with another count of larceny. The latest allegation stemmed from his alleged failure to turn over to the sheriff's department more than $1,600 confiscated during a 1974 narcotics raid. He had been arraigned and was free pending trial in a district court.

## Uncooperative County Commissioners

Dear Jay,

I issued a press release on October 27. (In an interesting turn of events, the commissioners I mentioned included James Lanni, who was convicted of rape in 1994 and placed on the sexual offenders list, which he considered cruel and unusual punishment.) Here are the highlights of my press release.

> As the Sheriff and chief peace officer of Oakland County, I feel that it is my duty and responsibility to you, the citizens of Oakland County, to make you aware of some very critical facts that have thwarted the Sheriff's Department in providing an effective and equal law enforcement effort to all citizens of this county.
>
> These political ostriches, who are afraid to improve the total quality of law enforcement for every member of this county, have attempted to relegate me and my department to the role of jailers only. The six so-called political leaders have hurt the effort to fight crime through mutual coordination and cooperation.
>
> As Sheriff in the last six years, I have repeatedly tried to serve each of you as your elected law enforcement representative. Each year these six commissioners have torn my budget apart and any expansion has been stymied.
>
> In 1973, this department prepared a grant for a Crime Prevention Bureau, which would have given us the ability to have several officers trained in Crime

Prevention and to work in the community showing citizens the best and most effective way to prevent them from becoming victims of crime. Once again, the Board of Commissioners rejected our request to help you, the taxpayer. This year those six commissioners voted not to renew the grant that has helped to provide education to thousands of schoolchildren about the dangers of strangers and how to avoid becoming a crime victim.

Youth crime is on the rise and we need more than one man to handle the burden. Counseling services and criminal casework have to be followed up and provided or these youthful offenders will become habitual criminals. Once again, the leaders of our community have cast aside these young people as hopeless cases and have refused to allow the Sheriff's Department to offer any kind of meaningful service.

In 1977, I proposed a patrol force of six officers who were experts in crime prevention and accident investigation. Because the concept proved highly successful during a several-month trial period, the Sheriff's Department proposed an expansion of this unit. This program was scuttled at the last minute by a group of commissioners who have no concern nor knowledge of modern law enforcement.

Particularly Commissioners Lillian Moffitt and Jack MacDonald in addition to Ralph Moxley, James Lanni, Wallace Gabler, and Dennis Murphy have done nothing but hinder effective, coordinated and cooperative law enforcement within this county by their repeated attacks on the Sheriff and his Department and denial of critically needed manpower and equipment.

I say these Commissioners are soft on crime and I urge you, the taxpayers and voters, to carefully examine their records and then vote for their opponents. If you do that, then you will have taken a step towards bringing the law enforcement community together and allowing all of us in law enforcement to serve you properly and professionally.

# *1979*

The Shah flees Iran
Iranian students storm U.S. embassy
Margaret Thatcher becomes British prime minister
Soviets invade Afghanistan
Three Mile Island partial meltdown
Ayatollah Khoumeini takes power in Iran

## Objections to Media Coverage

Dear Jay,

The *Spinal Column Newsweekly* was often critical of politicians and I was included. However, there finally came a day when I had to respond to their criticism and explain the facts of a situation they had described incorrectly. Here is what I wrote them on January 12, 1979.

> Normally I do not answer your diatribes and lies, as it is not worth the time and effort, but there comes a time when there must be an attempt to call a halt to your untruths, particularly when you talk of such a sensitive matter as the death of an officer and notification of his family.
>
> It is untrue as reported in your commentary that I called a Detroit TV station in reference to Officer Dehnke and the three unfortunate victims of a faulty furnace. In fact, just the opposite—the station called me at home and took me to task for withholding this information. Arriving at the scene of this unfortunate tragedy, I was met by this TV station, and I gave them the basic story of the tragedy, but I gave no names because I was not sure all family notifications had been made. So much for your first lie and my so-called insensitivity. I have been at many tragedies and many heroic officers' deaths, and I have never been insensitive.
>
> As for your second lie—that I am unwilling to negotiate during contract talks. It is true there is a department to run, but I have appeared at every negotiation session with POAM (Police Officers Association of Michigan). In addition, I have reminded the union several times that all they have to do is ask for any kind of a meeting they wish. I have granted this in the past to the prior union without any difficulty. There is an open door. If they do not choose to use it, that is the union's affair—not mine.
>
> Your invitation to "mutiny" within my department and your constant attempts to start controversies have not gone unnoticed and your recent low in newspaper journalism has been brought to proper attention for necessary legal action.
>
> Yes, I do believe in modern, professional law enforcement and I am proud of the fact that I am the national President of the American Academy for Professional Law Enforcement.
>
> One who does nothing, makes no statements, plans no programs, and makes no waves doesn't rock any boats. I have tried to do something—things I think are vitally necessary if this county is to survive—but politics is hell, at least in this county, controlled as it is.

# The Past and Future Sheriff

Dear Jay,

I contributed a chapter on the Sheriff to a book called *Crime and Justice in America*, edited by John T. O'Brien and Marvin Marcus. Pergamon Press in New York published it in 1979. It was a textbook in many law enforcement and police academy courses, and was referred to during the lawsuits against law enforcement agencies in 2000 for the Branch Davidian conflagration in Waco during 1993. I entitled my chapter "The Future Shire Reeve—Tribune of the People." I will include only excerpts here because it was a chapter of some 32 pages.

## Cost of Controlling Crime

Crime not being controlled means something to all of us—higher food bills, higher tax bills, higher business costs, etc. Crime has not been controlled and many large cities have seen an exodus of taxpayers. Smaller suburban and rural communities are coming face to face with problems of crime control and its cost.

There is no measuring of the psychic costs of crime to victims, the families of victims, and even the families of criminals themselves, and to our communities and our society in general. The great dollar impact of crime (as well as the psychic impact) creates a serious economic drain on all of us.

Professionalism in law enforcement offers new promise in solving many of our people problems, but it also can be costly under our present law enforcement non-system. The most promising and effective way to both more effective control of crime and improved professional personnel is to change the system and structure that is now cost inefficient and ineffective.

It is my firm opinion, after 37 years of study and practice of law enforcement, that the catalyst and coordinator for this better, less costly, more effective crime control can and should be the county sheriff. Yes, the future of law enforcement should be directed by a modern shire-reeve, a tribune of the people—a sheriff who will be the champion of the people's rights in a more effective county-wide cooperative law enforcement, with proper liaison between local agencies of his county and state and national law enforcement agencies.

## The Sheriff

Let's take a quick look at the ancient office of sheriff. Some interesting background on the sheriff was penned by historian W. A. Morris in his book on the medieval English sheriff of 1300:

> The office of sheriff is one of the most familiar and most useful to be found in the history of English institutions. With the single exception of kingship, no secular dignity now known to English-speaking people is older. The functions, status and powers of the office, like those of kingship itself, have undergone change, but for over nine centuries, it has maintained a continuous existence and preserved its distinguishing features.

Thomas Jefferson pointed to the office of sheriff as being the most important of all the executive offices of the county.

The office of sheriff dates far back in time. His role as a peace officer goes back at least to the time of Alfred the Great. The reeve of the English shire was the forefather of our sheriff of today. The shire-reeve (sheriff) has a fascinating history of over a thousand years.

The sheriff's job has many functions and many responsibilities. Unfortunately, he has been shelved aside with the growth of our cities and the rise of municipal police, so few people have adequate knowledge or appreciation of this important office. The sheriff has a most important power—the power of *posse comitatus* (the power to call together the people and resources of the community.) This gives him an important role in emergency preparedness and embraces coordination among local police agencies.

As regards corrections, a function growing in importance, the sheriff has exclusive jurisdiction over the county jail and prisoners in transit or in court.

The sheriff is the only office holder touching all the bases; i.e., law enforcement, court services and corrections, plus having the power of posse comitatus.

In the sheriff, we have the one individual who could make the unworkable system work effectively and at less cost to the taxpayers. A modern sheriff is a people's representative—the only elected peace officer in criminal justice.

The sheriff of tomorrow must stand before and for the people of his community as a seasoned, responsible representative with service and experience in law enforcement and criminal justice, not a newcomer to the scene or a person selected primarily for political reasons as has been the case so often in the past. He should also hold a non-partisan office, to have a better chance to deal with the problems of law enforcement and criminal justice by removing the factionalism and possible favoritism that could hinder professional efforts.

While a single county police department may be a good idea in some places, in many areas it is a political impossibility, especially in counties similar to Oakland County, Michigan. Mayors, city managers, townships supervisors, and police chiefs are reluctant to relinquish their power.

As an alternative, there is another possibility that should be considered, one that involves coordination and cooperation between all levels of law enforcement: local, county, and state, with coordination at the county level with state support. While the responsibility for combating crime should be with the local police who are responsible to their citizens, unfortunately crime knows no barriers, while local police do. The sheriff has countywide jurisdiction, shares the same responsibilities to the citizens as local police, and should be the catalyst for such coordination.

Michigan was specifically singled out in the 1967 President's Commission on Law Enforcement and Administration of Justice—*Task Force Report: the Police*, as a prime example of fragmentation in communities. Oakland County has 61 governmental agencies and some 43 separate law enforcement agencies. Little, if anything, has been done to implement the sound proposal of the Commission to consolidate. I have proposed a study to research, analyze, and implement consolidation of administration and operations. My invitation has been welcomed verbally but left unheeded due to the resistances of various small law enforcement agencies.

Robert DeGrazia, former Police Commissioner of Boston, urged that by 1985, all departments would have no fewer than 25 members and by the year 2000, no department would have fewer than 200 members. Obviously, this has not happened. Consolidation has been discussed for many years. Police chiefs of small departments argue that small departments provide the personal type of police service necessary and requested in their communities. Police administration experts counter with the more efficient and less costly law enforcement if small departments were eliminated.

As early as 1920, Raymond Fosdick argued in *American Police Systems* that the increase of crime in urban districts was traceable to small police departments and it would seem necessary to try some form of cooperation. In 1936, August Vollmer in *The Police in Modern Society* wrote that with 250 separate police units in Chicago, no wonder men like Dillinger were able to avoid police in that area. In 1940, Bruce Smith said in *Police Systems in the United States* that when every local government, no matter how weak or small, must maintain its own police facilities, interrelationships become burdensome and rivalries become destructive.

The 1967 President's Commission of Law Enforcement and Administration of Justice produced the Task Force Report called *The Police*, mentioned earlier. It described the lack of cooperation between law enforcement officials and agencies, and the lack of resources of many departments to provide basic police and patrol services.

The 1971 Advisory Commission on Intergovernmental Relations concluded that a 1967 survey showed that ¼ of 91 metropolitan areas had ten or less men. A ten-man force "has difficulty providing full-time patrol and investigative services, not to mention the essential back-up services of communications, laboratory, and records."

The 1973 National Advisory Committee on Criminal Justice Standards and Goals advised: "Police agencies that employ fewer than ten sworn employees should consolidate for improved efficiency and effectiveness."

I do believe that the American Sheriff should become the pivot man in a new criminal justice reorganization. The local department, when specialized support is required, should contact the sheriff, who would then provide it. If greater support and more sophistication are still needed, the sheriff may request additional assistance from state forces. If this were done properly and cooperatively, many criminals would be put out of business.

What is happening, however, is a constant struggle and jockeying for position among our many law enforcement agencies in America. The teamwork so necessary to really combat against crime is mostly nonexistent.

With revamping of structure, there must be a revamping of law enforcement functions and the leadership of those functions. Most importantly, we must revamp the office and function of the sheriff—the oldest and most continuous law enforcement and justice office in the history of the English-speaking world.

The office of sheriff is symbolic of the development of the law enforcement function—from something citizens did for themselves to something others were chosen to do for them. We must turn the wheel around and allow a structure and a leader through which citizens can again become involved in the system.

The sheriff can be an agent of change to make an ineffective system more effective. The sheriff can assist in defining law enforcement roles, providing law enforcement services by contract, and providing effective support and sophisticated services to the many small police departments of America.

The sheriff, as elected representative of the people of the county, has constitutional and statutory functions and should be concerned with countywide law enforcement services. These include the modern, humane custody of offenders as per the laws of the state and the proper administration of the county jail; general preservation of the peace, security of the courts, patrol services for unincorporated areas by either agreement or contract; and generally specialized scientific and supportive services that can be provided from the county level.

## Contract Policing

Contract policing will be the wave of the future for suburban and rural population areas. Contract policing is the term used by county sheriffs' departments for the law enforcement services provided by the sheriff's department through agreements with local agencies of government in exchange for annual, semi-annual, or monthly fees.

The objectives of this arrangement are to provide all necessary and effective police services where costs for policing are prohibitive or taxing for the local government unit trying to finance its own force. The contractual agreement still allows the local government to maintain control of the contracted force through its control of funds. Moreover, the local unit can cancel the agreement, and this can be done with or without cause.

Through contract policing, the local governmental unit receives not only the above-mentioned general services of the sheriff's department, but regularly assigned deputies to work directly within the local jurisdiction, often out of a local substation set up in headquarters of the township, village, etc. The contract provides the necessary funds to hire qualified and trained deputies for the local jurisdiction. This is at a cost savings to the contracted areas, since recruitment, testing, training, and equipping are provided for by the sheriff's department, plus supportive forces, including dispatchers and an established technical communications system.

On the other hand, where local units of government decide to have their own police force, it varies in size and quality of operations. To begin a force, it is necessary to execute a budget allotment, and then hire a chief or director, who in turn finds 4-6 subordinates for patrol. Later, perhaps, a radio dispatcher will be found. Training, qualifications, and technical services are dependent upon subsequent budget allowances by the local government unit. The duties, functions, and powers of the chief vary from community to community, depending upon political and governmental factors.

If contract policing is agreed upon, the community or township may experience a real cost savings, a greater potential for professionalism, backup forces, and the elimination of duplication in services.

Crime prevention and control demand teamwork, coordination, and expertise. Contract policing accentuates these qualities. An added payoff seems to be in the important area of good police community relations, as the contract officer realizes that the existence of his job depends upon the proper and professional delivery of police services to the satisfaction of the contracting community.

It will take a team—the concerned people of a county along with their police departments and their sheriff—to restore to the future the promise of the "blessings of liberty" and the "pursuit of happiness" in peace and security in this land. The future shire-reeve can be a modern "tribune" who can champion the people's rights—and that should include the right to relative peace, safety, and security in a more effective law enforcement system.

Sheriff Spreen and Crime Dog McGruff at ESCAPE program and Big Boy.

## Law Enforcement Coordination

Dear Jay,

I was asked to address the American Academy for Professional Law Enforcement in Chicago on May 17, 1979. I haven't mentioned to you that at the same time I was sheriff, I was also the Director of the Center for the Administration of Justice at Mercy College in Detroit. That was part of the reason they invited me to give this talk. My talk was entitled "Law Enforcement Coordination: Is the Sheriff the Key?"

I began by discussing how fragmented and overlapping the police system is and bickering and jealousy over jurisdictional power. I mentioned that personnel were the most costly item in the law enforcement system and then I got into the problems of the system. I described the problems in the child-killer investigation caused by fragmentation but since I have discussed them earlier, I will skip them here. Therefore, here is what I told them.

Managing a big system demands a top-notch law enforcement administrator—one who blends that happy combination of education, training, previous experience and managerial expertise to put it all into proper effect.

Yet, even when a large municipality finds such a person, we find that there is a factor in the big cities that negates all the above. That factor is the moving finger of time and the events that generally can be calculated to occur to reduce the time available for any continuity of planning and programs for effective law enforcement and crime control.

Tenure in office is the key problem in many of our major cities. In some cases, too long a tenure can also bring problems, such as J. Edgar Hoover, who probably would have continued to receive public adulation if he had retired ten years earlier, rather than the shafts of criticism now directed at his memory.

In the City of New York, since its consolidation in 1898, the average tenure of its police commissioners has been slightly over two years. For such a large city, this is much too short and this causes inability for its top management to provide a sustained and lasting direction for proper programs and progress.

In the City of Detroit, since 1963, there have been six police chief executives, averaging a little over 18 months in office. No city can really survive such a turnover in the office of its top police executive.

There are many problems that are engendered by such a "suitcase brigade" in our big cities. Causes, of course, are many times engendered by politics. Effects turn out certainly not in the best interest of the citizens of that community. Chicago is now without a top administrator due to recent political winds.

Are there better answers to be found in our smaller cities where the police chief executive's time in office may be somewhat longer? Perhaps, but here a top-notch police chief executive can be a most frustrated individual. He must work within a system that cannot work effectively with police of so many other jurisdictions. Whether capable or not, in most cases he cannot possibly have the territorial area impact to be an effective controller of crime.

Part of our problem is the existence and the proliferation of so many small police departments throughout our land—operating independently—sometimes almost in a vacuum. This immense fragmentation of law enforcement and law enforcement effort pleases criminals and frustrates the sincere police officer and executive.

What effective law enforcement we do have is due in good measure to the voluntary cooperation of concerned police executives at various levels of government. This has been in spite of the way the police function is organized in our country, not because of it. This has been in spite of the fragmentation of police into thousands of small agencies, not because of it.

America is fond of its local police departments. We want our police to be close to the people they serve. We want our police to know and to be known by members of their communities. Rapport between the police officer and the citizen at the local level is one of our chief defenses in curbing and preventing crime.

This is the great advantage of keeping police patrol services in the localities they serve. But, there are great disadvantages when the local agencies are too small and too fragmented. There are problems in recruiting, training, administrative expertise, purchasing, having, and maintaining the right facilities and equipment for use when you need them, sophisticated communication control, important backup services like evidence technicians, scientific labs, and special investigators and so on.

Are answers to be found in strong state police forces? I would say "yes"—but! Much help and support can come from modern, professional state police forces, but if local departments were done away with and we had only state police in the 50 states, that would be wrong. It would be tantamount to a "big brother" approach and would certainly be too distant and too remote. It would not be in the citizens' interest to displace local police authorities.

While strong support should be found from our various federal police agencies, one national police department would be completely contrary and abhorrent to the ideas of democracy, upon which our country was founded. It would lead to "big brother" law enforcement.

There are problems with our investigative system that result in ineffective and costly investigations. Our American law enforcement and investigative machinery has lumbered on with very little change in spite of a rising crime rate and a falling clearance rate.

From time to time, there is some public scrutiny of police agencies, when crime escalates. Editorials may be written and answers may be demanded as to why crime increases. However, in the main, we continue with a system that many now see severe defects in.

It is only when some vicious or sustained scenes of crime occur that the eyes and ears of the American public are sharply focused on what law enforcement is doing and how it is doing but only for a time and then we go back to business as usual.

Consider the public and media attention give to the scene of woundings and killings known as the "Son of Sam" case in New York recently, or the "Hillside Strangler" cases in Los Angeles. Public attention is riveted until something is done.

Those two cases concern two of the nation's largest cities with sizable police agencies arrayed with tremendous resources. Still these departments found such cases difficult to cope with.

In similar sensational type cases, we find that the system ensures inefficiencies and ineptitude and many times results in jealousies and bitterness among law enforcement agencies—local, state, and federal.

A few years ago, the Manson murders in California showed the problems of a system where the guns involved were actually being held in another police jurisdiction property unit unbeknownst to the investigating department.

The co-ed murders in Michigan some years ago exemplified the problems encountered when agencies, independent and working generally in isolation, are suddenly forced into a teamwork relationship that none is prepared for.

A striking example of unpreparedness for a large-scale, multi-jurisdictional investigation which epitomizes police fragmentation at its worst is the child-killer murders of Oakland County, Michigan. (See details elsewhere.)

While a single county police department may be an answer, politically in many areas it is impossible. Mayors, city managers, township supervisors, and police chiefs are reluctant to relinquish their power.

Another possibility is one that involves coordination and cooperation between all levels of law enforcement: local, county, and state, with coordination at the county level and support from the state. While the responsibility of crime should be with the local police who are responsible to their local citizens, unfortunately, crime knows no barriers while local police do. The sheriff has county-wide jurisdiction and shares the same responsibilities to the citizens and should be the catalyst for such coordination.

Consolidation (either of departments or of services) offers a possible solution. Police chiefs of small departments argue that their departments provide the personal type of service necessary and requested in the communities they serve. But national advisory commissions and state advisory bodies and police administration experts advocate elimination of small local departments.

I believe in the consolidation of police services more than in consolidation of police departments. And I believe that the sheriff's position (not necessarily the person) is the key to harmonizing and coordinating law enforcement.

Why the sheriff? The sheriff has become a modern, progressive law enforcement official. He has the authority to take the lead in innovation and to coordinate law enforcement efforts in his county. He has the power of "posse comitatus" (the power to call together the people and the resources of the community.) This gives him an important role in emergency preparedness and could embrace coordination among local police agencies.

As the elected people's representative, he can be the bridge between law enforcement and the people in society. As their representative, he can talk to them about the need for involvement in crime prevention, obtain their assistance for the development of modern police administration, for scientific advances in criminalistics, better crime detection, improvement in the correctional process, etc. He can operate within the governmental framework on a par with his peers—the other elected office holders in county government.

The emphasis for the election or selection of a sheriff must be on maturity and experience, rather than just potential. Job experience and law enforcement credentials are more important than raw ambition, because a manager's or executive's function is problem solving. Making proper decisions requires years of experience.

The office of sheriff must bring law enforcement a togetherness—almost like a marriage. We could use the bride's custom of wearing "something old, some new, something borrowed and something blue," to describe this needed marriage within law enforcement.

Yes, it will take a team—the concerned people of a county along with their police departments and their sheriff, bolstered by state and at times national support to restore the promise of the "blessings of liberty" and the "pursuit of happiness" in peace and security in this land.

The future sheriff can be a modern "tribune" who can champion the people's rights and that should include the right to relative peace, safety, and security in a more effective law enforcement system and at a cost we can afford.

Jay, if I were giving that talk today I would have to include some other things. Sheriffs exist now in every state except Alaska and Connecticut. In most states, sheriffs are elected. In Hawaii, the chief justice appoints the sheriffs, while in Rhode Island, the governor appoints sheriffs for each county. In Connecticut, towns were established so early that they never had county government, and they hire or appoint marshals to serve civil papers, transport prisoners, and handle the jails.

Many police departments have been disbanded and cities have turned to contracts with the sheriffs' departments to save money on manpower, facilities, communications equipment, investigations, and to run the jails. While that is expensive for a community, it is more expensive still for a small town to maintain a police force, however small.

Every time a small town eliminates their police force, it causes disquiet among citizens who fear the sheriff's deputies won't arrive from afar as quickly as local police could do. In the last year or two, Wisconsin police forces in Black Earth, Cambridge, Mazomanie, and Deerfield have been eliminated and the Dane County Sheriff's Office serves them. Middlesex, Pennsylvania, is considering axing their police force as other Pennsylvania towns (Aleppo, Haysville, Union) have done. Pennsylvania has more local departments than any state with well over a thousand.

Last year Mount Clemens Police Department in Michigan debated whether to contract with Macomb County Sheriff's Department to save money. The police department budget was $3.5 million a year compared to a sheriff's contract for $2.1 million. I believe they now have contracted with the sheriff.

Towns in many states have set up contracts with sheriffs' departments including South Carolina and California; however, some complain about rising costs. Del Mar, California, was hit with a 24% increase in costs for a 2006 contract compared to 2005. Council members are asking for research about policing alternatives. Del Mar will pay $1.5 million for the coming year, Solana Beach pays almost $3 million, and Encinitas pays over $10 million for sheriff department contracts.

# Reassuring My Deputies About Their Jobs

Dear Jay,

I learned that my deputies feared that their jobs, their hours, and their overtime pay were in danger because of the growing number of volunteer deputies who were coming in to the department. I wanted to relieve their concern. After negotiations with the POAM (Police Officers Association of Michigan) and Oakland County, I prepared new Guidelines for Oakland County Sheriff's Reserve Program. I called it "Letter of Understanding" on December 20, 1979, to be effective for two years. These five guidelines were the most important to my troops:

1. The reserves are an auxiliary force, which will be utilized, in force, only during extreme emergencies (riots, natural disasters, etc.) During these disasters, the reserves will be used only after all available regular deputies have been utilized. The purpose of the reserves is to aid and assist the regular deputy in his duties during these emergencies.

2. The reserve shall ride with a regular deputy, only when the regular deputy *voluntarily* allows the reserve to accompany him; except in those types of emergencies in #1. The reserve shall have special deputy status while in uniform and only while the reserve is under the direct control and supervision of the regular deputy. The reserve program will not be used to replace the regular deputy under any conditions or to perform any job a regular deputy would normally be paid to perform. The reserve will not be used to reduce overtime or fill minimum manpower requirement of regular deputies.

3. At no time will a patrol vehicle containing a regular deputy and a reserve deputy be considered a two-man patrol vehicle, and at no time will back-up cars be called off, on calls where a back-up is normally required, because the regular deputy is accompanied by a reserve deputy.

4. Deputies shall be afforded all protections and defenses by the County and Department, in connection with the reservist, as they would in their dealings with the County in their ordinary course of employment. Furthermore, the County shall give to the reservist a Waiver of Liability against the deputy for any and all liability that he may have against the deputy, which he must execute prior to participating in the program.

5. At no time will reserves function in their capacity as Oakland County Sheriff's Department Reserve deputies without being accompanied by a regular Oakland County deputy. At no time will a reserve deputy, or two or more reserve deputies, operate a patrol vehicle, for any purpose, without being accompanied by a regular deputy. There will not be any patrol vehicles in the Oakland County Sheriff's Department Reserve Program designated Reserve Patrol Vehicles, regardless of purchaser, except Brandon (one vehicle) and Orion (one vehicle) or unless mutually agreeable by the parties to this agreement.

# *1980*

U.S. boycotts summer Olympics in Moscow
U.S. suspends grain sales to USSR due to their support of war in Afghanistan
John Lennon assassinated by Mark David Chapman
President Carter fails attempting helicopter rescue of hostages in Iran
Reagan defeats Carter and later takes credit for freeing Iranian hostages
About 125,000 Cubans leave Cuba for America
Mt. St. Helens erupts, killing 60 people
ABSCAM, FBI agents pose as Arabs, bribe politicians
Richard Pryor is burned trying to freebase cocaine
Japan passes U.S. as largest automaker

# Law Enforcement Life

Dear Jay,

I was honored to make a presentation at the 1980 Society of Automobile Engineers (SAE) Congress and Exposition in Detroit on February 27, 1980. I decided to try to describe the life of law enforcement officers so they could appreciate the profession better. Here are some of the things I told them.

> I am very pleased and honored to be here this morning to talk before such a distinguished group of national and international business leaders.
>
> Law enforcement is big business. It is not only the business of catching criminals and preventing crimes, but it also involves the expenditures of millions of taxpayers' dollars in a myriad of services aimed at the nation's communities to make them safe places in which to live and work.
>
> Because we are "big business," law enforcement must be cost-accountable to the community and the people it serves. Inasmuch as over 90% of the budget of most police departments is both in current wages and deferred pensions it is most important that we realize the utmost potential and professional competence of our law enforcement officers in their service to humanity, and this professional performance is greatly influenced by the quality of work life.
>
> The quality of work life is extremely important for our patrol and corrections officers because how they deal with you, the general public, is highly dependent upon their attitudes and adaptation to various environmental factors.
>
> In a recent article, General Motors Vice President Stephen Fuller outlined some of the chief goals of the quality of work life. I find that they apply to all organizations and include such goals as more employee involvement in the operational levels and management decision-making process; improved relationships, especially between supervisors and the people reporting to them; better cooperation between union and management; innovative and more effective design of jobs and organizations; and improved integration of people and technology.
>
> In law enforcement, the work environment is extremely critical because it is often unstable and constantly changing. Being a law enforcement officer is dangerous, and the mental stress and fatigue of facing unknown danger day after day, year after year, builds up protective barriers. Can you imagine the tension faced by the officer during every traffic stop, family fight, neighbor dispute, not knowing if one of these people will try to take his life? More police officers are killed each year handling these types of calls than during armed robberies or burglaries.
>
> The whole role of police officers has changed for the last decade. A police officer is no longer just a guardian of the peace. He must be a sociologist, psychologist, lawyer, physician, marriage counselor, educator, and babysitter.

Compounding this, the public's attitude towards police officers has changed, and as a result, there has been a corresponding loss of respect for law enforcement and for laws in general. This loss of respect sometimes develops into open hostility against the officers themselves. Besides the physical injury that often accompanies this hostility, it may lead to high frustration levels in the police officers.

Many officers give up high paying jobs or go right from college into the law enforcement profession because they have a desire to serve their community and help their fellow man. Many look at it as a "calling," a service to others that most citizens are reluctant to accept. Law enforcement is considered useful—as long as it doesn't touch the individual person. It's all right for the other guy to get the ticket or be arrested for drunk driving, but if it ever happens to us, then the cop was out to get us.

Home life problems also affect the work environment of the law enforcement officer. The work hours and rotating shifts play havoc on his home life. There are late calls, emergencies, night shifts, and the never-ending court appearances. Marital problems start to surface because the spouse begins to demand that the officer spend more time at home.

A police officer can't just forget about work when he's done for a day. He's on duty 24 hours a day and no matter where he may be, he must be ready to enforce the law and to protect citizens. A physician may choose to respond to an emergency as he drives past a wreck on the street, whereas a police officer is required by law to stop and render service even if he's off-duty.

Because he deals with criminals constantly and also the problems of society, the police officer may develop a cynical attitude towards life and the public. Police officers feel that their hands are tied by liberal court decisions giving the criminals more of a break and little or no restitution to the victims of the crimes. Weeks of work put into solving a crime may go out the window because of some legal mistake the officer was not trained to recognize. Incompetent and lenient judges continually release criminals and lower bonds allowing dangerous criminals freedom once again to ravage the streets of our communities.

As in other fields, alcoholism, divorce, extra-marital affairs, and sometimes suicide are the emotional releases upon which a few frustrated police officers come to rely.

A police officer often feels isolated, not only from the community and management, but from other police officers in other neighboring communities. There is little coordinated police action across jurisdictional boundary lines and each community becomes like an island in a sea of surging crime. Lack of coordination between detective bureaus in major criminal cases often causes vital clues and information to be overlooked or never seen at all.

Part of the problem is that many have felt lost in the administrative shuffles. Their attitudes have been shaped because they feel they have no say in problem-solving or management operations. The Oakland County Sheriff's Department is now operating a new concept of team policing. Each member of the team is trained as a specialist in a particular area of interest and the members are working together as a unit. Cross-fertilization occurs as each trains the other in his unique specialty. The organizational rank structure is eliminated and direct communication between top management and team members now takes place weekly. I am an active participant with the three teams that have been established.

They are encouraged to make suggestions for new operational procedures and to experiment with new techniques in police operations. To make this new organization work, we are now in your communities listening to your problems, talking to you on a one to one basis, and working together to solve the problems with the people and their law enforcement agencies.

Our department is now using contract law enforcement services. We have developed a service that allows small communities or large townships to contract for police protection from our department. Under this agreement, we assign a specific number of officers to patrol that community. The community also has the back-up support services of investigators, crime lab, aviation, marine division, and administrative staff services.

Most of our officers are selected to serve in those communities in which they reside. This gives each officer a pride in his community because he and his family live there. Substations have been established in communities, which give officers a centralized location within the community to which they can report for work. This has eliminated the officer driving many miles out of his way just to fulfill manpower requirements.

One of our major problems was shift preference; and, working closely with the officers' union representatives, we reached an agreement to solve this problem. We now give officers the choice of selecting first and second preference of work shifts that best fit his home life pattern. This was important because constant shift changes were found to be highly disruptive for the officers' private lives.

Marital strife is highly prevalent in police work. Quite often the spouse has no idea what the officer does and the stress and problems that he faces daily. Our department is involved in an awareness program for the wives, which gives them a full orientation including the opportunity to go on patrol with their husbands to see exactly how they work. Tonight I will welcome the spouses of our corrections officers and walk them through the jail blocks to gain a perspective into what it's like on both sides of the bars.

To further improve the environment in which the officer operates, we are fostering more citizen involvement through educational programs to explain laws and the criminal justice system, and to become crime prevention conscious. I have entitled this program ESCAPE, which is an acronym for "*E*nlisted in the *S*heriffs *C*rime and *A*ccident *P*revention *E*ducation" program.

In a major new effort to improve the quality of work life of all police officers in Oakland County, U.S. Senator Donald Riegle is joining with us in developing a demonstration project, which could become a model for the nation. This will lead to the development of a centralized communications system for all police agencies, specialized training programs for all officers, centralized purchasing to eliminate duplication of efforts and wasted funds, centralized record keeping and coordination of major crime investigation teams.

I have outlined to you some of the programs our Sheriff's Department is implementing in an effort to help correct some imperfections. These programs are aimed towards bringing the community and its law enforcement agencies closer together in a true teamwork effort by improving the quality of life in the community and for the officer who serves that community.

## Comments by Opposing Sheriff's Candidates

Dear Jay,

Marylynn G. Hewitt of *The Oakland Press* wrote a story called "Stewart To Run Against Spreen" which was published April 16, 1980. Here's a bit of what she said:

> Huntington Woods Police Chief James Stewart was expected to announce his candidacy for Oakland County sheriff today at the city's police department ... Before Stewart can challenge Spreen, he must win the Republican nomination for sheriff in the Aug 5 primary ... If Spreen and Stewart face each other, the election is expected to be bitterly contested.

## Invitation for Schools to Participate in ESCAPE

Dear Jay,

Beginning in April 1980, I sent this invitation to Education Administrators.

> I would like to take this opportunity to invite you to join with me and the Oakland County Sheriff's Department in a bold new endeavor involving the young people of our community. I firmly believe that education and positive interaction between police officers and our young citizens is the key to effective law enforcement.
>
> As Sheriff of Oakland County, in order to reach this goal, I have begun a new program called ESCAPE. This is an acronym for ENROLL in the SHERIFF'S CRIME and ACCIDENT PREVENTION EDUCATION program.
>
> In an effort to improve the communication and interaction between members of this Department and the youth of our communities, this program is encouraging those youngsters to visit the Sheriff's Department to see "who we are," "what we do," and "how we can all work as a team." We are specifically interested in reaching those students at grade levels 5-9.

To acquaint you with this program, to have you evaluate its soundness, to encourage you to send classes in groups to our Complex, we would invite you as educators and administrators to share the same experience.

This program will allow the youngsters to visit the Law Enforcement Complex for a tour of the Jail, Gun Range, and Communications Section, and to see the various types of equipment used by the men and women of this Department. Members of the Sheriff's Department will meet with the tour group to explain to the youngsters how the patrol cars and patrol boats work as well as the helicopter, radar units, and the K-9 units tracking and recovering lost persons or property primarily through a new slide presentation. Included in the presentation of slides are some areas of the Department that are not accessible on the tour.

Our program will be available for a morning and an afternoon tour on Monday through Thursday, and a morning tour on Friday. Reservations must be made at least one week in advance. Please limit your group size to a maximum of 30. This will benefit the students as well as accommodate our daily operations.

## New ESCAPE Program

Dear Jay,

I was happy to get some news coverage for our new ESCAPE program. A local newspaper published a story about our tours on April 16, 1980.

> Kids are involved in half of all crimes and fatal accidents according to Oakland County Sheriff Johannes Spreen.
>
> Many kids, he said, have no respect for the law.
>
> "Ten percent like and respect us, and 10 percent hate our guts," he said.
>
> Peer group pressure has a strong influence among the young, and the Oakland County Sheriff's Department (OCSD) has plans to equalize that pressure.
>
> A new program Spreen instituted this week, "Enroll in the Sheriff's Crime and Accident Prevention Education" (ESCAPE), is targeted toward educating young people about the workings of the police department, but people of all ages are encouraged to participate.
>
> Spreen said the program will last three hours, and will consist of lectures by trained department specialists and a tour of the jail and complex.
>
> By Thursday of this week, Spreen said he plans to send letters to teachers and school administrators in the county, informing them of ESCAPE and inviting their participation with class trips.
>
> The program is geared toward explaining a deputy's job, and why that job is necessary.

The program is also aimed toward explaining what the Sheriff's Department is doing to help the community, and how they have helped in the past.

The public will have the opportunity to examine police cars and boats at close range, view a slide show, and witness a special police sniper unit scale walls.

Spreen is also planning to offer a trace and retrieve demonstration with a police dog.

"Most importantly we want to bring these kids into the lecture room and engage in a dialogue," Spreen said. "So that when those kids leave here they will have a new respect. I want to hear them say, 'I would like to be a member of the OCSD.'"

## Auto Theft Training Seminar

Dear Jay,

I don't have to tell you what a problem auto theft is. We designed a full day training seminar in April for 250 road patrol and traffic officers called "Auto Theft Recognition and Recovery."

We intended to show them the various methods of detecting stolen motor vehicles. We offered the program at no cost to departments who sent their personnel. We also prepared a 25-page manual with many illustrations for the seminar. It was quite successful. We had speakers on the following topics:

- National Auto Theft Bureau Presentation
- Stolen Vehicle Registration
- Fraudulent Documents
- Prosecution and the Law
- Workshops on Vans and Pickups, Passenger Vehicles, Motorcycles, and Proper Legal Documents

## Improvements in the ESCAPE Program

Dear Jay,

We asked every group to evaluate their experience with the ESCAPE Program and to give us feedback. I would then forward that information to the ESCAPE team to improve the program. By the end of the summer of 1980, we had made some improvements. In general, these were points made by schoolteachers and administrators:

- Initiate the program at the fifth or sixth grade level in the formative stage in their attitudes toward authority figures.
- Try to get students involved in some activities—limit the "talking at."
- Give students an opportunity to give their suggestions and ideas.
- Break up into small groups (5 or 6 students to one officer) during refreshments to relate to an officer and have an exchange.
- Make slide program action-oriented or use video.
- Offer tours and discussions to high school students but focus on earlier ages.
- Offer in-service programs for teachers and administrators. They are more likely to send students if they are informed themselves.
- Involve service clubs by making presentations about the program and gaining their support.

Sheriff's posse of Shriners around 1980.

## The Day I Nearly Got Shot

Dear Jay,

On May 3, Willie W. Payne wrote how I nearly got shot in "Gunman's Sights Set on Spreen" in *The Oakland Press*.

> A Pontiac man carrying a Bible, a .30-06 caliber rifle and 200 rounds of ammunition was overpowered Friday by two sheriff's deputies on the Oakland County Courthouse lawn. Asked after his arrest what he was there for, he replied, "Kill me a cop ..."
>
> Police identified the man as Louis Grousnick, who was released six months ago from the Center for Forensic Psychiatry in Ypsilanti. Authorities said Grousnick had a long history of arrests on charges ranging from firearms to assault and that he signed death threats with the name "Butch."

Jay, my deputies learned of the man's attempt after an unidentified vending machine service man told someone in the kitchen area of our law enforcement complex that a man was lying on the lawn with a telescope-equipped rifle near the south information sign. My undersheriff told me that when they arrived, the man was lying on his stomach reading a Bible with the gun and a full bag of shells lying nearby.

I had received a letter the previous month that said, "This is the last letter you will receive from me Spreen. So get your deputies, judges and the prosecutors together, because I am going to kill you all." I guess it was this guy.

## Criticisms by Opponents Running for Sheriff

Dear Jay,

As things heated up for election time, newspapers ran articles about my opponents and me. I had much respect for Huntington Woods public safety director James Y. Stewart, who later became Marshal for Eastern Michigan. However, some of his comments to reporters about me were in error. This article ran in a local newspaper on July 30, 1980.

The reporter asked Stewart if he would have the sheriff's department work in cooperation with the strike force. He said, "An area in which there has been an apparent general lack of cooperation has been between the sheriff and county prosecutor L. Brooks Patterson. At least I could sit down at the same table with Brooks and talk. We might not agree but we could talk."

Stewart told the reporter that the sheriff's department should return to the basic services such as the coverage of the jail, road patrols and contracted services, secondary road patrols, the grant-funded alcohol enforcement team, and the water safety division. He had spent 32 years as a cop in Oakland County and over 16 years as a chief, but had only a 16-man department in Huntington Woods.

## Problems with Organized Crime Strike Force

Dear Jay,

August 7, 1980, a local newspaper began a series of interviews with people about the "warring factions" between certain local police units, the County Prosecutor's office, and the Sheriff's Department over the past few years. Here were the main points of my interview with a reporter, which covered a whole page. I will just add that in the same issue was a story about a jewelry store robbery that may have been partially set up by the Oakland County Organized Crime Strike Force.

Reporter: Would you say that Oakland County has quality law enforcement at this time?

Spreen: I think we have many quality police departments throughout the county. I believe our own agency measures up to the very high standards we have set for the Sheriff's Department.

However, I must say that I don't think this county will ever again have overall quality law enforcement as long as the Prosecutor of this county is directing his own police department. He and his organization all too often attempt to interfere with the work of the professional police officers of this county.

Reporter: Will you explain?

Spreen: I'm happy to explain. I see the prosecutor's job as a job that is done in the courts. He should not be leading a police force because he has no qualifications for the job by education or by training. Neither does the Chief Assistant Prosecutor have any qualifications to lead a police unit of any kind. These fellows are lawyers, not policemen.

Reporter: You are, of course, referring to L. Brooks Patterson, the Prosecutor, and his Chief Assistant Prosecutor Richard Thompson. Correct?

Spreen: Yes. The Prosecutor is in conflict of interest when he is placed in a position of running his own police unit. He is then in competition with every police unit in Oakland County. His job is to find the truth. When his office decides what will be investigated, then carries out the investigation, then does the interrogation and brings about the arrest as well, he must feel an enormous pressure to bring a conviction regardless of the merits of the case. When election time comes around, he wants to show that his police unit has done a better job than all the others. Would he not be under pressure to prosecute more of his own cases than those of other police units? Would he not be under pressure to be more aggressive in his prosecution of his own cases and less aggressive in the cases of those police agencies he competes against?

Frankly, Patterson is trying to be a dictator in Oakland County law enforcement. He actually told me in front of several creditable witnesses that the only way to fight organized crime is under a dictatorship. In my opinion, L. Brooks Patterson is probably the best friend to organized crime Oakland County ever had.

Reporter: What evidence do you have to support such an allegation?

Spreen: In my opinion, he actually prevents organized crime from being properly investigated in this county. Organized crime investigation is pretty much in their hands now. It's all under their jurisdiction so the rest of us have to sit around twiddling our thumbs while he spends his time trying to get publicity from his dirty movie raids and his prosecution of a few welfare fraud cases.

In the meantime, real organized crime sits safely around Oakland County laughing up their sleeves at law enforcement because they know the rest of us have been neutralized and they know Patterson and his Strike Force can't get the job done.

Reporter: How would you go about attacking organized crime in Oakland County?

Spreen: The first thing I would do is recognize the fact that organized crime is not a local situation. It is statewide and interstate wide. It can only be attacked on a massive scale by a statewide police agency such as the state police and the FBI. It should not be directed by some tiny Strike Force that is incapable of seeing the whole picture. His tactics are those of the Gestapo. We now have "Big Brother" in Oakland County and his name is "Babbling Brooks Patterson."

I think Brooks Patterson uses his office as a political tool to eventually achieve higher office.

Reporter: Other than attempting to gain publicity for his Senate campaign, what other political moves have you seen Patterson making?

Spreen: Look at who he has running against me. He has handpicked James Stewart who serves as Chief of Police of Huntington Woods. Now that's a town that is one-mile by one-mile. Stewart is the husband of the former Jackie Rice who headed up Patterson's past campaigns. She is presently the treasurer of his campaign fund and she used to work in his office. Now, if Stewart takes over my job, Patterson will then be running the Sheriff's Department, too. This would totally destroy any semblance of separation of powers.

Reporter: What do you think of the big jewelry store robbery up in Lake Orion that has revealed the fact that the armed robber, himself, was being paid by the Strike Force?

Spreen: It's really shocking, isn't it? I guess we all have to be grateful that no one got hurt, thank God. What I can't figure out is, since they had that car staked out in advance, how they ever lost it. (Editor's Note: The robbers went around the block, the police headed straight down M-59 toward Pontiac—so the police car was in front of the robbers and that is why they lost sight of the car they were tailing.) The whole thing sounds like the Keystone Kops!

## Jail Overcrowding—No Simple Solution

Dear Jay,

I wrote about some problems with a reporter for the *Oakland Press*. I wondered if they would print an article against one of their own. They printed it on August 18 under the title "Sheriff Says Writer Ill-informed." I'll just include the essence of the article.

> This letter is in response to a column in *The Oakland Press* on July 28 of this year by John King. While I greatly respect the freedom of the press, I feel there comes a time when a professional law enforcement administrator must respond to irresponsible and ill-informed remarks by an irascible individual who knows next to nothing about law enforcement and the corrections system.
>
> When I took office in January of 1973, the jail had adequate space to house the prisoners, although sufficient staffing hadn't been given my predecessor, and I fought an uphill battle to gain enough officers to staff the jail. I have repeatedly brought these problems before the Board of Commissioners and the county executive.
>
> Today we are faced with the reality that a federal court may indeed render a decision ordering Oakland County to expand the jail or limit the number of prisoners being held. The court will also in all probability order the county to hire additional officers to staff the jail. Jail expansion will take time, so the immediate problem is how to limit the number of inmates. As sheriff, by statute, I must receive those prisoners committed by the district and circuit courts. You can see the problem; on one hand, a federal judge may say stop taking new prisoners, and on the other hand, a circuit judge may order me to take new prisoners.
>
> Fortunately, not everyone is like Mr. King, who like an "umpire sitting in the bleachers" call balls and strikes from centerfield. Mr. King refers to several "Band-Aid" approaches in solving the overcrowded conditions, but *first aid* is better than *no aid*. I accept the challenge of my office, but we must be realistic when it comes to funding. The board allocates the money, and I optimistically await their decision.
>
> The Oakland County Jail has a reputation as one of the finest county facilities in the nation. I am proud and Oakland County can be proud of this facil-

ity's operation and the dedication and professionalism of the many men and women of Oakland County in the Corrective and Court Services Division. Working under the handicap of space and staff, we still offer a secure humane facility. Mr. King fails to mention the thousands of dollars saved by utilizing several innovative methods such as inmate labor, work release, food subsidies, in-house baking, and energy conservation, to name a few.

I might add with great pride that Oakland County is one of the few correctional institutions in the nation to receive the American Medical Association accreditation, that we offer a very comprehensive corrective guidance program which includes post-release follow-up and an on-going program with the Pontiac school system to improve the capabilities of inmates once they are released.

Finally, Mr. King's suggestion that the office of sheriff has outlived its usefulness and the powers should be transferred to the county executive is ludicrous. I'm sure the county executive would be the first to decry the folly of forming a countywide Public Safety Department. The office of sheriff belongs to the people, as he is the only law enforcement officer responsible to the people, and elected by them, not appointed by a politician, and is susceptible to removal at the polls if he is not living up to the expectations established. I am proud of my record during the almost eight-year tenure in Oakland County. I am proud of this Department which has been lauded time and time again and very much looks forward to another term to serve the people.

As for your columnist, Mr. King, if he really and truly wants to be part of the solution then I invite him to spend some time in the jail as our guest and find out the truth for himself. We would be happy to provide some fine "jailhouse" coffee and a slice of bread, which we now bake ourselves for approximately 9 cents per loaf instead of paying on the commercial market 69 cents, or we might even come up with a couple of doughnuts which we bake ourselves now at great savings. I would suggest to Mr. King that he keep his eyes upon the doughnuts—and not upon the holes.

Johannes F. Spreen, Sheriff

## Organized Crime Task Force Subsidized

Dear Jay,

The Organized Crime Strike Force was funded for another year. The board had considered my criticisms and those of others about the Force operating under the Prosecutor. Some of that was covered in an article of November 8, 1980, in *The Oakland Press*. Cindy Goodaker wrote "Strike Force to be Funded Another Year." Chief Assistant Prosecutor Richard Thompson, mentioned in the article, later served as Prosecutor from 1989-1996. He is now with the Thomas More Law Center in Ann Arbor, Michigan.

Goodaker began by saying that the Organized Crime Strike Force will be funded for another year, but the board of commissioners still didn't give the prosecutor's office much reason to rejoice at Friday's budget hearings. That was because the board declined to approve a request for 13 more positions and spent most of the afternoon debating whether the strike force should be a part of the prosecutor's office.

She said that Alexander Perinoff, D-Southfield, questioned why they need an organized crime strike force operating as a police agency to create more work for themselves. Chief Assistant Prosecutor Richard Thompson responded that if the prosecutor doesn't do it, organized crime is going to be running around the county doing whatever it wants.

## Should I Get Involved with the Strike Force?

Dear Jay,

I received this December 9 letter from Captain Robert H. Robertson, Commanding Officer of the Criminal Investigation Section of the Department of State Police. I was flattered by his comments and felt the need to consider his request since the Strike Force had been funded for another year.

> Dear Sheriff Spreen:
> I read with regret the article in the *Detroit Free Press* written by John Castine regarding the reorganizing of the Oakland County Organized Crime Strike Force.
> I have long felt the unit should be governed by a Board of Directors. The Board should have representation from the Sheriff's Department, City Police, Prosecutor's Office, and State Police. I am asking that you set aside your personal displeasures toward the Prosecutor's Office and personally serve, or have a representative of your department serve on the Board.
> I believe your fine department should participate in the staffing of such a unit, but that is a management decision that only you can make. Even if you do not assign an investigator(s), the input from your department would be a valuable asset to the Board.
> Please feel free to call me any time to discuss this issue.
> Sincerely,
> Captain Robert H. Robertson

# *1981*

First launch of a space shuttle (Columbia)
Reagan fires striking air traffic controllers and breaks up their union
Pope shot by insane Turk
Sandra Day O'Connor becomes first female Supreme Court Justice
Prince Charles and Diana Spencer marry
Polish government crushes the Solidarity movement
First reports of homosexual men dying due to AIDS
52 American hostages released after 14 months of captivity in Iran
Assassination attempt on Ronald Reagan by John Hinckley

# Involving Citizens in the Sheriff's Department

Dear Jay,

I noticed that among your duties, you are in charge of the Reserve officers in your county. You may be interested in what I tried to do in Oakland County. I've always believed that more crime can be prevented when the public is better informed and prepared, so I worked to create ways that we could educate and use citizens.

Most law enforcement agencies of any size have at least one reserve program. The Oakland County Sheriff's Department had four reserve programs (Mounted, Patrol, Marine, and Administrative) which totaled 184 volunteers during December 1981. These Reserves donated 26,704 hours to the Department. Other persons (student interns, department employees, citizens, and Boy Scouts) volunteered 9,966 hours to the department during 1981.

I began the Reserve program in 1976. The Mounted Reserves participate in crowd control, parade detail, special civic events, and area searches for fugitives and missing persons. It, of course, appeals to those who like horses and horseback riding.

Patrol Reserves rode with full-time deputies on patrol, participated in parades and special civic events, provided security at school athletic events, and were readily available to assist at any emergency.

Marine Reserves supplemented the full-time Marine Deputies in the busy seasons by patrolling lakes, conducting livery inspections, and teaching safety courses in boat and snowmobile usage. This Division housed 21 patrol boats and 12 Search and Rescue Team members. With 25 Marine Deputies, the division was able to respond to calls regarding Snowmobile and Water Safety anywhere in Oakland County. Training of children in the Snowmobile and Watercraft areas enabled them to conform to current state statutes while operating these machines. Our training programs reached a great number of youth on these topics.

Administrative Reserves worked directly for the Sheriff and Undersheriff. Their duties were to assist command officers in the planning and development of Department policies, growth patterns, and establishing future goals.

Prior to becoming a Reserve Deputy, a person received a Basic Police Training Course which included orientation of policies and procedures, Traffic Accident investigation, Criminal and Civil Law, Report Writing, First Aid and C.P.R., Firearms Training and Qualification (for those who chose to be armed), and

Arrest Procedures. We held these training classes at the Oakland County Law Enforcement Complex.

I began an experimental program in September of 1981 called the Eyes and Ears Patrol. This program worked in conjunction with the Crime and Accident Prevention Patrol but consisted of volunteers only. The purpose of this Patrol was to prevent crime through a highly visible and flexible business and neighborhood patrol and to build a better rapport between the citizens and their police.

In a two-month period, the Eyes and Ears Patrol checked 70 homes of people on vacation and found 12 homes open and unsecure. They checked 259 businesses, assisted 15 citizens, assisted deputies on major occurrences 30 times, and found 46 suspicious activities ranging from malicious destruction of property to the breaking and entering of a dwelling. Based on these facts, I approved the continuation of this program.

Like your reserves, these volunteers were unpaid for their service. They did not operate county vehicles. The vehicles, gasoline, insurance, and license plates were funded through the ESCAPE program and donations and therefore did not cost the taxpayer additional monies.

One of my major goals was to expand the size of the Reserve force to better serve the citizens through cost-effective law enforcement, education, and crime prevention. These days, such programs are used in many counties. In those days, it was more unusual to make so much use of volunteers and to attempt so much education of citizens.

## Reorganized Crime Unit Still a Problem

Dear Jay,

Hank Schaller of *The Oakland Press* wrote "Spreen Won't Join County Crime Unit" on April 15, 1981. The article referred to Commissioner James Lanni. Some time after this, Lanni was convicted of raping a female. He made history when in 1998, he challenged (and lost) the 1994 Michigan law that convicted sex offenders must register with the police agency where they live.

Schaller's article described how Committee Chairman James Lanni, R-Royal Oak, had asked me to attend a meeting about the Reorganized Crime Unit and explain why I had decided against participating in the crime unit. Lanni also asked for a report on what would have to be done so the Oakland County Sheriff's Department would participate in crime unit investigations. He wrote that several commissioners were angered that I refused to participate in the crime unit, despite reorganization efforts. The reorganized crime unit was now being supervised by the Michigan State Police instead of the prosecutor. My undersheriff and I had attended reorganization meetings and found that it was the same old operation, same old standards and all they intended to do is impose a board of directors over the organization.

Some of the commissioners told the reporter that if the five investigators assigned to the prosecutor's office concerned me, perhaps some of those investigators could be assigned to the Sheriff's Department instead. It was something to consider.

## Closed Schools Could Be Minimum Security Prisons

Dear Jay,

John A. Basch wrote a story for *The Daily Tribune* of Royal Oak on April 15, 1981, called "Use Closed Royal Oak School for Jail—Sheriff."

He described my proposal to turn vacant schools into jails for minimum security prisoners. I made that recommendation before the Public Services Committee of the Oakland County Board of Commissioners using a soon-to-be-closed Royal Oak school and others in Farmington Hills, Pontiac and Waterford Township as examples.

I thought that would help solve the overcrowded conditions at the Oakland County Jail in Pontiac while saving taxpayers the cost of expanding it. The taxpayers could expand the jail, but that would cost about $10 million. That's about $1 million more than the jail cost originally when it was opened in 1973. We didn't have a minimum security facility. I proposed using various schools around the county to solve that problem. I was talking about finding a place for persons arrested on drunk driving or divorced fathers who fail to pay child support and housing first-time offenders convicted of minor crimes. It would be a hell of a lot better than putting persons aged 17 and 18 in the same cell as vicious criminals.

I told the county Board of Commissioners that if we had expanded the jail five or six years ago as I suggested, it would have cost only about $3 million. I explained if we don't do something to solve the problem, we're going to be forced to release prisoners into the community when they should be locked up.

I informed the Board about the recently-passed Emergency Powers Act, where the governor must release prisoners from state prisons when they exceed the maximum rated capacity of the state's prison. That release was blocked temporarily by an Oakland County Circuit judge after Patterson filed a lawsuit challenging the legality of the release program.

## Our County Jail Was Full

Dear Jay,

The overcrowding problem continued and the *Detroit News* ran a story on May 28, 1981, entitled "County Jails Face Crowding." They described how I had refused to accept new prisoners and the Wayne and Macomb lockups face overcrowding in the wake of rioting at Jackson State Prison. I could not accept new male prisoners from municipal police agencies unless they had no lockups of their own. Our Oakland County Jail was 100 prisoners over its rated capacity of 485.

## Overtime Deputies Raised Concerns

Dear Jay,

A nice reporter for a local paper wrote "Discussion Runs Overtime" on June 4, 1981. I will tell you privately, Jay, there was an additional reason I decided not to run for governor but I was not about to announce it publicly. After the mother of my child died, I remarried. My wife at that time, Mona, finally told me she had accepted a $15,000 loan from a bookmaker, a gambler. He died and his wife had the note signed by Mona. This knocked me for a loop. I knew this could come out and hurt me, even though I had known nothing about it and wasn't responsible for what Mona did on her own before I met her. The reporter was there to cover overtime concerns but she included my announcement not to run for governor.

In 1979, overtime hours in the sheriff's department numbered 66,694. In 1980, this figure increased 23 percent to 81,950 for a cost of $1,077,808. I explained to the Board of Commissioners why the overtime had been necessary. First, the department was supplying 56 hours to townships under county contract instead of the 40 hours paid for.

There are 53 township contract positions. Different commissioners disagreed. I was grateful to one who said, "You know that if the Sheriff didn't have someone there on the sixth day and there was an emergency, I guarantee you they would hamstring him ... His problem is money and staff. Spreen is a poor guy trying to provide a service. He didn't create the problem. We did."

Other overtime, said Nyovich, my undersheriff, came from requests for special services at events like festivals and parades. Here we were discussing overtime but the real problem was the overcrowding in the jail which wasn't being addressed. When I called that to the attention of the Board, the reporter quoted my words, "This is like Nero fiddling while Rome burns."

# Police Chiefs and Sheriffs—Partners

Dear Jay,

On June 30, 1981, I addressed the Michigan Sheriff's Association and the Michigan Chiefs of Police. It was historic because it was the first time that the State's law enforcement community (all sheriffs and chiefs) met in a joint conference.

I had been chosen because I had been a police chief (commissioner) and was currently a sheriff. Obviously, I wanted to do a good job. However, I felt changes were needed to work together and effectively reduce crime and costs.

At that time, only a few places had consolidated sheriff and police facilities. It often had to be consolidated in bits and pieces and one of the first consolidations was in your area, Jay. Parker County and Weatherford, Texas, recommended a single building for the records system and booking procedures back in 1972.

However, some places like Indianapolis and Marion County, Indiana, entered into a unified government plan in 1971 but never consolidated police and sheriff departments despite favorable public opinion polls. The obstacle was a political struggle between the Mayor of Indianapolis and the Sheriff of Marion County, according to a San Francisco legislative analyst who was studying the possibility for San Francisco in 2001.

Needless to say, this wasn't an easy plan or talk to prepare.

> It is heartwarming to see the cooperation and coordination that this meeting signifies.
>
> As I enter my fifth decade in this law enforcing calling of ours, I believe that our emerging profession has within it the finest of men and women exemplifying the best in America.
>
> Recently, I returned from the 40$^{th}$ reunion of the class I entered law enforcement with. Conversations with old classmates reaffirmed my feelings that law enforcement must change to meet the changing economic needs of a society burdened by crime and recession.
>
> If there is to be change, then we, as chiefs and sheriffs, must be innovative and progressive in leading our new breed into a new world, lest we be passed by and inherit the fate of the dinosaur. We must examine that which we offer our public—service and protection—asking ourselves, "Can we do these things in a better way?"
>
> Services and protection can be translated into our success in doing two really important functions (in addition to generally preserving the peace). Those are the control of crime and the control of accidents. This attempt at control is costly—not controlling is even more costly. From a society who must ultimately pay the price comes our challenge. I hope that once hearing

that challenge, we will realize that it transcends that which has separated us in the past.

Law enforcement in our state is fragmented, and nowhere is the problem more acute than the tri-county area which surrounds Detroit. There are 103 police departments which encircle the City of Detroit in the counties of Wayne, Oakland, and Macomb.

The existence of so many small departments throughout our land—operating independently—presents a tremendous problem for us and hampers us in solving our crime and accident problems. This immense fragmentation is a delight to the criminal mind and a frustration to the sincere police officer and police executive.

We have good law enforcement today but it could be great. Most concerned police executives at various levels voluntarily cooperate in spite of the fragmentation of police into thousands of small agencies. Nevertheless, islands of isolation exist where there should be bridges of understanding.

Each of you represents one sovereign entity—one department. Our careers—our very lives—are tied to the destiny of our individual departments. But our similarities far outweigh our differences.

I see before me a group all bound to the same common public trust of protection for the citizenry. Everyone here wished to protect not only his career, but also the people he is sworn to protect. We are gathered together but we are divided by our lack of trust for each other.

This lack of trust is a natural defense that we, as administrators, have developed in a time of change and financial cutbacks. We all sense that changes are imminent, that overlapping and fragmented services face elimination, and consolidation efforts could eliminate our positions. We become jealous of our positions, and we see other chief and sheriffs as possible threats. We covet information, rather than share information. We become further fragmented, rather than united.

We are a group that, when viewed by the public, represents a unified body of law enforcement personnel. A citizen sees the police as one body of people (whether the uniform be brown or blue) cooperating, fighting crime and preventing accidents.

More and more, as Michigan is immersed in financial recession, people look to their police for not only increased protection (for the threat of crime is never more real than during hard times)—but for us to be effective; to not only fight crime, but to do so with less and less resources.

I am here today to ask that we all work together to see that each policing agency secures a role in this mosaic. The public does not understand overlapping and fragmented policing services. By remaining fragmented and competing, not cooperating, we are setting the stage for our own extinction.

I wish to make my own position clear before I continue. I personally do not believe in one large county police department. Unfortunately, because of two papers in Oakland County taking the position that I am pushing for county policing, I have had eight stormy years trying to dispel the image that I advocate such a concept. I am here because I, like you, face a clear and present threat to all that I have worked for.

Daniel T. Murphy, Oakland County's executive, illustrates my point in the *Detroit News* on April 19, 1981, when he talks of consolidation. He states, and I quote: "The Oak Parks, the Ferndales, the Hazel Parks are still fine communities. Is there a way that we can get three, four, or five of our cities together and decide that maybe they don't need individual police and fire departments?"

In this interview, I quote again: "Murphy predicts that the county role will increase at the expense of local control, which is jealously guarded by individual suburbs."

We stand on the threshold of change with men such as Murphy advocating a county police authority. How many of us will be standing after this proposed change? If Oakland, Wayne, and Macomb County go executive, there may very well be three large county police departments with three chiefs and one hundred of you police chiefs will not be at these meetings in the future.

If we work together to free ourselves of the jurisdictional, budgetary, and manpower constraints that impede solving crimes (such as arson, auto thefts, and homicides like the child killer), then do we not invite consolidation by another hand? How long can crime outstrip our abilities before county, state, or local governments step in with consolidation programs that we have no hand in?

We must not allow the erosion of trust between agencies to continue. We need trust to be effective, to share information, and make the best use of our scarce manpower. Nothing remains static; we must work to fight distrust lest it become more pervasive and divisive.

We must meet and talk in a spirit of cooperation in order to project effectiveness to the public that employs us. We must complement each other's efforts. We must clearly demonstrate effective use of manpower and an ability to overcome the sophisticated problems that confront us.

In dealing with sophisticated problems, fragmentation ensures inefficiencies, and many times results in jealousy and bitterness among law enforcement agencies—local, county, state, and federal.

The co-ed murders in Michigan some years ago, the child-killer investigations, both in Oakland County and now in Atlanta, and the Jimmy Hoffa disappearance are striking examples of unpreparedness for large scale, multijurisdictional investigations.

There ought to be a shared-power concept, a shared-responsibility concept with the sheriff providing certain law enforcement functions of a type that could not be provided as economically and effectively at the municipal or small department level.

It is my firm belief that we must have proper role definition in the State of Michigan. The State police have a very important job to do and that job transcends highway patrol, although I believe they should patrol the major freeways and highways of this state. They should also be heavily into control of the narcotic traffic, control of white collar crime, certainly into heavy lab and identification assistance to local and county departments.

The people in the community want and like their own local police. The concept of local police protection has become an inalienable American concept.

We want our police to be close to the people they serve. We want our police to know and be known by members of their communities. Rapport between the police officer and the citizen is one of our chief defenses in curbing and preventing crime.

The problem is that local police cannot do the whole ball game, cannot do everything required today in solving sophisticated crime, brutal crime, and terrorist crime. The best job done by local departments is that constant reassuring protective patrol provided by their officers in their local cars, the immediate response to calls for assistance from their citizens and the immediate, initial investigation. If they need additional assistance, there should be some defined way for them to request it.

That may be where the progressive sheriff comes in. The modern sheriff should not carry the burden of a partisan political label. I have asked the Michigan Sheriff's Association to pursue the possibility of non-partisan elections for sheriffs in order to have a better chance to deal with the problems of law enforcement by removing the politics, factionalism, and possible favoritism that could hinder professional ethics.

The sheriff's role should be that of specialized, scientific assistance to the individual community, usurping no department's authority, and threatening no department's sovereignty. A sheriff's role is to provide policing where there is no policing, and to provide supportive assistance to each department within the county.

We have instituted some programs in Oakland County dealing with cooperation between local police departments and the sheriff's department. We call one program S.H.A.R.E. (Scientific Homicide, Arson, and Rape Effort). I recently deputized a number of local police officers who completed 40 hours of training in homicide investigation, and we now have a team prepared to investigate any major homicide in a participating jurisdiction in Oakland County.

Oakland County has a comprehensive county-wide arson program. Through the Oakland Community College Police Academy, data is compiled on all arsons which occur within the county. Members of the Sheriff's Arson Unit, several members of local police departments and other local agencies work together on major investigations and the sharing of data.

Our county and cities have entered into a contract whereby the cities pay the salaries of five sergeants whereby professional correction services are provided to the city at the city's jail. This has been mutually satisfactory.

For the last six years, we have provided prisoner transport for all departments within the county to and from the county jail. This takes the burden off the local department, freeing manpower for protective patrol in their own communities.

For many years, Oakland County has been sharing effort and resources in our Narcotics Enforcement Team (NET) operation. Here, State police and local cooperation is exemplified to fight narcotics proliferation among our young people and our schools.

I feel that the modern sheriff's department could and should provide to local jurisdictions specialized traffic programs, accident reconstruction, police driver training, and other programs.

We have a pilot program whereby members of the Michigan State Police, local police departments, and the Sheriff's Department work as a team five nights a week in a concentrated alcohol enforcement program. We have the first mobile breathalyzer operation in the state. Such a program couldn't have gotten off the ground without the effort of all agencies involved.

Other supportive services could include crime lab services, a comprehensive juvenile delinquency prevention program, marine program, canine, and other types of specialized training and aviation services.

Our solutions lie in educating the citizenry, reaching out to them and their youth, letting them see who we are, what we do and that we can be their friends. This teamwork will do much to reduce crime and accident rates.

I have no single solution to solve our problems nor do I expect any one chief or sheriff to propose such an end-all solution. I ask that we recognize that our collective problem can be solved by our collective efforts.

I see before me a group of professionals, a brain trust, capable of waging a protracted conflict or coming together to solve our current problems. To fail to coordinate is to fail to progress. To remain fragmented is to invite reorganization. For any one sheriff or chief to ignore the needs of fellow law enforcement executives is to further fragment and further divide.

Our common dilemma is that immediate action is needed. If we take no action and fail, we fail our families who have stood by as we built our careers, and we fail ourselves as we fail to be all that we could be. We fail our departments who look to us for leadership and guidance. And we fail the citizens as we do not give them their dollar's worth in service and protection, in cost-effective crime and accident control.

Let us pull together for progress, or continue on divisive paths and fall victim to the consolidation efforts of efficiency experts that will do for us what we should do on our own.

Jay, I'm happy to say that there have been many efforts to reduce fragmentation and to consolidate sheriff and police departments. Some I know about include Jacksonville, Florida; and Tongue River, Illinois. St. Paul, Minnesota, and Ramsey County co-located a police and sheriff facility. The Pueblo, Colorado, City Council rejected a proposal to combine police and sheriff dispatch centers in 1992 but in 1994, Colorado was studying consolidation for Denver.

Sarpy County, Nebraska, conducted a feasibility study for consolidating in 2006. It's clearly a very tough thing to agree on and then to execute.

## Politicians, Jails and the Mentally Ill

Dear Jay,

I'm sure you've had the experience of addressing a group of very qualified people who wonder whether you know what you are talking about. I addressed the Michigan Psychiatric Society on August 29, 1981. I was a little worried about getting the right information across to this prestigious and influential group, so I thought I would get it off with a laugh. As it turned out, I didn't need to worry because they received my address very well indeed, and the discussion and comments following the talk were quite productive.

Good morning. It is a privilege to address the Michigan Psychiatric Society and I know I am in the right place. I need help. I think I need to have my head examined. Why, oh why, did I ever run for sheriff?

You know, as Gilbert and Sullivan so aptly and lyrically put it in the *Pirates of Penzance,* "When the constabulary duty's to be done, a policeman's lot is not a happy one."

But that was in the good old days. When you are sitting at the top of a law enforcement agency in today's troublesome times, you sometimes wonder if you have a masochistic tendency.

Perhaps I have. Who else would have taken the job of Police Commissioner in the City of Detroit in the hot summer of 1968, after the most serious riot of this century in America? Especially after about nine other guys turned it down. When I told friends in New York City that I was going to accept the job, they all responded with the same gesture and exclamation: "NOT DETROIT!"

During those interesting days in Detroit as Police Commissioner, I remember one day when I was helping to promote the department's Police and Youth in Sports Program, I turned out to "do my thing" dressed in sweat clothes and sneakers.

I noticed that a boy about 10 or 12 was inspecting me with a puzzled look in his eye. As soon as he realized I was looking at him, he said, "Are you really the commissioner?"

"Yes," I said, "I really am."

He stared at me again: "Well, you sure don't look like a commissioner."

I asked him: "Why do you think that?"

"The commissioner in Batman doesn't dress like that."

I laughed and said that I dressed differently on different occasions to do all the things that a commissioner had to do. "After all," I said, "I don't have Batman to help me." However, many times, I wished I did.

The boy's question was a provocative one. What would a modern day urban police commissioner really look like if he had all the personal equipment he needed to deal with the problems of crime, accidents, and community tensions?

He'd need at least two heads—one to accentuate the positive, another to counteract the negative. Hey, that reminds me of a song. He'd have to wear many hats, and be prepared for quick changes.

He'd need about six arms—to keep in touch with the white community, the black community, the police, the mayor's office, the city council, and civic organizations.

He'd need a magician's wand and a bag of tricks to make bad turn into good, and to make essential resources materialize out of thin air.

He'd need the sense of balance of a tightrope walker, and the patience of Job, and a sense of humor to fall back on when everything else failed. At times, a disappearing act would be most appropriate.

He might also wonder sometimes whether he had something he didn't need—a hole in the head!

Nevertheless, even if he had—he probably would run for sheriff as a Democrat in a Republican county—and find out his problems have doubled. Seriously, ten years ago, I really did not know much about what a sheriff does—at least a sheriff in a metropolitan county, comprised of over one million citizens, serviced by 61 governmental units with over 40 separate, independent police departments among them—plus 11 townships under contract with the county for sheriff's road patrols.

Today we are concerned with jails and the sheriff's responsibility for those in our jails and the increasing number of persons in them who are mentally ill.

Before we get further locked into these remarks, understand that we are focusing on jails today rather than prisons—and there is quite a difference.

The jail is operated by a unit of local government for the detention of unsentenced persons—no matter what the charge—and for sentenced misdemeanants where the punishment is one year or less. Most jails are county jails and are managed and operated by sheriffs in most of our 3,000 counties in the U.S. The prisons are operated by the state for sentenced prisoners, generally for felonies punishable by over a year.

Historically, the local jail is one of the oldest components of the criminal justice system. In 1166, Henry III of England had parliament pass an act providing for construction of jails at the Assize of Clarendon. Their purpose was to provide a detention capability for suspected or accused persons until they could be brought before the proper court. These facilities were inadequately heated, improperly ventilated, and provided little or no ancillary services. With some exceptions, the same could be said of most jails in this country until recently.

When the English colonists came to the New World, "gaols, lockups, and stockades" which doubled as warehouses were used as places of confinement for those who broke the law. These structures also housed the insane, the poor, vagrants, orphans, and sometimes the ill.

The jails in the U.S. eventually gave birth to the American innovation of the penitentiary at the state level. However, the local jails at the county level continue to pose major problems for the sheriff and administrators throughout the country.

These problems encompass escapes, riots, dangerous contraband material being introduced into secured areas of the jail, physical and sexual assaults upon inmates by other inmates, suicides, and even murders. In addition, many facilities are badly overcrowded and undermanned, which adds to the tension of the inmate population.

Most jails in the country are dangerously overcrowded these days. Jails are the intake point for the entire criminal justice system. Jails are the catchall for social and law enforcement problems. The jails feel the effect of community, police and court problems, but can do very little to control the population confined therein.

Jails contain a population more varied than any other type of correctional institution. Large numbers of people come into contact with detention facilities and can be greatly affected by the confinement experience.

Our jail in Oakland County is dangerously overcrowded these days. The jail is only eight years old and was constructed to hold 484 inmates. Today, we average 650 in our system—last week several days we were holding over 700 in the system.

We understand that personality dynamics and traits are molded (if not fixed) in the first few years of child development. Does it not follow that perhaps the institutional personality is first set in the jail—(the point of first impact in the incarceration process)—and not in the prison? By then, it's probably too late.

The basic goals of the jail are the safekeeping and welfare of the prisoners, the protection of society, and the safety of jail personnel.

Those things must be done while achieving a proper balance between security and correctional objectives. This balance must be maintained under pressure of a really diverse prisoner population with a wide range of security and correctional needs. Within this population are drunks, aggressive homosexuals, fearful first offenders, sophisticated criminals and increasingly—the mentally ill. The first offenders as well as the mentally ill are profoundly affected by their first experience in a jail and are often used and abused by other inmates. Often, the mentally ill are in jail only because they have gone off their medicines, and jail personnel have no idea what medicines, if any, they were on.

The sheriff must walk a narrow road as he tries to satisfy the requirements for humane treatment and inmate rights. He must balance that with the sometimes forgotten rights of correctional personnel, plus meet his sworn obligation to produce the inmates in court as they are summoned by the judge, to also protect the public, and to release the inmate when ready—preferably a better person than before the incarceration.

This is a tough assignment. It requires the training and upgrading of present jail staffs and the professional recruitment of individuals qualified and willing to introduce and enforce modern concepts of inmate behavior and treatment and to be trained in the theory and practice of these concepts.

This means extra costs of jail operations. In doing so, he needs public support through his governing bodies, the news media, the schools, related agencies, and professional groups such as yours.

The problem of housing the mentally ill in jails isn't new. Over the years, they have been a police concern. They often exhibit behavior that is viewed by the public as dangerous or bizarre.

Sometimes situations arise because group homes are unable to provide the necessary care and protection a mentally ill person needs.

I was at the scene of a tragic death of a young boy in such a home. I wondered if even well-meaning citizens in charge could provide the necessary care the disturbed boy apparently needed.

Of course, many times actions of the mentally disturbed are not criminal in nature, but a police officer is left with no choice but to remove the person because of bizarre behavior. The officer then has to decide what course of action to take. The subject may be taken to a hospital where he may or may not be admitted. However, often he is taken to jail where he will be accepted, usually on a disorderly person charge.

All cases aren't this simple because many serious crimes are attempted or committed by disturbed people. There was a man who recently shot his psychiatrist in Bloomfield Hills—he is not lodged in our jail. Another case is Louis G ... who wanted to shoot the sheriff and was found 100 yards outside my window with a newly purchased rifle with scope and 200 rounds of 30-06 ammunition outside my non-bullet-proof windows.

After the arrest, a person enters the criminal justice system and the process to resolve his case is usually lengthy—thus his jail stay lengthens and lengthens.

The impact of housing the mentally ill in a jail has been taxing to the sheriff and his deputies, creating even more problems for the jails.

While many sheriffs' departments have adequate medical care, few jails are able to provide full-time professional care for mentally disturbed inmates. These inmates may, for their own safety, be stripped of clothing and held in isolation. This type of handling makes them manageable, but does little to improve their condition. Most jail officers aren't trained to handle and understand these people, so unfortunately the tendency is to ignore them except for basic needs. The courts haven't devised any system to speed up the process as it relates to the mentally ill; consequently, those charged with felonies usually wait nine months to a year before they are processed through the court.

With the knowledge that as many as 10% of all prisoners have identifiable mental problems, jail personnel must receive the necessary training to deal properly with such people. As the State wrestles with the mental health programs, the ripple effects will continue their impact on jails. Most sheriffs and their staffs are ill-equipped to deal with this problem, and get little support from those who control their budgets.

The professionals in mental health aren't always able to agree, so while they debate and experiment, the problem will still be felt by law enforcement. There may be many answers for the mentally disturbed, but jail isn't one of them. The sheriff, by statute, is obligated to receive those accused of crime and committed to jail as well as convicted people sentenced to jail, but the system must be rearranged to properly handle or divert those accused of crime that have obvious mental conditions. A jail wasn't really intended to be a mental institution, but in the meantime the problem is there and is exacerbating.

It is clear that the recent changes in the mental health system have prompted an uncommon marriage between law enforcement and mental health. The stringent requirements for involuntary hospitalization do, in fact, result in the jailing of persons who might otherwise be housed in mental hospitals.

The movement towards community placement of mental patients and the lack of success in self-medication and self-maintenance of these community placements effectively results in the jailing of those placed on after-care status from state hospitals. Additionally, the incidence of untreated mental health problems in the community at large underscores the role of law enforcement as the modifying, controlling agent and it is the police officer that becomes the first line of response for mental health problems—as he is for most social problems—being the government representative out there 24 hours daily.

The two systems have come, it seems, irreversibly united in terms of public service; the "public" that we mutually serve represents a difficult community problem—the needs for solution are immediate. Yet this "union" is too often limited by communication problems and perceived philosophical differences.

In viewing the traditional relationships between mental health professionals and law enforcement personnel, we sometimes first consider the apparent differences. These two groups speak in different languages—for the law enforcement professional, the problem is legal—or criminal—the "problem" can be assault, or theft, or vagrancy. For the mental health professional, the "problem" is clinical and is described as psychosis, or depression, or character disorder. For the law enforcement professional, the "solution," as prescribed by his code of ethics, requires public safety—requires confinement. For the mental health professional, the responsibility is individualized and necessitates treatment or medication of the individual.

Therefore, this "marriage" not of convenience, not always of love—this marriage of necessity involves two partners who perceive the needs of their "wards" from two different—often opposing—philosophical perspectives. The challenge is clear: It is important that we identify a system which will provide the required level of public safety through the appropriate detention of offenders and at the same time, insuring humane confinement through the provision of adequate mental health care. It is also important that this system functions to place persons appropriately—the mental patient who is not a criminal should not be placed in jails; the mental patient who is a felon must be securely detained.

Meeting the "challenge" requires that we maintain communications, that we provide for balance between correctional goals and treatment goals. We should not seek to re-define jails and to make them mental institutions, rather as correctional institutions; we are required to be responsive to the mental health needs of the persons remanded to our custody. Conversely, we cannot expect that mental institutions at the community level will become prisons.

At this time, I would like to present our Oakland County Program as a model which we feel approaches meeting this challenge. The Oakland County Jail Mental Health Program provides for the application of mental health treatment within a correctional setting, provides for the expedition of movement of those persons who should not be confined in jail, and provides for the secure detention of persons who are criminals, but also mentally ill.

The Mental Health System provided within the Oakland County Jail represents a unique and effective response to the increasing numbers of offenders requiring special mental health services. Over 70% of the persons exhibiting signs of mental illness in the jail are felons. In this classification, the crimes range from murder, to rape, to armed robbery, to breaking and entering. They are felons and require confinement; they are ill, and require treatment. The remaining persons are misdeamants or those who have committed lesser crimes termed misdemeanors. Persons within this group may not need jailing, and may instead need hospitalization or community mental health treatment.

It is clear though, irrespective of the goals of correction, that we must address mental health problems. We cannot rid ourselves of these problems for to do so would require abandonment of our public safety responsibility. Most of the mentally ill coming into our jail must be retained in order to protect the public.

The system of service delivery includes close coordination of my department and the psychiatric team provided through the Oakland County Community Mental Health. In addition, essential to this system is the direct support provided through community mental health professionals. The system which we have designed serves these following purposes:

**1. The prompt and accurate identification of mental illness in the jail.**
The identification function falls first on the road officer. When an individual is mentally ill, but not a threat to the community, direct transport to a state mental institution is essential. If the individual does threaten public safety, the road officer is required to charge that individual and bring him to the jail. If the person is brought to the jail, corrections officers and inmate services counseling staff provide for the identification of mental illness and work as a team to identify housing, management and treatment needs during confinement.

**2. Immediate response to mental and emotional crises.**
This response capability provides for further identification, provides management support, and has significantly reduced incidents which threaten general jail security.

**3. Appropriate and comprehensive referral.**

Through using trained mental health counseling personnel and correctional personnel, inmates requiring specialized attention receive that attention. Inmates who do not require additional help are diverted.

**4. Appropriate treatment.**

Treatment may include referral to programs, housing recommendation, administration and monitoring of psychotropic medications or transfer to outside mental health facilities.

**5. Time review and monitoring of treatment and behavior.**

This review and monitoring is especially indicated when the treatment includes medication administration.

**6. Information sharing.**

The transfer of clinical information from the Mental Health Community to the Forensic Center and to community/state mental health systems is essential to maintaining responsibility to the correctional system.

The comparison of mental health services between 1979 and 1980 reflects a dramatic increase in the numbers of offenders which the system services. The need for mental health services within the county jail has continued to grow within recent years and we expect acceleration because of state and local cutbacks in mental health dollars. We are fortunate that we have put a system into place in Oakland County. Most jails in Michigan have nothing comparable and yet their needs far outweigh the resources which are available.

In 1980 in Oakland County, we saw a 46% increase in the persons requiring mental health intervention when compared against 1979. Already in 1981, we have seen again close to a 25% increase in mental health requirements of the jailed population. I employ a psychiatric team of only five for a correctional system which houses 650 people per day or more. The psychiatric team conducted 888 reviews in 1980 and we need more help here.

Over my last several years as sheriff, I made numerous requests to the Oakland County Board of Commissioners to no avail. However, relief came for staffing due to a class action suit commenced in 1978 and we were finally to get some new staff positions plus additional medical, psychological, and psychiatric help.

I believe law enforcement personnel and mental health professionals should propose the following steps:

1. Continue to develop integrative systems such as Oakland County which meet the requirements of the correctional function and the requirements of mental health.

2. Continue to address the needs for balance within the system by providing for appropriate levels of staffing with funding from the State Board of Mental Health and County Boards.

3. Continue to work with local courts to address the appropriate placement of persons; diverting those who are not criminals and confining those who require correctional care.

## Our New Scooter Patrol

Dear Jay,

A weekly newspaper had this story on September 16, 1981, "Trial Run Begins for County's New Scooter Patrolmen."

> A trial program utilizing Oakland County sheriff's deputies, reserve officers, and motor scooters was recently initiated in 3 townships including Commerce, according to Sheriff Johannes Spreen.
>
> The new scooter patrol is a crime preventive measure, Spreen said, rather than strictly responding to crimes after the fact. A small scooter is utilized for patrolling residential areas, he said, coupled with a standard patrol car and crime prevention van.
>
> The residential scooter patrol will be utilized in subdivisions to flush out criminals, such as potential breaking and entering perpetrators, according to Spreen.
>
> Larger scooters will be used for patrolling the areas citizens frequent when they leave their homes, Spreen said, such as places of employment, schools, and shopping areas.
>
> "These units will offer crime responses and prevention possibly with the assistance of citizens," he said. "We will use trained reserve officers and citizen radio watches. For little more than the price of one car we can get 3 scooters with 3 people patrolling."
>
> The 4 scooters utilized in the patrols were donated by Anderson Honda of Farmington, according to Spreen; with an automobile for citizen patrols donated by Bob Sachs Olds of Farmington.
>
> Gasoline for the donated units is paid for through the enrollment in the sheriff's crime and accident prevention education (ESCAPE) program.
>
> Deputy Ken Hurst said the scooter patrols of subdivisions are aimed at stopping daytime breaking and enterings.

Volunteers working at Elias Brothers Restaurant to raise money for ESCAPE program around 1981. My wife, Mona, is standing next to me.

## Resignation of My Undersheriff

Dear Jay,

On November 17, 1981, I issued the following newsletter to our deputies explaining that I let Nyovich go because he had an agenda that was not mine or ours. You might be interested to know that Robert Nyovich, a lawyer and graduate of Wayne State University, has been practicing family and criminal law in Oakland County for the last several years.

> On November 16, 1981, I requested and received the written resignation of Undersheriff Robert Nyovich. I know there must be many rumors as to this change and other pending changes.
>
> I believe that any differences between Robert Nyovich and myself are, at this point, academic. What is important is that you understand that I intend to double my efforts in steering our department toward the brightest possible future.
>
> What does this mean? It means that I intend to evaluate all past orders and eliminate, modify, or replace with new orders any orders not in the best interest of the smooth operation of this department.
>
> It means that I will demand professionalism and accountability and will not tolerate negativism and indolence. I will evaluate all personnel and strive to insure that each man and woman is placed in a position to enhance his or her productivity. There may be future changes in order to bring this department in line with these goals.
>
> I am proud of the men and women who make up this department and, contrary to popular belief, I am aware of the difficulties that confront you in the performance of your duties.
>
> I ask that you have confidence in me and believe in both my ability and intent to remove the roadblocks that presently stand in the way of the maximum harmony in the operation of our Department.
>
> I look to each and everyone of you to provide the input for maximum effectiveness. I will accept each and every suggestion presented to my office for consideration of merit whether signed or unsigned.
>
> I ask you to be patient and to work hand in hand with me toward a higher standard of professionalism. I further ask that we all stand behind Interim Undersheriff Harry Jones, and do everything we can to make his transition as smooth as possible.
>
> I remain,
> Sincerely,
> Johannes F. Spreen

# My Wife Was a News Item

Dear Jay,

The information about my wife, Mona, hit the press on November 21, 1981. *The Oakland Press* ran a front page story by Albert C. Jones called "Sheriff Cries Foul Over 'Smear.'" Not only did I have to fire Robert Nyovich but also my secretary. They were in a romance together even though he was married, but they were colluding and making the most of a little bad news about my wife. In the end, my marriage with Mona did not survive.

> A confidential Michigan State Police intelligence report which mentioned Sheriff Johannes F. Spreen's wife was leaked to Undersheriff Robert Nyovich, whom Spreen fired early this week.
>
> Although neither man would specify it was the direct cause of Nyovich's forced resignation, Nyovich left within days after receiving the report and giving it to Spreen.
>
> Spreen, then a widower, married Mona Hemmerling last year. She was part owner of a tavern in the Eastern Market section of Detroit, and her name was among those mentioned in the five-page 1979 report which mysteriously got out of state police files.
>
> The tavern, called the Butcher's Inn, and its ownership were among items discussed in the report. Mrs. Spreen has since given up her ownership interest, an aide to the sheriff said.
>
> Friday, Spreen called for a full investigation.
>
> "I have requested the head of the FBI and head of the state police to look into certain improprieties in my department," Spreen said.
>
> "There appears to be an effort on the part of some to undermine me and my department, to slander me through allegations against my wife, and the spreading of a document from unknown origins that appeared to be several years old.
>
> "And I'm absolutely positive they are without foundation.
>
> "I have full confidence in my wife, and I love her very much."
>
> Spreen said an agent for the FBI took statements from several employees and concluded by saying the investigation is not over.
>
> John Anthony, special agent for the FBI in Detroit, refused to confirm or deny if any investigation was being conducted.
>
> Mrs. Spreen could not be reached for comment.
>
> Nyovich, asked Monday by Spreen to resign, told *The Oakland Press* that he received the intelligence report by mail Nov. 13, three days before he was fired, and gave it to Spreen the same day.
>
> It came in a Detroit Police Department envelope, he said.
>
> Capt. Robert Robertson, head of the Michigan State Police Criminal Investigations Section, confirmed that the report is authentic.

However, Robertson said late Friday, "I got my copy today from the *Detroit News.*" He indicated copies had been distributed to many members of the media.

"We'd like to know the answer" about how the report was leaked, he said. "I don't know where it first started circulating."

Thursday, Oakland County Commissioner James E. Lanni, R-Royal Oak, also asked for an investigation of the Sheriff's Department. In a letter to the county's Organized Crime Unit, he ended:

"There is a police report from the Detroit Police Department which will aid you in your inquiry."

Lanni said Friday night he believed he was referring to the same report that Nyovich received, but that his knowledge was limited to sections "read to me over the phone."

The case referred to in the state police report "is a closed case," Robertson said. "Its origin is out of a booze smuggling investigation involving Customs."

Much of the report tells of associations among various people. Asked about these, Robertson said, "Associations are not a violation of law."

Both Nyovich and Spreen have declined to say publicly why Nyovich was fired.

Nyovich, reached Friday at his West Bloomfield Township home, would only say, "When and if the time comes for me to talk, I'll be straightforward and have everything documented."

Nyovich said he didn't solicit the state police report, and that it was sent to him anonymously.

Capt. Harry A. Jones, formerly in charge of Administrative Services Division and 28-year veteran of the Sheriff's Department, was appointed interim undersheriff Tuesday. His appointment will become permanent with Nyovich's final separation from the department Dec. 16.

The 34-year-old Nyovich, a lawyer, said he was considering several job alternatives but hasn't decided.

Oakland County Executive Daniel T. Murphy all but confirmed offering Nyovich another position within the county.

"He hasn't been hired," Murphy said. "He is a Sheriff's Department employee until Dec. 15 ... he can volunteer to do work here, but we can't pay him while he's still on the county payroll.

"It's our intent to find something for him. He's a good employee and I'd hate to lose him."

Following Nyovich's resignation, Spreen began to dismantle and reassemble his command staff. His personal secretary, Jacqueline "Jackie" Cey, resigned Wednesday, refusing to accept another position within the jail.

"If I'm subpoenaed, then I'll make my statement, but for now, I've said I'm going to remain silent," she said.

Mrs. Cey said she is looking for another job with the county and anticipates she will be offered one because, "I have a good work record."

Mrs. Cey's resignation was followed Thursday by reassignment of Capt. Bill J. Nolin from head of the department's Protective Services Division to "captain in charge of overtime for all segments of departmental operations."

Nolin was also ordered by Spreen to clear out of an office in the front of the building to one in back of the jail.

Capt. James Curtis was reassigned from command of Community Inspection and the Government Services Division to Nolin's former post.

The sheriff said there may be additional changes next week.

## My Wife's Problems Became My Problems

Dear Jay,

Albert C. Jones printed the story "Spreen's Wife Blasts 'Low' Blow" in *The Oakland Press* on November 22, 1981. And I'll just add this was the beginning of the end of my short marriage to the ever secretive and mysterious Mona Jo Hemmerling, whom I divorced later.

> Mona Jo Hemmerling didn't marry Oakland County Sheriff Johannes Spreen a year ago to become a central figure in a political brouhaha.
>
> But now she has, and she's not happy about it.
>
> "I think this is all disgraceful and as low, dirty and cheap as any group of individuals can go," she stated Saturday, referring to a police intelligence report that apparently touched off the forced resignation of the undersheriff last week.
>
> A wholesale shake-up of the sheriff's command structure has followed.
>
> The 1979 Michigan State Police report named her as part-owner of a Detroit bar that was suspected of selling smuggled liquor.
>
> Mrs. Spreen has since given up her ownership interest in the Butcher's Inn, but said she still holds the land contract to the property.
>
> The 1979 investigation is a closed case, state police say, and no criminal charges were issued.
>
> However, the five-page report leaked out last week, and Undersheriff Robert Nyovich said he received a copy anonymously through the mail.
>
> Nyovich resigned Monday, just three days after he said he showed the report to Spreen.
>
> By week's end, the mysterious report had apparently been widely circulated to the media.
>
> In an angry statement Friday, the sheriff had stated, "There appears to be an effort ... to undermine me and my department, to slander me through allegations against my wife."
>
> Saturday, after portions of the report appeared in area newspapers, he didn't take kindly to a reporter visiting his ranch-style home in the rustic Quaker Valley subdivision of Farmington Hills.

A few seconds later, Spreen relented, and the couple agreed to a brief interview.

Asked if she was aware that she was being investigated, the sheriff refused to allow her to answer.

Commissioner James Lanni, R-Royal Oaks who last week asked the county's Organized Crime Unit to investigate "possible improprieties" in the sheriff's department said Saturday that there are "many questions about activities" in the department.

But when pressed to name them, Lanni did not mention the controversial intelligence report which he says he has not seen.

Instead, he said the finance committee of the Board of Commissioners plans to "go over an audit of the sheriff's gasoline supply" on Monday. He said a preliminary audit showed about 5,000 gallons of gas were unaccounted for from the department.

The intelligence report did say the Michigan attorney general was investigating the bar and "attempting to uncover ownership by persons alleged to be organized crime figures," but apparently no illegal ownership ties were discovered.

Oakland County Prosecutor L. Brooks Patterson, a longtime political adversary of Spreen, refused to be drawn into the controversy when queried Saturday.

"Everyone knows how I feel about Spreen, but I'm not going to kick a man when he's down," Patterson said.

Jay, I'll just add that James Lanni did. I feel he was one of the worst, most vicious politicians I have ever encountered. Now he is a registered sex offender. Yes, what goes around, comes around.

## My Posse Rode Again

Dear Jay,

The year ended with a December story by Albert C. Jones in *The Oakland Press* called "Spreen Welcomes Posse Back." After the County Executives and the Board of Commissioners dropped 27 deputies, this result came as very good news.

The sheriff's posse will ride again. About 20 members of the estranged Mounted Division last night decided to return to Sheriff Johannes F. Spreen's stable during a meeting held at the Oakland County Jail.

Last Monday, in a letter written by Mounted Division spokesman Murray J. Chodak, a Detroit lawyer, Spreen was informed "that the membership had determined that they could best serve the people of Oakland County by withdrawing ... and affiliating with the (county's) Safety Division."

Members had met Dec. 3 at the Bloomfield Hills home of Chodak and it was later announced that all 25 members were going to join the Safety Division amid promises that County Executive Daniel T. Murphy would provide additional funding.

But several members, saying they have at least $6,000 in the division's treasury, said the additional funds were unimportant because they could raise the money themselves.

Twenty-one members were in attendance, including five former members who said they were forced to resign two years ago by Chodak and his legal association, former Undersheriff Robert Nyovich.

Nyovich was fired Nov. 16 by Spreen.

A smiling Spreen also showed the membership a copy of a telegram sent by a member from Texas, saying he refused to leave the sheriff department's posse.

"We will ride in the Super Bowl," declared Spreen. "We have applications on file. We will increase the numbers that we already have. We will assign a liaison officer to work with the Mounted Division.

"All this is very heart-warming," Spreen continued. "I'm proud of the Mounted Division. I think there were some scurrilous remarks made at Mr. Chodak's house that weren't true. I've always supported the communities involved in law enforcement. We want more citizens involvement and we're accepting applications for our Mounted Division and several other programs where citizens can work with our deputies."

"I felt there was an unhealthy situation that existed between Nyovich and Chodak," said Roy Lewis, a deputy and former liaison person for the Mounted Division. "It was apparent that it was coming down to a two-man operation. When Chodak wanted things for the posse ... if he wanted to change things, he would approach the posse. If he didn't get an agreement, he would come back with an order from Nyovich. Supposedly, the order came from the sheriff.

Also in attendance at the meeting was County Commissioner James A. Doyon, D-Madison Heights. Doyon said there is an effort on Murphy's part to reduce Spreen's role to that of only a jailer and giving more police authority to the Safety Division.

Jay, you might be interested to know that Murray Chodak was in business with the son of missing Jimmy Hoffa. That son, Jim Hoffa, is now president of the Teamsters Union.

# *1982*

President Reagan introduces "Star Wars"
"Just Say No" is new tool to combat growing U.S. drug use
USSR shoots down and destroys South Korean flight 007
U.S. invades Grenada after coup on island
Sally Ride becomes first American woman in space
U.S. Embassy in Beirut is bombed, killing 40 people
Hackers invade military computers in Los Alamos
Tylenol murders happen in Chicago

# I Could Add 38 Positions

Dear Jay,

The year began well as I received complimentary comments for our services to many communities and businesses. One example was from William Krupka, Vice President of Corporate Security for Perry Drug Stores. He wrote me on January 14, 1982, saying "Allow me to congratulate you and the personnel of your department for exemplifying the highest degree of police professionalism in the discharge of your duties. Whenever the need for assistance was required of your personnel, they responded without delay and rendered what service was applicable to the particular situation. Thank you again for your assistance and should I be able to serve you in any capacity, please feel free to call."

I was also gladdened by a consent judgment that allowed us to add 38 jail positions. I wrote this news release to my troops on February 25, 1982.

> After nine years of documented correspondence and studies, there has at long last come a day where we can begin to alleviate the twin evils of overcrowding and understaffing at the Oakland County Jail.
>
> It is certainly ironic that this day has arrived because of court actions brought by jail inmates and their lawyers (a class action suit brought four years ago, March 17, 1978, against the County.)
>
> This has cost the taxpayers $76,500 alone in their attorney fees and costs, not counting the overtime costs over the years necessitated in the jail.
>
> The Honorable Patricia J. Boyle, presiding in United States District Court, has signed a Consent Judgment which will add 38 positions to the jail staff. Surely, the Judge would not allow 38 positions if I had not been right all along. This indicates that the Oakland County Jail has suffered a severe staffing shortage.
>
> Under court order, we must now limit the jail population to 450! (A reduction of well over 100 inmates a day from present figures.) Where will they go?
>
> I strongly suggest that Executive Murphy move on to the problems of the need for expansion before we end up in court again and the cost to the citizenry becomes overwhelming.
>
> If the County Executive (Mr. Murphy) is a good administrator, then why did it take a Consent Judgment to meet the basic needs of staffing that I requested nine years ago?
>
> Regarding our officers, I would like to express my deep appreciation to the men and women of the Corrective Services Division, and their supervisors, for the tremendous job done over the years in the face of great odds.

# Honoring Our Volunteers and Employees

Dear Jay,

A delightful female reporter wrote a nice article on April 22, 1982 entitled "Sheriff's Department Wins National Awards."

It is National Volunteer Week this week, and in this spirit, the Oakland County Sheriff's Department honored over 200 volunteers and spotlighted recent national recognition at the First Annual Recognition and Awards Banquet held April 13.

The Pontiac Silverdome was the location for the dinner, and appropriately so, as it was here that the volunteers worked to raise monies for the ESCAPE (Enroll in the Sheriff's Crime and Accident Prevention Education) Program.

"It was a thought and a dream a year ago," said Sheriff Johannes Spreen. "Now, it's a reality. You made the dream come true."

The sheriff called the volunteers the "champions of the Super Bowl program and hot dog sales," noting the sale of 67,000 programs at the end, more than have ever been sold before, anywhere. A Rose Bowl game saw 55,000 sold.

Gabe Kassab of Elias Brothers told the group he would be renewing his contract with the department, and presented the sheriff and Crime Dog McGruff with a check for $15,775.41 for their efforts. The monies will be used for the ESCAPE program.

McGruff, the well-known detective dog symbol association with the department's "Take a Bite Out of Crime" programs, is just one portion of an advertising campaign organized by the National Ad Advisory Council.

The department also was honored with an award from the National Citizens Crime Prevention Campaign supported by the Crime Prevention Coalitions for their crime prevention efforts.

Many government officials attended the banquet and helped in the presentation of the awards. In attendance were Oakland County Prosecutor L. Brooks Patterson, and county treasurer C. Hugh Dohany.

Some ten county commissioners, and supervisors from those townships contracting for sheriff deputy services were also at the dinner.

The monies collected for ESCAPE will be used in such areas as preparing pens, pencils, coloring books, a safety belt program, curriculum guide notebooks, township hall and substation information stands, and perhaps on-the-scene video taping of operators stopped for driving under the influence of alcohol, said the sheriff.

Selling hot dogs to raise money for the ESCAPE program.

Sheriff's deputies dressed as Crime Dog McGruff and his two offsprings—Ruff and Reddi at 1982 Superbowl—Ready to take a bite out of crime!

# An Audit Cleared Me Again

Dear Jay,

Sandra Combs of *The Oakland Press* did a story on April 23, 1982 called "Audit Clears Spreen of State Funds Misuse."

> Michigan's auditor general has found no basis for charges of misuse of state grant funds by the Oakland County Sheriff's Department.
>
> The audit was conducted after allegations were lodged against the department in December 1981 concerning the use of Secondary Road Patrol grant funds. The funds totaled about $350,000 annually in 1979, 1980 and 1981.
>
> Auditor General Albert Lee in a four-page letter to Gerald H. Miller, Department of Management and Budget director, recommended that some changes be made in record-keeping of expenditures of the state grant.
>
> The allegations charged that:
>
> - A clerk paid from grant funds worked on tasks not related to the SRP program.
>
> - The department reassigned certain sergeants to supplant SRP funds for county funds.
>
> - Patrol officers paid from SRP grant funds worked on non-road patrol activities.
>
> - The department conducted road patrols in incorporated areas contrary to provision of the SRP statute.
>
> "Our review did not disclose misuse of SRP grant funds for the allegations regarding the clerk position and the supplanting of (those) funds for county funds through reassignment of sergeants," Lee's letter said.
>
> The audit indicated, however, that there was a lack of adequate documentation at the Sheriff's Department to support patrol hours charged to the SRP grant for two of the three years under the grant.
>
> It also noted that SRP-funded officers "conducted patrols in urban areas from time to time without Sheriff's Department compliance within applicable SRP statutory provisions."
>
> Meanwhile, Oakland County Sheriff Johannes F. Spreen said he doesn't know why the documents about the patrol hours were inadequate but he plans to find out.
>
> "I'm asking Capt. James Curtis, who worked with the former undersheriff (Robert Nyovich), for a full report on the patrol hours," Spreen said. "I want to find out why there wasn't adequate documentation."
>
> Nevertheless, Spreen admits that it's possible the SRP patrol officers may have been in urban areas without going through the proper channels.

"I did assign some officers to Southfield after we received a request for help from the chief there," he said.

Spreen said when there's an emergency call from a chief, there isn't always time to get approval from the Oakland County Board of Commissioners and the other municipality's governing body.

"We've done nothing wrong," Spreen said. "The man who made the allegations is the man who put the people out on the streets."

Spreen said Nyovich was responsible for knowing what SRP patrol officers were assigned.

## We Were Given a Bus

Dear Jay,

I was delighted to receive the donation of a bus. A local paper covered on May 6, 1982.

> A 1978 Rts Transit coach was donated by GMC Truck and Coach to the Oakland County Sheriff's Department last week.
>
> This bus, presented by Ed Boehmer of the Service Development Department will eventually be equipped with extensive communication and emergency equipment to be utilized near the scene of disasters and other crises, according to police spokesmen.
>
> This will include situations where it is necessary to provide continuous 24-hour emergency service. This might mean serving as a vehicle for communication with on-the-scene emergency squads, auxiliary equipment, phone hook-ups, officer relief, and a type of "mobile office" for supervisors.
>
> Examples in which this bus might be brought into use encompass natural disasters, train derailments, missing children searches, and hostage negotiations.
>
> The radio equipment installed in this vehicle would make it a central communications center which would be available to all areas and police agencies in Oakland County, where the situation demands, such as a cooperative command effort.
>
> Sheriff Johannes Spreen received the coach for the department.

## Our ESCAPE Program Won Awards

Dear Jay,

I was asked to make a presentation at the National Sheriffs' Association annual meeting in Las Vegas June 20, 1982. I entitled it "E.S.C.A.P.E. from Crime and Accidents" so I could feature our ESCAPE Program. Here are some highlights from that presentation.

Crime and the economy are our greatest public concern—they seem to be inextricably entwined. Crime and/or fear of crime blights a community, causing losses to business, industry, school upheavals, and an exodus of people.

Citizens are being murdered, raped, robbed, and assaulted, homes are burglarized at an ever-increasing tempo. Shoplifting, larceny, vandalism seem to be regarded as a way of life—and the police who respond are not only laying their lives on the line constantly—but are being sued with ever-increasing success when they take action.

We have an ever-increasing contentious and litigious society. We have lawyers advertising for business in T.V. guides and in newspapers. Pay only if you collect!

Can you blame an officer in these times? Who wants to lose all they have worked for all their lives to a "criminal" and his lawyer?

Right now, I have a $2.2 million judgment against me because of "vicarious liability" as a result of action taken by a former undersheriff and at the direction of the prosecutor, no less.

I often ask myself the question—Are we better off now than when I entered the law enforcement profession? The answer is "No!" Why? To me, the only answer, and please don't think me ridiculous, is love! Yes, if you translate love into care and concern and consideration for your community, your loved ones, your neighbors, crime would not exist.

Today, the citizens who really care and the police who really care are fighting apathy, fighting politicians, fighting with each other. What we have is law enforcement agencies battling among themselves instead of real cooperation.

To really turn things around and win the war against crime and accidents, we need citizens on our team and we need the funds to do what must be done.

In Oakland County, through a program called ESCAPE (Enroll in the Sheriff's Crime and Accident Prevention Education program) we are earning our own money to put in crime prevention patrols and do many other things in the prevention of crime and accidents.

The other day, I went to a seminar on home breaking and enterings. The key speaker was a convict from Jackson Prison, who was the "hit" of the program. It is sad to see this because we need the best young minds in order to make law enforcement a noble profession it must and could be. We in law enforcement must compete with their "peer groups" in the education and socialization of young people.

Unfortunately, teachers and cops have become the enemy. We must turn this around by involving young people with law enforcement activities at an early age. Let's show these young people they are the "good kids" before they are exposed to the problems of delinquency.

Our Sheriff's Department has enlisted the National Crime Fighter "McGruff" and has deputized him to work with deputies on school talks, community gatherings and social functions. In Oakland County, we also have two crime puppies, "Ruff" and "Reddi" in a pilot program authorized by the Advertising Council and the National Crime Prevention Coalition.

The ESCAPE program is also bringing groups of people into the Oakland County Sheriff's Department and the jail through the front door so we don't have to deal with them later as clients through the back door. We have a slide presentation of the department and then a complete tour of our complex. There is a most important question and answer period and an informal group discussion with refreshments.

We are exploring the concept of "police omnipresence" which falls very close to the concept of Citizens' Watch, but works within the department.

We have also purchased motor scooters with monies earned by our volunteers, reserves and posse members.

In our history, when a crime occurred, the sheriff rounded up the able-bodied men of his county and pursued the evildoer and brought him to justice. But that was always after the fact. The crime had been committed. Today we need a posse that can be rounded up and assist the sheriff before the crime is committed and before the accident occurs.

We have won an award from the National Association of Counties for our ESCAPE program. None of this could happen without volunteers. This is "love," isn't it?

## Our Jail Was Busting

Dear Jay,

On August 30, 1982, my top men wrote a letter that was published in *The Oakland Press* about the overcrowded jail situation. I was very grateful to them for their explanations to the public.

> As members of the Sheriff's Jail Consent Judgment Ad Hoc Coordinating Committee, we feel we must respond to some of the inaccurate and irresponsible statements made by William Spinelli, a subordinate of the county executive.
>
> - As to the claim that we are not accepting the recommendations of the Jail Study Subcommittee, this is simply not true. We have followed most recommendations with the exception of a concept which would remove convicts from our jail to be mixed with our work release residents. This was deemed not feasible by the sheriff and the undersheriff.
>
> - The proposed use of credit cards for posting bond was researched and suggested to the Jail Study Subcommittee by sheriff's personnel, but ruled illegal by the prosecutor's office. We are awaiting direction from a higher authority before any further movement on this will be made.

- We have installed phones in nearly every prisoner area of the jail, contrary to Spinelli's statements.
- We are prepared to house overflow prisoners in the Circuit Court detention area as new staff becomes available.
- We must accept certain prearraigned prisoners from various police departments. Sheriff Johannes Spreen is in Circuit Court because we refused one such arrest. We are refusing most prearraigned new arrests as a means of controlling our population.
- The courts determine who is work release eligible, not the sheriff.
- Our Trusty Camp, contrary to Spinelli's charges, is operating as close to capacity as the number of eligible low-risk prisoners allows.

In summary, Spinelli is either (a) woefully uninformed as to what is really happening in the jail, (b) embarking on a political mission to embarrass Spreen by his attacks on the credibility of our Corrective Services Division officers, with little concern for truth and accuracy, or (c) both of the above.
Harry H. Jones, Undersheriff
Charles L. Cooper, Captain
Lewis M. Doyle, Captain
Carl G. Matheny, Captain
Jail Consent Judgment Ad Hoc Coordinating Committee
Oakland County Sheriff's Department

# My Wife Kept Making News

Dear Jay,

A reporter wrote an article published on September 9, 1982, called "Oh, Mona! The Sheriff's Beautiful but Controversial Wife is Modern in an Old-fashioned Way."

> She likes to cook her own jams and jellies, likes to turn out homemade cakes from scratch and her candy is so delectable she has boxed it and sold it at fundraisers. She is devoted to her daughter, Kelly, believes in family togtetherness and is fiercely loyal to her husband. All in all, Mona Spreen could be described as an "old fashioned girl" ...
>
> The only thing modern about Mona Spreen is her political viewpoint. She has become an outspoken advocate for her husband. She's been very active in a group called "Political Office Watchers" (POW) who have appointed themselves to supervise political activities in Oakland County government ...
>
> Mona Spreen married Johannes Spreen, Oakland County's Sheriff, unaware that this union would vault her name to the headlines in an attempt

to discredit him politically. In city newspapers, her past acquaintances as owner of a restaurant located at Eastern Market in Detroit were described as "shady" and with "Mafia connections."

... Since the wedding, however, the Spreens have been barraged with criticism. Not only have Mona's affiliations been suspect, but Spreen himself has been the target of several accusations ...

Mona said, "You know, they can talk about intrigues and political corruption in other places if they want. But I think Oakland County is a hotbed of corruption. The things that go on here are unbelievable! If only people knew what goes on!"

By the light in her eye, one perceives that Mona Spreen does not intend to just sit back and be an observer ...

## Short-handed and Over-crowded Jails

Dear Jay,

Here we were overcrowded at the jail, short-handed already, and then a simple political struggle to cut my troops occurred. *The Daily Tribune* summarized it in an article on November 20, 1982, called "Will Sheriff Marshal his Forces in Bid to Repeat Lucas' Feat?"

... Democrat Spreen and Republican commissioners are fighting again, only this time it's serious. The Republican-dominated board wants to save $1 million by laying off 27 members of the sheriff's 50-man road patrol division.

The move, led by Royal Oak Republican James Lanni, has cleared the board's finance committee and goes before the full board on Dec. 2. The measure is likely to pass, despite the sheriff's cries that it's a vendetta by Lanni and a "step toward destroying law enforcement in Oakland County."

Lanni and the GOP counter that the cuts are necessary to hold the line on county spending and make the sheriff toe that line. The layoffs, they say, will not cut into the force of deputies under contract to specific Oakland County townships, and are a fair way to reduce the amount Southeast Oakland taxpayers—who already pay for their own cities' police departments—subsidize the north Oakland patrols ...

Spreen isn't talking about his political plans, but a run for county executive is not out of the question ...

Spreen has a talent for drawing the attention of television cameras, and it's not hard to see him becoming a hero in the media ... In his remarks to the board Thursday he warned that township residents will be "in grave danger" because of the cuts and he appealed for unity. "Our concerns," he said, "should be with the public's safety—not the North against the South, Democrat against Republican. We are a county government!"

It sounded almost like a campaign theme.

## My Wife's Political Group Was Disliked

Dear Jay,

John Basch wrote an article about the group called Political Office Watchers (POW) that my wife, Mona, championed in the *Daily Tribune* on December 24, 1982. He wrote:

> It's no secret that most commissioners don't like the Political Office Watchers ... The group's secretary, Mona Spreen, wife of Democratic Sheriff Johannes F. Spreen, even offered to resign in an effort to purge the group of any undeserved label. The group rejected Mrs. Spreen's resignation.

# *1983*

Leonid Breznev dies, Yuri Andropov takes over
Rev. Sun Myung Moon marries 4,150 of his followers in New York City
Princess Grace of Monaco dies in car accident
John Belushi dies of cocaine and heroin
Prince William is born to Charles and Diana
Mexico's economy collapses
Telephone Company breaks up into 22 district phone companies
Vietnam Memorial is erected in Washington, D.C.

## My Request to Regain 27 Deputies

Dear Jay,

The *Tribune* published an article January 7, 1983 by John A. Basch called "Criminal is the Winner, Says Smarting Spreen." Judge Templin died in 2004 at age 83, having served as a judge for some 30 years.

The article reported the Circuit Judge Robert L. Templin denied my request to put 27 deputies back on road patrol duties.

> ... The Board of Commissioners last month voted to eliminate 27 deputies and supervisors from the sheriff's road patrol ...
>
> "I think we presented a good case," Spreen said. "But in the meantime we have a terrible state of affairs in this county by having so many deputies out of work at a time when we need them most. It's a terrible injustice to the citizens who live here."
>
> In additional to Spreen's suit, the Police Officers Association of Michigan, the union which represents the deputies, also has filed a complaint seeking to reinstate the laid off deputies.
>
> In that case, Judge James S. Thorburn also denied a request for a temporary restraining order to prevent the layoffs.

## My Wife Tried to Help

Dear Jay,

Mona's group, the Political Office Watchers (POW), put out a newsletter in January/February 1983. One article was "Proposed 'Agreement' with Sheriff's Department from the County Executive." I don't know who she had write it but here is the article.

> Following the vote to lay off 27 Sheriff's deputies at a time when crime is increasing and the county has a $2.3 million dollar budget surplus, the County Executive proposed an "agreement" with the Sheriff, Johannes F. Spreen, under which he promised to suggest reinstatement of the laid-off deputies.
>
> The agreement asks the Sheriff to contract away certain obligations that are imposed on him by statute or the constitution. For example, the Sheriff is obliged to accurately report the jail population and cannot divorce himself from this obligation by contact because he remains ultimately responsible.
>
> Following is a news release put out by the Sheriff on December 21, 1982.
>
> Regarding the Oakland County Sheriff's Department budget cuts and the so-called "Agreement" between the County Executive and the Sheriff—many

reporters have been misinformed. Obviously, the County Executive and his political aide, Patrick Nowak, have blatantly lied to many reporters.

There were not several meetings or weeks of planning to come up with this "agreement," if there was such intensive planning. I, the Sheriff, had no knowledge or participation in such.

The hastily drawn agreement was presented to me 24 hours before a press conference was to be held by the County Executive. I was told by the County Executive, and his political aide, Nowak, that I had until 3:00 p.m. that day to sign and "take it or leave it—that's it."

The so-called "agreement" was a maneuver and manipulation by the County Executive and his aide, Patrick Nowak, to assert power and control improperly over the Sheriff's Department. The only other meeting I have had with the County Executive was on December 3, 1982, after a crucial vote by the Board of Commissioners the night before.

If any citizen would like a copy of this so-called "agreement" and my response to it, please call or write me at the Sheriff's Department.

## Facts About Losing My Deputies

Dear Jay,

I decided to write a commentary to *The Oakland Press* about all this. They printed it on February 11, 1983, under the title "Let's Finally Set the Record Straight."

> There seems to be a one-sided media presentation recently on the part of some media, relative to the Oakland County Sheriff's Department. A serious distortion of the facts has, unfortunately, been perpetrated.
>
> In fairness to the members of the Sheriff's Department, myself and your readers, allow me, as their elected representative for law enforcement of Oakland County, to present what are the true facts.
>
> It has been reported that only one Sheriff's Road Patrol officer and 14 Jail Detention officers have been laid off as a result of recent controversial actions by the Oakland County Board of Commissioners. That is only the tip of the iceberg of truth, but conveniently covers up the rest of the story, one that has caused so much destruction and damage to a top-notch, professional Sheriff's Department.
>
> Here is the whole truth—not just the tip—and what a difference!
>
> While it is true that only 15 people lost jobs, the process that resulted in that was as follows:
>
> - Twenty-seven officers were laid off from the countywide Road Patrol. We were able to save jobs for five of them.

- Twenty-two officers were removed from the countywide Road Patrol Services.
- Nineteen of these officers then used seniority rights to bump 18 newly hired officers out of their jobs in the jail.

While five officers were saved, four of these are no longer in a countywide support position. They must work in the townships that pay for their services. Therefore, 26 officers have been lost to the over one million citizens of this county. This is the real tragedy for all of us.

The bottom line: There are no more countywide services that the people are paying taxes for, nor are the people getting any tax dollars back because of these reductions. And worst of all, we are probably going to lose 13 persons in our Secondary Road Patrol services and five persons in our Alcohol Enforcement Patrol program because the county has violated the law in failing to maintain conditions as they existed in 1978 when we received these grants.

Because of these layoffs, the Deputies' Union agreement provides for no reserves being utilized to replace laid-off deputies. Therefore, we now will lose the services of 109 trained reserves who patrol communities with and in assistance to our deputies. We've had a total of 154 individuals lost to protective patrol in our county. Along with that, eight patrol cars were removed, which results in a loss of 400,000 miles of protective patrols.

That's the truth.

I would hope that the people in Oakland County would be concerned enough to contact their county commissioners. Please let them know how you feel.

## Prosecutor Uses Tricks to Reduce Debt

Dear Jay,

A few days later, the *Daily Tribune* carried this little story by Thomas B. Scott called "Patterson Raffles Cars to Cut Debt." I could not believe that a politician would take advantage of government opportunities to reduce his own personal debt.

Oakland County Prosecutor L. Brooks Patterson has come up with a politically novel scheme to wipe out his $130,000 campaign debt. He told delegates to the state GOP convention he plans to raffle off two new 1983 Chevrolets on July 4.

At $1 a ticket, Patterson figures the giveaway will be a big success—unless other candidates jump in with their own raffles. Ticket sellers also get a shot at a $1,000 bonus raffle.

Patterson should have been peddling his tickets next door to the convention site. Several thousand Detroiters, each hoping to win one of 52 abandoned houses being raffled off by the city for $1, crowded into the Cobo Hall exhibition area beside the GOP Saturday morning.

A house and a car for $2 isn't a bad buy. If you can find a better deal....

## Competition for the Sheriff's Job

Dear Jay,

My troubles were in the newspapers so I was not surprised that others decided to enter the race to be the next Sheriff of Oakland County. This story appeared in *Spinal Column* on March 16, 1983, and was called "Stewart Returns to Sheriff Race."

James Stewart, chief of public safety for Huntington Woods, announced he will run again for Oakland County sheriff in 1984 ...

"You don't have to run several thousand dollars over budget habitually," Steward said. "One of the things you can do as a good professional administrator is to present your budget to them (the board) and get them to do the essential things and then you can live with it as nearly as you possibly can."

... If elected, Stewart said he would alleviate the ongoing feud between the sheriff's department and the county executive with good leadership.

"The feud really has come about because of the lack of confidence in the leadership in the sheriff's department and the mismanagement in reference to overtime and what the deputies were allocated," Stewart said. "That would be a real easy situation to resolve. I would live within the budget set by the board of commissioners."

## My Wife Becomes News—Again!

Dear Jay,

*The Oakland Press Sunday Magazine* published a very long article by Al Adler on March 20, 1983, called "Mona Spreen: She's Caught in the Middle."

Mona Spreen admits she's made some "mistakes" over the years ...

Her first "mistake" might be traced to the job she took, at about age 20, in the Turf Lounge, a tavern in southeast Oakland County ...

A second mistake, she admits, was her first marriage ... Then there was her friendship with Howard and Elaine Dixon of Troy and her co-ownership of the Butcher's Inn, a Detroit tavern.

The Dixons loaned her $15,000. It was a generous action that would turn sour and cause more problems than it solved ...

Mrs. Spreen, the thin, attractive 39-year-old wife of Oakland County's 63-year-old sheriff, Johannes Spreen, looks back over her life and concludes she did many things not because she wanted to, but because that's what circumstances dictated.

However, when she married Spreen Nov. 15, 1980, she was thrown into a public spotlight that puts anything she does—or did—under a magnifying glass ...

She met Spreen in the summer of 1980.... at the tavern ... The sale of the bar and restaurant was finalized in December of that year.

The key element in the controversy is a 1979 Michigan State Police report that named Mrs. Spreen as a partner in a business allegedly selling smuggled liquor from Canada. It was also alleged that Mrs. Spreen was having private liaisons with known organized-crime figures and that there was hidden ownership of the bar-restaurant by known crime figures ...

Dixon died in January 1980 and Mrs. Dixon, to Mrs. Spreen's surprise, filed a lawsuit seeking complete repayment.

"I'm willing to pay so much a month, whatever I can afford," says Mrs. Spreen, "but she won't accept that. She wants payment in full." The civil suit is still pending ... She says her biggest regret is not having told Spreen immediately about the $15,000 loan.

"I didn't tell him because I wanted to protect our relationship," says Mrs. Spreen. Upon urging of a friend, Mrs. Spreen says she finally did tell her husband and he has accepted the situation.

"I wouldn't have married her had I not been impressed," boasts Spreen. "I wish she wouldn't be involved so much," says Spreen.

## Informing Commissioners of Overcrowded Jail

Dear Jay,

On July 14, 1983, I was scheduled to make requests of the Board of Commissioners but they permitted me only five minutes. Therefore, I informed them that I would send them a presentation by mail. During my five minutes, I made these remarks.

> Soon our doors to the Oakland County Jail will burst open due to overcrowding. Something must be done. I have been patient and persevering, pleading, exhorting, writing letters, asking for studies, meeting with National Institute of Correction people, and over these years working with our Jail Study Committee, but we still have the problems.
>
> Our neighboring counties have built or are building new jails or extensions to their jails. I have complied with the 19 requirements of the Consent Judg-

ment but I cannot comply with the requirement for additional space. That is your job. I have requested that you act for nine years now, but to no avail.

Accordingly, I have requested my attorney to start legal action against you on my behalf.

Do we allow politics to become petty and destructive or do we join forces together as Americans to work in bi-partisan teamwork? I beg you now to help me in my endeavors.

In my written presentation, I will detail points about the Sheriff's Department:

- Service and Support Role
- Paid Services to Townships Policy
- Posse Concept
- Avon Project to Develop "Vigilant" Citizens
- Use of Reserve Officers
- Request for a Professional Career Ladder

Ladies and gentlemen, let us put aside bi-partisan bitterness. I stand ready to work with you. Let us work together for the safety and welfare of all the people of this county and the police departments that protect them. Our citizens deserve no less.

## Jail Inmate Sues Sheriff's Office

Dear Jay,

On July 25, 1983, this article called "Inmate Files $2 Million Lawsuit" appeared in *The Oakland Press*. Our problems with overcrowding were multiplying by the day.

> An 18-year-old Oakland County Jail inmate who alleges he was sexually assaulted by two other inmates in April has filed a $2 million civil rights suit against the county and Sheriff Johannes Spreen. In the suit filed in U.S. District Court, Louis McClure of Madison Heights alleges that the county and Spreen had a duty to separate him from high-risk, violent offenders while he was imprisoned at the county jail in April awaiting sentencing on a drug charge.

## Volunteer Gets Praise

Dear Jay,

Mike Martindale wrote this for the *Detroit News* on September 7, 1983. He called it "For Retiree, Job's Worth More Than the Money." I was glad for one of our many volunteers to get some praise for their work.

> Meet Oakland County's $1.25 man—Lou Marsh. At 77, he couldn't be happier.
>
> ... He puts in a full day in the bureau's major crimes division, sorting through incident reports from the night before, often fielding telephone calls, whatever is necessary.
>
> And he does it for—this is no typographical error—$1.25 a year.
>
> ... It was Marsh who first approached Oakland Sheriff Johannes Spreen about a job 10 years ago. And he's been on the payroll since.
>
> ... Lt. Henry Hansen, who heads the detective bureau, said, "He helps us out in so many ways—tracking down information, scanning those reports. He is able to do a lot of the nitty-gritty that others don't have the time to do."

## Crime Dog McGruff

Dear Jay,

One of our deputies, Marc J. Cooper, wrote this letter to the editor of *The Oakland Press* entitled "McGruff Prevents Crime" and it was published December 20, 1983.

> In response to the article written by Randall MacIntosh on Nov. 20 ("Paying for Crime Doggy gets taxpayers by the tail"), I would like to set a few facts straight.
>
> The program which Mr. MacIntosh called "goofy" is a national program. The FBI, the attorney general's office in Washington, the Army, Navy, and Air Force, the Detroit Police Department and the Farmington Hills Police Department, among others, support the McGruff Program. McGruff is the national symbol for crime prevention. The McGruff symbol was developed by the National Coalition for Crime Prevention.
>
> The deputy who portrays McGruff donates many hours to this program to help reduce the jail population ... This deputy and Sheriff Spreen feel that working with young people, as well as adults, is very important. We must remember that over half of the crime committed in this county is committed by young people.
>
> Marc J. Cooper, Deputy.

# Judge Beer's Double Life

Dear Jay,

Judge William Beer, who had put me in jail when I refused to reinstate a bad employee in 1976 and served as my defense in a lawsuit that lingered until 1982, had been leading a double life. I could not have been more shocked when I heard about this in 1983. Here is one article about it called "Oakland's Judges Made News in 1983" by John A. Basch in the *Daily Tribune* on December 28, 1983.

> There were a number of important stories told in 1983. Some marked the end of long-standing disputes, others just the beginning ...
>
> It was the revelation that former Oakland County Circuit Judge William J. Beer led a "double life" complete with two families while serving on the bench that grabbed the biggest headlines in 1983.
>
> Beer, a controversial figure during his judicial tenure, was barred from ever serving as a judge when it was revealed that he fathered several children by his sometimes courtroom secretary while married to the former Dora Lambert of Royal Oak.
>
> He maintained two households, one in Berkley with his wife and their three sons, the other in Detroit with the woman he called "Mrs. Meyers" and his nine other children. "Mrs. Meyers," turned out to be the former Barbara Santimo, whom he later married.
>
> In November, Beer was in the headlines again, the target of a million-dollar lawsuit accusing him of mishandling the trust fund of a heiress to the Vernor's soft drink fortune.
>
> The suit, which Beer denies, claimed the 74-year-old former judge wooed a third woman, while concealing his marriage from her.

# *1984*

**Indira Gandhi is assassinated
Geraldine Ferraro becomes the first woman Vice President running mate
President Reagan re-elected in landslide election
The AIDS virus is discovered
Soviet Union boycotts summer Olympics in Los Angeles**

# I Decided to Run For County Executive

Dear Jay,

Well, here comes the end of my career in law enforcement. *The Detroit News* ran a little story under the title "Will Spreen Run Again?" on May 31, 1984.

> Oakland Sheriff Johannes F. Spreen is keeping the folks guessing, but the rest of his colleagues at the county courthouse have filed for re-election ... Apparently content to let the suspense build, the sheriff has a stock answer—"I don't know whether to run for re-election, for executive or for cover." There's no shortage of candidates to replace him as sheriff ...

The next day, the *Daily Tribune* ran a little article entitled "Sheriff Spreen Seeks Election as County Exec," by John Basch.

> Using the building he has occupied for nearly a dozen years as a backdrop, Oakland County Sheriff Johannes Spreen announced he will run for county executive, ending speculation about his political future ...
> Two others already have filed for the post—incumbent Daniel T. Murphy and fellow Democrat Billy J. Nolin, a sheriff's department captain.
> ... Spreen, who wants to streamline county government, said the current administration, "doesn't fulfill its responsibilities to the people."
> ... Noting that if he's elected he'll be "operating from a different vantage point," Spreen said he expects to "get along" better with the Republican-controlled board of commissioners than he has as sheriff.

The following day, June 2, 1984, Randall MacIntosh of *The Oakland Press* wrote a story, "Spreen Joins the Race for County Exec."

> Oakland County Sheriff Johannes Spreen announced Friday he will enter the race for county executive.
> ... Spreen met to discuss strategy recently with Gov. James Blanchard and two of the governor's leading fund-raisers, Ronald Thayer and Donald Tucker.
> Thayer was an aide to Blanchard while he was in Congress and the finance chairman of his gubernatorial campaign.
> Tucker is an attorney from Franklin, chairman of the 18th District Democrats and a Walter Mondale delegate to the national convention.
> ... "In the past 10 years, Oakland County government has become more and more narrow in its focus and more and more partisan in its actions," Spreen said.
> ... Murphy said he is not taking the sheriff's challenge lightly.

"He's known throughout the county, but not everybody knows what kind of slipshod operation he's run for the past 12 years. Nothing is for sure," Murphy said last week.

Spreen accused Murphy of "not being accountable to the people."

... In 1983, county commissioners cut 27 positions from his budget because they contended Spreen was instituting unauthorized programs and he had exceeded his overtime budget by more than $500,000.

The next day, June 3, 1984, Randall MacIntosh of *The Oakland Press* wrote another article. "Spreen Tackles All-out Battle with Murphy."

... Sheriff Johannes Spreen, who entered the race as a Democrat Friday, said he does not expect an endorsement from Gov. James Blanchard during the primary, but said he "expects to get his vote."

But even with the help of the governor, and the state party, unseating Republican incumbent Daniel Murphy is a formidable task ... Murphy's most serious challenge came in the November 1974 election for the first executive ... But Spreen is a proven vote-getter. He has received an increasing number in each successive election.

... In 1976, the year Democrat Jimmy Carter was elected president, Spreen outpolled Murphy ... Tables turned as Republican Ronald Reagan was swept into office in 1980 when it was Murphy who outpolled Spreen ... Murphy easily defeated Thomas Lewand, 236,372 to 181,869 as Spreen beat his Republican opponent, James Stewart, 225,490 to 194,000.

Murphy has already raised $100,000 and said he will spend $300,000 or more to retain his seat. Spreen enters the race with $1,400 in his campaign treasury ... But before he can get to Murphy, Spreen must first obtain his party's nomination by beating a man from within his own department who has also entered the Democratic primary.

Capt. Billy Nolin, a former Spreen ally who has been at odds with the sheriff over the past several years, entered the race Wednesday.

"Stimulating" is how Spreen described the primary challenge from Nolin.

## Heat Builds for County Executive Race

Dear Jay,

June 7, 1984, was a big day. Several newspapers had stories about the race for County Executive but I'm not sure I wanted this kind of publicity. Neil Munro wrote an editorial for the *Oakland Press* called "Spreen-Murphy Race Should Be Colorful."

... Whatever else you may think of Spreen, it must be conceded that he is a colorful character, so the campaigning should be equally fascinating.

The sheriff's path to high office is not utterly strewn with roses. Bill Nolin, one of his aids, had already decided to try to get the Democratic nomination for county executive.

Therefore, Spreen will have him to contend with in the primary ... The contest will cost the sheriff money and energy that he no doubt would rather spend going after Murphy ...

Though Gov. James Blanchard has not endorsed Spreen, he has lent him the services of two of his leading fund-raisers and political operatives ...

Then there is the real possibility that Spreen could defeat Murphy. That would suit the governor even more ...

On the same day, June 7, 1984, Tom Walsh, editor of the *Detroit Free Press*, wrote a column called "Don't Count the Sheriff Out."

Leave it to Oakland's maverick sheriff, Johannes Spreen, to breathe some life into an otherwise ho-hum election campaign for county offices ...

He filed to run for county executive against Murphy, a gamble no other big-name Democrat was willing to take ...

With President Reagan heading the ticket, and Michigan Democrats saddled with fallout from the state income tax hike, 1984 is widely viewed as a can't-miss year for the GOP ...

The man does have Name Recognition, capital letters intended. With the exception of Patterson, no politician in the county has a higher profile than Spreen.

Murphy doesn't come close. A low-key guy who rarely calls a press conference, Murphy's reputation as a sound fiscal administrator springs partly from shunning things like chauffeur-driver limousines and other trappings of the politically powerful that are commonplace in a nearby city that begins with D. For the record, Spreen drives himself to work, too.

Another plus for Spreen is that he's good on the airwaves. At 6-4, he's an imposing television figure. He speaks well and oozes sincerity. Often in politics, delivering the message with authority is as important as the message itself.

Another article of that day, June 7, 1984, came from Robert Roach, a *Detroit News* staff writer and was entitled "I'll Slash Executive's Salary—Spreen."

Oakland County Sheriff Johannes F. Spreen opened his campaign to replace County Executive Daniel T. Murphy with a promise, if elected, to cut the executive's "excessive" $76,665-a-year salary by 10 percent.

The sheriff's campaign against incumbent Murphy—and the six-man race to succeed Spreen—promise to make the 1984 county elections the liveliest in years.

"No county executive should make more than the governor," charged Spreen yesterday, apparently unaware that Gov. James J. Blanchard's authorized salary is $78,000 ...

Spreen said he would enact 10 percent pay cuts for the executive, and two deputy executives paid about $60,000 each, and "probably" do the same for Murphy's seven "super chiefs," or department heads, who draw $54,000 a year.

Even with the salary reduction, Spreen, if elected, would still get a $22,000 pay raise. As sheriff, his pay is $48,000. He also makes another $13,000 a year from his New York police pension. He would also qualify for an $8,000 pension from his stint as sheriff, but couldn't collect that while still on the county payroll ...

Murphy reacted angrily to Spreen's claim that his pay was excessive and claimed Spreen would change his mind, if he's ever elected and learns what the executive's job involves ...

Murphy's authorized pay is less than both Blanchard's and Detroit Mayor Coleman A. Young, who gets $79,685, but more than Wayne County Executive William Lucas, who makes $72,500.

The same day, June 7, 1984, a *Detroit News* editorial came out called: "What? Spreen for County Exec?" This was the most damaging of the articles—possibly because I had sued the *News* for libel and slander. I won my first case against them but lost on appeal. It's difficult to prove "malice."

> Oakland County Sheriff Johannes Spreen's announcement that he will get out of law enforcement and seek the nomination to run against County Executive Daniel Murphy is good news—unless he defeats Mr. Murphy. That prospect is appalling ...
>
> As county sheriff for more than a decade and as Detroit police commissioner prior to that, he has developed a lot of name recognition.
>
> As county executive, Mr. Murphy must make department heads unhappy, principally by not giving them everything they want in the way of budgets. He has done this in particular with Mr. Spreen ... As sheriff, Mr. Spreen is primarily responsible for putting up prisoners in the county jail, though he has constantly sought to expand his role ...
>
> In personnel matters, as we have noted, Mr. Spreen has had a succession of undersheriffs, many of whom departed in acrimony ... In 1977, he became engaged in a dispute with the South Oakland County Chiefs of Police Association over what one local chief said was his tendency to "travel around the county knocking local police departments."

## Support for Me as County Executive

Dear Jay,

I received much support by citizens and colleagues. An example is this letter from Dennis M. Aaron, Oakland County Commissioner for Oak Park published June 17, 1984, in the letter to the editor section of the *Detroit News*. It was entitled "A Vote for Spreen." Obviously, I was very grateful for this letter, and wrote Aaron telling him so.

> The June 7 editorial, "Spreen for County Executive," was an excellent example of "poison pen journalism." *Detroit News* readers are entitled to an editorial based on facts—not political partisanship.
>
> For 12 years, I have watched County Executive Murphy and his Republican-controlled board of commissioners systematically destroy Sheriff Spreen's efforts toward better law enforcement and better jail management.
>
> Under Mr. Murphy's leadership, staffing the jail was reduced below nationally recognized standards. The sheriff's pleas for more jailers and for increased jail capacity went unheeded. Finally, the Federal Court in Detroit interceded and ordered Oakland County to do what the sheriff had been asking for over the years. Murphy's indifference to the problems at the jail, unfortunately, results in the taxpayers paying for his poor judgment.
>
> Millions have been wasted over the years in grandiose political schemes. Food disappears from county-managed cafeterias, meaningless jobs done by the administrative staff are constantly being added to the budget, contracts are awarded to the "high bidders" instead of to "low bidders"—and *The News* remains silent, ignoring obvious waste and management on the part of Oakland County Executive Murphy.
>
> I have watched my fellow Republican commissioners abdicate their responsibilities and simply vote the way that Murphy wants them to vote. The Murphy machine may be good politics for him, but it is bad government for Oakland County.
>
> Yes, I think that a change is needed in Oakland County and I am proud to cast a vote for "Spreen."
>
> Dennis M. Aaron, Oakland County Commissioner, Oak Park.

## No More Room

Dear Jay,

I continued to run the department with a terribly overcrowded jail. I finally had to announce that we could not accept most misdemeanor prisoners into the county. I notified local police chiefs via police teletype that we would stop accepting most misdemeanants who had yet to be bound over to circuit court as of midnight Wednesday, August 22.

I explained that severe overcrowding at the jail and an attempt to stay within prisoner guidelines established by a court order led to my decision.

Certain misdemeanants would still be accepted at the county jail. Prisoners charged with drunk driving, assaulting a police officer, or those who have already been bound over by the courts will be allowed into the facility.

I wrote that it would be up to local police chiefs to make other arrangements for their prisoners. For example, they could send prisoners to other communities that have their own cells or release people on bond after the suspects are processed.

I added that this decision would stay in effect until the overcrowding situation improved.

## Overtime Hours Became an Issue

Dear Jay,

Randall MacIntosh did a story about our overtime hours and budget problems called "Spreen Shifts Staff to Cut Out Overtime" on September 21, 1984, for *The Oakland Press.*

> Oakland County Sheriff Johannes Spreen saying "I have no desire to go to jail" told county commissioners he has canceled overtime in his department, except for extreme emergencies.
>
> Spreen was called before the County Commission's finance committee Thursday to explain why his department exhausted its $570,000 overtime budget in eight months ...
>
> Because the account is exhausted, it is technically a violation of state law for the sheriff to assign any more overtime.
>
> Spreen blamed the problem on complying with a federal consent decree that establishes a minimum number of deputies on duty in the jail.
>
> To cut back on the overtime assignments, Spreen returned 11 officers to law enforcement programs approved by the county commission. Most of the 11 had been working on special projects for the sheriff.
>
> Accident prevention, canine training, public education, and deterrent patrols have been canceled because of the reassignments, Spreen said ...
>
> "My only choice is to accept that from now on I am to be only a jailer, not a sheriff in the modern understanding of that word," Spreen said.
>
> Deputy Management and Budget Director Russell Martin said Thursday, "We simply informed him that he would be in violation of the law if he kept spending money he didn't have. Now the ball is in his court," he said.

# I Lost the Election for County Executive

Dear Jay,

I lost the election for County Executive to Daniel Murphy. I finished my term as sheriff and retired.

I decided to make one more run at improving government in Oakland County. I ran for commissioner on the Oakland County Board of Commissioners.

On October 9, 1986, a reporter wrote two articles about the election which was to be held on November 4, 1986. One article was about me and the other was about my opponent, Board incumbent Jack McDonald. The two-year term as a commissioner has a base pay of $16,089. I lost the election but I'll include a few comments from both these articles.

The article about Jack McDonald was "McDonald Points to 12-year Record." The article about me was "Spreen Calls for a More Regional Approach." I'll start with the article about McDonald and then go into mine.

> "He (Spreen) has name recognition. And yes, I am going to work hard," said McDonald, seeking his seventh two-year term as county commissioner from the 27$^{th}$ District.
>
> Despite his opponent's notoriety, McDonald is convinced his experience on the county board of commissioners is a plus.
>
> In a county that has attracted unprecedented growth and development, roads—as far as McDonald is concerned—are one of the major issues today.
>
> Other alternatives McDonald believes should be considered include a bonding issue for road projects or a gas tax in Oakland County ... Imposing fees on developers to help finance road improvements is another alternative that is before the state Legislature, he said ... Reviewing the county government's structure, McDonald opposes any size reduction in the county board of commissioners. Landfills and solid waste are issues that will increasingly draw commissioners' attention as work continues on the county's planned incinerator system, MacDonald said ...
>
> In law enforcement, McDonald supports involvement of the sheriff's department in specialized areas, such as arson investigation and scientific criminal analysis, to relieve local departments of developing such costly services ...
>
> Spreen is running for the county commission seat in the 27$^{th}$ District. "With a county government, a regional approach is so necessary to approach the problems of crime, roads, and solid waste," he said.

At monthly meetings with interested residents, Spreen plans to keep residents up-to-date with county business, as well as solicit opinions to take back to the board of commissioners.

Crime, including prevention of it, is a top issue in Spreen's campaign. "I would like to see a consolidation of services rather than of departments," Spreen said....

While Spreen lauds the county's tri-party road improvement agreements, he is flatly opposed to a county-wide tax for improvements. If financial waste in the county government was eliminated, there would be enough money available to improve roads.

He believes developers should pay their share of road improvement. "Those who use the roads or profit from the roads should pay for the roads," he said.

Spreen would like to see a centralized waste disposable service and plant, such as is currently being planned at the county complex in Pontiac ...

To further streamline county government, Spreen would like to reduce the number of county commissioners from the 27 to perhaps 15 to improve efficiency, accountability, and reduce duplication. "If the city of Detroit can do it with nine council members ... I think we can be safe to drop them from 27 to 15."

# PART III
## After Being Sheriff

# A Legacy?

Dear Jay,

In my retirement, I have often been asked to give talks. I've written articles and books, and taught many groups. I have many interactions in various clubs and activities with old friends and new friends. People still write about me from time to time.

I was delighted with a nice story that a reporter for a Michigan newspaper did about me on July 10, 2003, called "Big Fellow Spreen Has What It Takes to Be a Great Police Officer."

> It's been more than five years now since the "Big Fellow" and I competed against each other in a race-walking contest at Port Huron High School's track and field area.
>
> The walk-off took place during an early spring St. Clair County Senior Citizen Olympic meet. If memory serves me right, I was 63 and the "Big Fellow," 6-foot-5-inch Johannes F. Spreen of Marine City, was 78. There were eight of us senior citizens (55 years and older) in that race.
>
> That beautiful senior citizen Olympic moment was recalled for me recently when I received a letter and book from Johannes who said: "John, I remember well that nip-and-tuck race we had a few years ago."
>
> Johannes is affectionately called the "Big Fellow" because of his height, his extraordinary athletic prowess and stamina, and for being an octogenarian. He is 83 now, and there are few in his competitive age bracket that can hold a candle to this incredible force.
>
> In 1985, Johannes retired from a career in law enforcement that spanned nearly 45 years. He was a role model for police officers across the country. His enthusiasm, wit, and literary brilliance continue to shine as a beacon of light for everyone. And who would have thought that this one-time beat patrol officer would one day help to restructure the New York City Police Academy training to a college program. The academy, a West Point for officers, is now John Jay College for Criminal Justice.
>
> Where did Johannes Spreen come from, this gifted person who became a college professor and newspaper columnist after taking his talent from New York to Detroit as police commissioner and later as sheriff of Oakland County?

He was born in Germany, Sept. 28, 1919, in a village outside the city of Bremen. He arrived in New York in 1923 aboard the ocean liner *S.S. Seydlitz* with his mother and sister. They joined his father and brother and settled in Brooklyn. The rest is a matter of record.

Johannes has a bachelor's, master's, and doctorate (all but his dissertation) degrees in law enforcement. He served as a lieutenant bombardier in the Army Air Corps during World War II.

He rose through the ranks of the New York Police Department to eventually become Inspector and Commander of Operations. After 25 years, he retired from the NYPD. In 1968, he became police commissioner in Detroit. Later, he was elected sheriff of Oakland County, and for 12 years, he was the only Democrat at the county level.

As police reporter for the *Times Herald*, I met the "Top Cop" when I was on a police-scooter assignment story back in the 1970s. You see, it was Johannes who started scooter patrols in New York City and Detroit. He also assisted Washington, D.C., police with their scooter program.

I covered several stories with him when he was sheriff, too. Our admiration and respect for each other were real. He was a class act then and he still is.

The book Johannes sent me, *American Police Dilemma—Protectors or Enforcers?* is a series of letter chapters dedicated to his daughter, Elizabeth Diane "Betty" Spreen, his late wife, Elinor, his wife, Sallie Ann Spreen, and their grandchildren. It could be a bible, a working tool of information today, for every police officer throughout the country. The book describes how policing has gradually emphasized law enforcement over the protection of people.

Johannes pulls no punches when he looks at politics, crime control, leadership, mental and physical conditioning, morals and rivalries that reduce the effectiveness of the police officer on the street. He definitely presents a convincing case for community-oriented policing.

Who said Johannes is retired? Why, even in retirement the Big Fellow has always been the tip of the spear in every challenge that has come his way.

Laura L. Newsome, executive director of the St. Clair County Council on Aging, Inc., said Johannes is a model for growing older and a teacher in "How to Age Positively."

He was named St. Clair County's Outstanding Senior Citizen in 1999. At 83, he still teaches body recall, memory improvement and conversational German. He is also a substitute teacher at Algonac High School.

By the way, he gave me one of those life lessons of his in that race-walking competition I mentioned earlier. Johannes took the gold. I came in a bruised second. But like he said, it was nip and tuck all the way, a great race.

Maybe it's time to see if a rematch is in order for the Senior Citizen Olympics next year. Surely at 84, he can't keep up the pace that he's set for himself. Top Cop, Tip of the Spear—ahhh, who am I kidding? Johannes was born to lead. And he does.

Johannes Spreen was assisted in writing his book by Dr. Diane Holloway, a psychologist and member of the American Psychological Association. She is an associate member of the International Association of Chiefs of Police.

## Community Policing: It Takes a Team

Dear Jay,

Some nice things happen to an old ex-sheriff and ex-lawman. I still give talks and speak to groups. I spoke to some local law enforcement chiefs in 2006 and one of them was nice enough to write the following story in a Phoenix area newspaper. The article called "My Turn: Community Policing Seeks to Bring People Together" by Buckeye Police Chief Dan Saban was published in 2006. Dan has become a good friend and sent me this article he wrote.

> Community policing has evolved since the late 1970s when I was a patrol officer in Mesa. Then, we started a program called Beat Profiling, which had as a goal connecting officers with residents.
> 
> It failed.
> 
> The program asked officers to reach out to citizens within our neighborhood beats. We would get out of our cars, talk with at least five residents a week, and hand out brochures about social services and crime-prevention programs.
> 
> I was anxious about engaging citizens in non-police matters, and so were my peers, because we weren't familiar with how to do it. My greatest fear was realized on my first attempt.
> 
> While on patrol, I noticed an elderly woman working in her yard. I pulled up, got out of my squad car, and walked toward her with a stack of pamphlets. I introduced myself and started to explain some of the programs. She quickly interrupted me, "No thank you, I give to my church." I walked away feeling rejected and discouraged.
> 
> Fortunately, today's community-policing concepts are nothing like they were 30 years ago. Chiefs of police recognize the importance of building relationships with the communities they serve. This is because community policing has been proven to reduce the crime rate. We also know that the bonds made between citizens and their officers develop feelings of trust and security.
> 
> Chiefs need to be innovative in creating their programs. Not everyone will be willing to support these efforts with time or money. What's partially to blame for this is that for many years police business became too inward-looking instead of forward-looking.
> 
> Another factor has been that team-policing concepts are often discussed but not always practiced. This must change if we are to build sustainable communities that are safe.

I'm inspired by legendary police commissioner and former sheriff Johannes Spreen, who, while working in Detroit during the tense racial times of the late 1960s, stated, "It takes a team, you and your police." His community-partnership approach encouraged people to work together, and it was successful.

In Buckeye, we've recently created the Community Partnership Bureau, which will focus on the three pillars of a community: businesses, schools, and churches.

Our bureau operates to bring people together. With guidance, police officers will know how to connect as a community team to serve and protect.

## Politics Today

Dear Jay,

The year is 2007. Will it be any different than 2006? It could be a year of political change and a year of opportunity.

Nancy Pelosi is the first female Speaker of the House. She pledges a "partnership not partisanship." (I wish that had prevailed in 1973, my first year as sheriff.)

Pelosi stated: "I accept this gavel in the spirit of partnership, not partisanship, and look forward to working with you on behalf of the American people." (In 1972, my aim was to work on behalf of all citizens of Oakland County, giving them the benefit of my law enforcement experience.)

Pelosi stated: "In this House, we may belong to different parties, but we serve one country." (It would have been great if the political leaders felt that way in 1973-84. Is she as naïve as I was?)

Yes, it should be US in the U.S.A., not US vs. THEM as it was in Oakland County then. Politicians spend too much time sparring with each other and not enough time solving problems. They try to destroy each other using the media.

I felt I could work with both Democrats and Republicans as sheriff. Little did I know then how politics could get downright dirty.

They say there should be no politics in law enforcement or in police work. I believe police officers should not engage in politics, but they become affected tremendously.

Police officials, chiefs, are appointed at the pleasure of the mayors and/or city managers. When they change, often the top command of police agencies change.

Politics began to affect me when I reached a top position in the New York City Police Department. I decided it was time to remove myself so I retired. The politicians appalled me when I was Police Commissioner in Detroit. I removed my name from consideration to be Police Commissioner under the newly elected mayor. Moreover, politics affected me greatly after I was elected Sheriff of Oakland County.

Too bad the Republicans could not listen to and heed the words of the new Speaker of the House.

I felt in 1973 that I could be the law enforcement representative of the people of Oakland County. I discovered that would not be easy. I felt that I could work with the Republican Commissioners and certainly with Brooks Patterson, who supplanted Tom Plunkett as prosecutor. I was naïve!

Some years later at a function in Washington, D.C., I spoke with President Reagan's Attorney General Ed Meese about my political troubles. I stated that I ran as a Democrat, thought more like a Republican, and acted like an Independent. And that is what I did for 12 years.

After a few years as sheriff, I asked my now deceased wife, Elinor, a New York cop's daughter who served as an officer herself, this question. With all the political nonsense and trouble we've been through, would it not have been better to run as a Republican. She looked up at me from her wheelchair (suffered from multiple sclerosis) and said, "Yes, John, but you are still your own man." I remember that remark with pride—but it comes at a price.

I finally became an anathema to the Republicans. That was wrong. I believe what Nancy Pelosi said is great. Let's hope it works that way for the sake of our country.

# *Epilogue*

I'm going to indulge in some musings about politics through my lifetime.

I was naïve. I was sincere. One reporter wrote that Sheriff Spreen "oozes sincerity." The same was said about me as Detroit Police Commissioner. I told that reporter, "Damn it, I *am* sincere." And I always have been. I care about police. I care about people. I even like and respect the media—or most of them, anyway. I'm not as sure about politicians, however.

In politics as Sheriff, I was attacked at times wrongly and at times unmercifully. In New York Police, and as Police Commissioner in Detroit, though those were not political positions, I still became a victim as many do in the political storms of the times. For example, there was a battle between Commissioner Vincent Broderick with Mayor John Lindsay that involved the New York Police Department. There was also a battle between Mayor Jerome Cavanagh with the Common Council involving the Detroit Police Department.

I'll also mention three big mistakes I made.

The first was endorsing Gene Kuthy for the new County Executive's position against Republican Dan Murphy.

The second was endorsing Sheldon Toll for County Commissioner in the District where I lived against Republican Pat Nowak.

The third was not following one good Republican's (Donald Quinn), advice to have lunch from time to time with individual Republicans.

In Detroit as police commissioner, I had only 17½ months to do the impossible. I said I didn't have time for a lot of lunches with 27 commissioners, 19 or 20 of the Republicans in Oakland County.

I believe this was a tale about a decent, nice, sincere guy caught in the whirlpool between politics, the press or media, and police politics, trying to sincerely serve the people with good police work, proper law enforcement that he had studied and practiced for many years.

Politics is necessary in a democracy but does it have to be so dirty, so barbaric, and so vicious? I guess it always has been since the days of the "penny press."

Our last national election was really bad. People got tired of the attack videos, the vicious attack sound bites, the mud-slinging, commercials, etc.

Now Internet searches are made constantly to dig up damaging videos or news clips to besmirch and shatter images. And it involves both sides of the political spectrum. The candidates on all sides are looking for and indulging in these smear politics. Attacks are directed to the character issues—trying to bring down the other person—attempting to turn his words against him.

Every candidate running for office, particularly national office, faces major risks. That cannot only cause a loss of his election, but a label for one's life.

For example, the hopes of Republican George Allen of Virginia were dashed by a Web video when he called an Indian American a "macaca" or monkey. He lost his November 2006 Senate re-election.

Attack videos range from the critical to the ridiculous. It makes one wonder why anyone would subject himself or herself to all this. How many capable, qualified people are lost to public service because of all this? It becomes a question of whether "to speak or not to speak," because in politics, your words can come back to bite you.

Yes, indeed, one must beware the "ides" of any month, particularly the October before the election. We now have the Presidential rollout of candidates for 2008. It is only the spring of 2007. The American citizen will have to bear up or brace up for many more months until November 2008. And two candidates may have already bitten the political dust. Senator John Kerry already has, with his ill-worded statement: "You know education, if you make the most of it, you study hard, you do your homework, and you make an effort to be smart, you can do well. If you don't, you get stuck in Iraq."

In February, the *New York Times* had a page one headline "Biden Unwraps His Bid of '08 with an Oops!" His spoken words may indeed have derailed his "presidential train" at the very start, before the wheels have even started to roll. These were his words at the kickoff as a candidate for the presidency, describing Senator Barack OBama, the Illinois Democrat running for president, as "the first mainstream African-American who is articulate and bright and clean and a good-looking guy."

Immediately Jesse Jackson and Al Sharpton, both African-Americans who have run for president, took issue with Mr. Biden's remarks, particularly over the words "clean" and "articulate" and "first."

Yes, as Rudyard Kipling wrote, "Words are, of course, the most powerful drug used by mankind." And like a bad drug, words can end one's political life. John Kerry knows that! Now Senator Joe Biden knows! And remember Howard Dean who let his emotions get the best of him when speaking in public?

And we all remember former President Bill Clinton's impeachment trial with his statement about the definition of "is." What is "is"??? His political career barely survived.

Everyone running for office must beware. Sheriff candidates must beware. Even once in office, people must beware of words spoken. Really, today with tape recordings, cell phones, and cameras, we all must beware, and those in the political process or cesspool must beware. It can be and unfortunately is a dirty business.

Yes, as I said before, words can come back to bite you. In my case, before I ever ran for Sheriff or even knew much about the function and duties of a sheriff, I had served as consultant to Prosecutor Plunkett at his request. Later, as Sheriff, I found some of those words used against me, but wrongfully.

I was accused by some, and some of the media, of wanting to become chief of a county police force, doing away with many small police departments where I had never stated that to be my desire.

In the report to Prosecutor Plunkett, which is in this book, I pointed out problems in policing, in law enforcement, and I recommended an Oakland County Law Enforcement and Justice Improvement team which I coined LEJIT. To me, it was composed of representatives of policing, law enforcement, prosecutor's office, the judiciary, and processes of rehabilitation and correction.

I advocated better training, better communication, better coordination, and more citizen involvement. I did mention other alternatives being used elsewhere, some initiatives suggested in U.S. government studies and reports, and suggested that some form of consolidation of police services be explored.

Later as a new Sheriff, I felt that LEJIT (which had not mentioned the sheriff because I knew little about the sheriff's role) could be implemented with the Prosecutor and the Sheriff as team members.

I felt I could work well with Brooks Patterson who defeated Tom Plunkett and who had asked me to serve with him.

Unfortunately, that did not happen for more than about one month. But I then found that Patterson was excluding me.

He had a copy of my report to Plunkett and used some of the comments improperly. He gave them to *The Oakland Press* which was a prime mover in slanting what I had reported to use against me. This bastion of so-called responsible news media was an adversary for twelve years.

If I could do it over, I would do something differently—changing those three mistakes—and still adhere strongly to my ideas and principles.

I did resent some of the political slings and arrows directed at me from politicians who had little background or knowledge of police work, now called criminal justice, compared with my (then) over 30 years of study and practice in three separate police agencies.

Well, so much for the good, the bad, and the ugly of a sheriff's life. I will end now with some comments about politics by California Governor Arnold Schwarzenegger and with my Love and Crime Credo, which was published when I was Detroit's Police Commissioner and Oakland County's Sheriff.

In Schwarzenegger's second inaugural address on January 5, 2007, I liked these comments.

> Post-partisanship is not simply Republicans and Democrats each bringing their proposals to the table and working out differences. It is Republicans and Democrats actively giving birth to new ideas together.

## Love and Crime

The problem of crime is complex and difficult and requires competent, well-trained, acceptable, professional police and sheriff's departments to cope with it. But, if I had to pick one thing that could really do the job and solve the problem—it would be love.

Love—what is it? It can be called a hundred different things—and the young don't have a monopoly on it. We seniors over 30 know about love also, and we are, hopefully, balanced by our experience. Maybe we can teach the younger generation a few things about love and work together for a pleasant and peaceful future.

What is this love that can cut down crime and cancel community tensions? What is this love that can do more about crime than all your law enforcement agencies, vigilantes, guns, and tanks? Let's try to define it.

- If it's caring about your neighbor so you report an assault you witness upon him or his home, that's love.

- If it's caring about your community so that you don't want to see it suffer, that's love.

- If you care about your fellow citizens no matter what their hue, that's love.

- If you care enough to willingly serve your country and your community, that's love.

- If you are concerned about the conditions which can tempt man to harm his neighbor and you want to see them alleviated, that's love.
- If you get concerned about crime and do something constructive about it, that's love.
- If you feel that there are things wrong, injustices, evils in this world, and you earnestly wish to do something about them, that's love.
- If you want to change things that do not seem right to you, calmly, coolly, with considered judgment, rather than with a destructive "to hell with it all" attitude, that's love.
- If you do your thing well, within the law and within the bounds of propriety, that's love.
- If you put your personal desires and politics second to your concern for your community, that's love.
- If you concentrate more on helping to professionalize your police than to complain about or ignore your police, that's love.
- If you follow the principles of honesty, truthfulness and fairness, that's love.
- If you use consideration, care, courtesy, and compassion in your dealings with all you meet, that's love.
- If you live according to the Golden Rule, the Commandments, or your moral, ethical or religious beliefs, that's love.
- If you consider the feelings of the other person as an individual who is with you on this small spinning speck of dust called earth, that's love.
- If you have faith in people and in your police, that's love.
- If you have hope that we can all live together in a better world, that's love.
- If you offer charity to all your fellow men, that's love.
- If you believe there may be a spot in heaven for all—regardless of their race, color or creed—that's not only love but heaven on earth.

# Synopsis

This is a summary of the major considerations in this book: Is the sheriff viable, under what conditions, and the concept of prevention as the best protection for all!

## Is the Sheriff Viable?

Where or what is the solution to the problems addressed in this book? My co-author and her husband asked this question. I'll leave it up to you—the reader—and law enforcement and police practitioners of today. Parts or pieces of solutions do permeate this book.

However, my first question to you is this: "Is the sheriff in America viable?" I'm not sure.

In England, where he started, the sheriff is mostly ceremonial today.

In America, in the Eastern part of the United States, the sheriff is not too strong. In the South and West, quite strong. In the Midwest, questionable in some areas—neither fish nor fowl.

In America's past, Thomas Jefferson pointed to the office of sheriff as being the most important of all the executive offices of the county. Attorney General Ramsey Clark asserted, "The policeman is the most important man in America today" in *The Democratic Policeman* by George Berkley, published in 1969 by Beacon Press in Boston.

Unfortunately, this is true in a positive as well as a negative sense. I know—I have been both policeman and sheriff.

My question now is this: Is the American sheriff capable today of functioning and developing as a law enforcement representative of the people? Can he or she be a positive force for good in the political milieu that exists in America today? I'm not sure!

In today's political milieu, people are fed up with political corruption and lack of ethics. People are fed up with our systems of politics and game playing. Just look at our front-page headlines of today.

We must put away bi-partisan bitterness and work together for the safety and welfare of all. Citizens deserve no less.

To be told by a Republican County Commissioner, "We can't make you look good—you're a Democrat," says it all, doesn't it?

## Under What Conditions Might a Sheriff Be Viable?

I feel the American sheriff could be very important—as you readers may already have discerned.

A modern sheriff supposedly is the people's representative—the only elected peace officer in the criminal justice system.

The sheriff is the only office holder touching all of the bases: law enforcement, court service, and corrections, and has the power of *posse comitatus*.

I believe the sheriff can be the key and the hope for better law enforcement in the United States—as the peoples' representative, but only:

- If the sheriff was qualified with enough years in law enforcement or police work
- If the office was preferably non-partisan (If the mayor can run non-partisan, why not the sheriff?)
- If the election of sheriff was held in a non-presidential and non-gubernatorial year
- If the media was fair, balanced, non-partisan in news coverage, with adequate publicity given to all candidates
- If adequately funded (Sheriffs can do little without proper funding.)
- If incumbent politicians and candidates would conduct campaigns with good character, honor, respect, and responsibility—citing their experience and their goals, striving for decency and integrity.

The concept should be Adversaries—yes! Enemies—no! The concerns of county officials should be with the public safety—not North against South, East against West, Democrat against Republican. We are a county government!

## The Concept of Prevention is the Best Protection

Here are two different concepts: Joe Arpaio's book *Toughest Sheriff in America* and Johannes Spreen's book *Nicest Sheriff in America*. Arpaios's concept is locking up criminals, no matter the costs. My concept is that prevention, education, and treatment cost less and may be better protection.

The sheriff should certainly arrest and incarcerate criminals who commit serious or heinous crimes. In addition, the sheriff, as the people's representative for law and order in a just society, could be a change agent, and catalyst for crime prevention. The sheriff could coordinate efforts with other police agencies and with the citizens of the county.

Prevention (if no crime occurs) saves the most money. Education (teamwork between police and citizens) saves lots of money. Reaching the hearts and minds of our youth would save money because young people commit almost half of our crimes. Treatment and incarceration costs the most—generally $23,000 to $25,000 yearly per prisoner.

Other methods should be explored. If Martha Stewart can wear ankle bracelets for six months to serve out the rest of her sentence, so can others. Fines, restitutions to victims, and other avenues should be considered. Violators of the law that can pay or provide restitution to victims should do so.

Finally, here is a 6'5" guy who talks about love and living by the Golden Rule—"Do unto others as you would have them do unto you." That is really as good an answer as any. Love engenders harmony and teamwork relationships between sheriffs, other agencies, and people affected by crimes. Really, what is the more important? Perhaps that is the only answer!

"It takes a team: You—your police—and your sheriff."

"The hope of tomorrow lies with the youth of today." Johannes Spreen

# *About the Authors*

Johannes Spreen, B.S., M.P.A., and Ph.D. (all but dissertation) was in law enforcement and police service from 1941 through 1984, interrupted by service in the U.S. Army Air Corps from 1943-1945 as Lieutenant Bombardier.

He was a career officer with the New York City Police Department, rising through the ranks to Inspector and Command of Operations.

After he retired from the NYPD, he became Police Commissioner of the City of Detroit. Later he served as sheriff of Oakland County, Michigan, for twelve years, and was the only Democrat elected at the County level.

Spreen was also Associate Professor at John Jay College in New York, as well as Professor and Director of the Law Enforcement and Protection Program at Mercy College of Detroit. He was a columnist for the *Detroit News* and the *Port Huron Times Herald.*

Johannes Spreen instituted Scooter Patrols in New York City and Detroit, and assisted the Washington, D.C. police with their scooter program.

He has written *American Police Dilemma: Protectors or Enforcers?* in 2003, *American Law Enforcement Does Not Serve or Protect!* in 2004, *Who Killed Detroit? Other Cities Beware!* in 2005, co-authored *Who Killed New Orleans? Mother*

*Nature vs. Human Nature* in 2005, and co-authored *The Saga of Thundercloud and Dancing Star* in 2006.

Diane Holloway, Ph.D. was a Dallas psychologist, and was appointed the first Drug "Czar" of Dallas by the Mayor. She also helped the Dallas Police Department develop their first police assessment center for upper ranks in 1987-1988, was an associate member of the International Association of Chiefs of Police, and was a member of the American Psychological Association, and served as a consultant to fire, police and city governments across the country. Earlier she was a management consultant and trainer on personnel selection with some of America's largest corporations.

She writes her own books and helps others write. She wrote and co-authored books with Johannes Spreen, Ken Jacuzzi, James MacLeod, Judge Joe B. Brown, Dr. Don Farrior, Fred Brown III, Lois Gentry, Nancy Bishop, Bob Cheney, and many others.

She wrote *Before You Say 'I Quit'* in 1990; *The Mind of Oswald* in 2000; *American History in Song* in 2001; *Dallas and the Jack Ruby Trial* in 2001; *Analyzing Leaders, Presidents and Terrorists* in 2002; *Jacuzzi: A Father's Invention to Ease a Son's Pain* in 2005; *I Did Not Burn the Church Down ... I Only Started the Fire* in 2005. She and her co-authors, Johannes Spreen and Bob Cheney, won first place for non-fiction in the Arizona Authors Association Annual Contest for *Who Killed New Orleans? Mother Nature vs. Human* Nature published in 2005.

978-0-595-44462-5
0-595-44462-8

Printed in the United States
93470LV00003B/124-141/A